E-Business

Issues and Challenges of 21st Century

E-Business
Issues and Challenges of 21st Century

Editors

B.B. Tiwari
Professor
Shri Ramswaroop Memorial Group of Professional Colleges, Lucknow

Bobby W. Lyall
Professor
Shri Ramswaroop Memorial Group of Professional Colleges, Lucknow

ALLIED PUBLISHERS PVT. LTD.

New Delhi • Mumbai • Kolkata • Chennai • Bangalore • Hyderabad

ALLIED PUBLISHERS PRIVATE LIMITED

1/13-14 Asaf Ali Road, **New Delhi**–110002
Ph.: 011-23239001 • E-mail: delhi.books@alliedpublishers.com

17 Chittaranjan Avenue, **Kolkata**–700072
Ph.: 033-22129618 • E-mail: cal.books@alliedpublishers.com

15 J.N. Heredia Marg, Ballard Estate, **Mumbai**–400001
Ph.: 022-42126969 • E-mail: mumbai.books@alliedpublishers.com

No. 25/10, Commander-in-Chief Road, Ethiraj Lane (Next to Post Office)
Egmore, **Chennai**–600008
Ph.: 044-28223938 • E-mail: chennai.books@alliedpublishers.com

P.B. No. 9932, No. 15, 3rd Floor (Next to Vijaya Bank), 5th Cross, Gandhinagar,
Karnataka, **Bangalore**–560009, Ph.: 080-41530285 / 22386239
• E-mail: bngl.journals@alliedpublishers.com / apsabng@airtelmail.in

Sri Jayalakshmi Nilayam, No. 3-4-510, 3rd Floor (Above More Super Market)
Barkatpura, **Hyderabad**–500027
Ph.: 040-27551811, 040-27551812 • E-mail: hyd.books@alliedpublishers.com

Website: www.alliedpublishers.com

ISBN: 978-93-89934-21-2

Published by Sunil Sachdev and printed by Ravi Sachdev at Allied Publishers Pvt. Ltd.,
1/13-14 Asaf Ali Road, New Delhi–110002

Preface

The capability of E-Commerce is not any more a matter of discussion. From the universe of promotion and dream, it has moved to that of digital reality and it has released one more transformation. Electronic Commerce affects a huge segment of the world, on business, and obviously, on individuals. We are on the verge of a revolution that is just as insightful as the change in the economy that came with the industrial revolution. Very soon big electronic business houses will permit individuals to rise above the boundaries of time and separation and exploit of worldwide business sectors and business openings not even believable today, opening up another world of financial chance and progress. Truly, this new advanced economy is majorly affecting the worldwide economy. E-Commerce business has enormous development potential and furthermore produces economic development in the country. We must recognize that E-Commerce will be the main impetus of economic and financial progress in country, particularly in India.

World faces an uncommon test and obligation to structure an E-Commerce procedure that, from one viewpoint, considers the advancement of E-Commerce and, then again, guarantees the social goal of giving access and advantages to the individuals who can't manage the cost of it. Electronic administration, open internet terminals, rural access subsidized cost and mindfulness are a part of the activities that must be considered as an aspect of this system which ought to guarantee that the administrative methodologies are straight-forward, fit, and free of explicit innovations.

Considering the way that E-Commerce helps in encouraging a positive business and regulatory condition, the book investigates the mechanics and usual way of doing things of E-Commerce. Additionally, it demonstrates how different components identified with E-Commerce add to the development of a lively and dynamic electronic network, bringing about financial and economic growth. It covers a wide range of issues under the umbrella of E-Commerce and the information based economy. In doing as such, it dives deep into the applicable issues and incorporates all advances associated with it. The sections of book further inspect the current and possible degree of E-Commerce exercises and recognize the difficulties and open doors for Indian business and the administration in the rising new economy.

Contents

Multi-Business Model Innovation in a World of E-Business, Omnichannel and Artificial Intelligence

Per Valter[1], Peter Lindgren[2] and Ramjee Prasad[3]

ABSTRACT: Very few people would argue against that e-business and its virtual nature has been a very successful business model in general and not only been a serious competing business model to the more traditional physical location-based retail business model, but to some extend threaten its very existents. Furthermore, the hole marked today, is not only divided into either virtual e-business or physical retail stores, more holistic business's trend has taken it even further with cross-channel content omnichannel strategies whereas the Latin word "Omnis" implies all/every channels shares a unified customer experience and thereby erasing the boundaries between the physical channels and the virtual channels from a customer experience perspective. Interesting this holistic view is not only pressured by the physical retail stores trying to defend their marked shares by entering the virtual e-business domain with a holistic approach, but also from virtual e-business domain trying to expand their marked shares by entering physical retail stores domain, the latter is usually done with a very high technology mindset, like when Amazon started the cashier-less grocery store concept called Amazon go, using machine learning and image recognition from hundreds of cameras within the store to eliminates the need for cashiers. In this context, this paper will examine if and how multi-business model innovation with its models and its relating digital innovations tools, would be able to create clarity, alignment, traceability and visualize potential business model ecosystems opportunities for today's business.

---

[1]CTIF Global Capsule, Business Development and Technology, Assistant Professor, Aarhus BSS, Aarhus University, Birk Centerpark 15, 7400 Herning, Denmark. E-mail: valter@btech.au.dk

[2]Professor of Innovation and New Business Development, Center for Industrial Production, Aalborg University, Denmark. E-mail: peterli@btech.au.dk

[3]Professor of Future Technologies for Business Ecosystem Innovation (FT4BI), Department of Business Development and Technology, Aarhus University, Denmark. E-mail: ramjee@btech.au.dk

Keywords: Multi-business Model Innovation, e-Business, Omnichannel, Artificial Intelligence, Business Model Ecosystems, Customer Experience, Digital Innovations Tools, Digitalization.

1. INTRODUCTION

In the first section of this article we will firstly examine the multi-business model innovation phenomena and secondly, we will examine the multi-business model innovation process. In the second section of this article the focus is shifted firstly towards e-business, omnichannel and secondly towards possible usage of artificial intelligence in combination with e-business, omnichannel and multi-business model innovation. Finally, in the last section with conclusions and future scope we list our conclusions and layout our suggestions for the future research scope with the combined fields of e-business, omni-channel, artificial intelligence and multi-business model innovation.

2. MULTI-BUSINESS MODEL INNOVATION AND PROCESS

In this first section of the article we will firstly examine the multi-business model innovation phenomena and secondly, we will examine the multi-business model innovation process. It's important to mention that we specifically going to examined multi-business model innovation and not just business model innovation, therefore we accept and believe the one organization can have many business models and not just one. If we look at previously proposed conceptual models[1, 2, 3] within the field of multi-business model innovation that supports digitalization and encompass artificial intelligence, then we would find the model advanced business model innovation supported by artificial intelligence and deep learning in Figure 1, this model have the business model ecosystem with its interrelated business models centralized and clearly distinguish between any human intermediary and machine intermediary that's either relay their perceptions of the business reality into the business models or apply the business model into the reality. Furthermore, the model's artificial intelligence part with business model patterns analysis and deep learning evaluate and make suggestions to changes within a business models or even the change of entire business models.

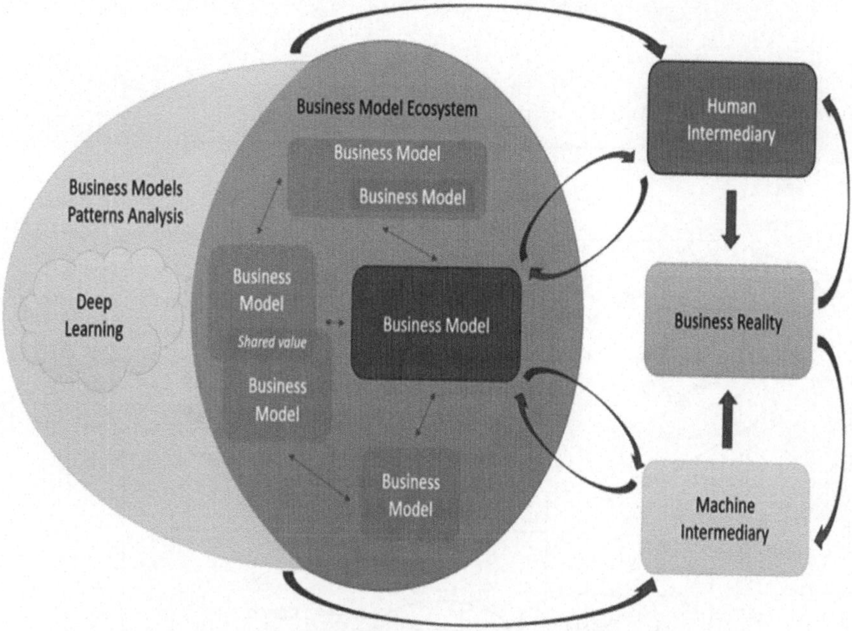

Fig. 1: From Advanced Business Model Innovation Supported by Artificial Intelligence and Deep Learning[3]

Other previously published result based on empirical experiments have looked more into the actual process of conducting multi-business model innovation,[4,5] where sensors where measuring various parameter like Temperature, CO2 level, Pressure, Humidity, 360-degree video recordings, emotion detecting and heart rates of the participants within serval multi-business model sessions, based on these results the model Valter's Seven Forces[6] in Figure 2 was later published, this model shows the seven categories of dominating forces that influence the results of the business model innovation process in either at positive or negative way, the seven categories of forces are as follows: emotions forces, group forces, individual forces, environments and tools, coach, process space, competition space. It's important to remember that the multi-business model process is a complex system with many dependent variables, therefore even if you have the most skilled and qualified participants in the world it not a guaranty for good results if for example other forces like the process space and the completion space are highly negatively affected with lets say insufficient time and high competition in the marked by large companies with huge funds available at their disposal.

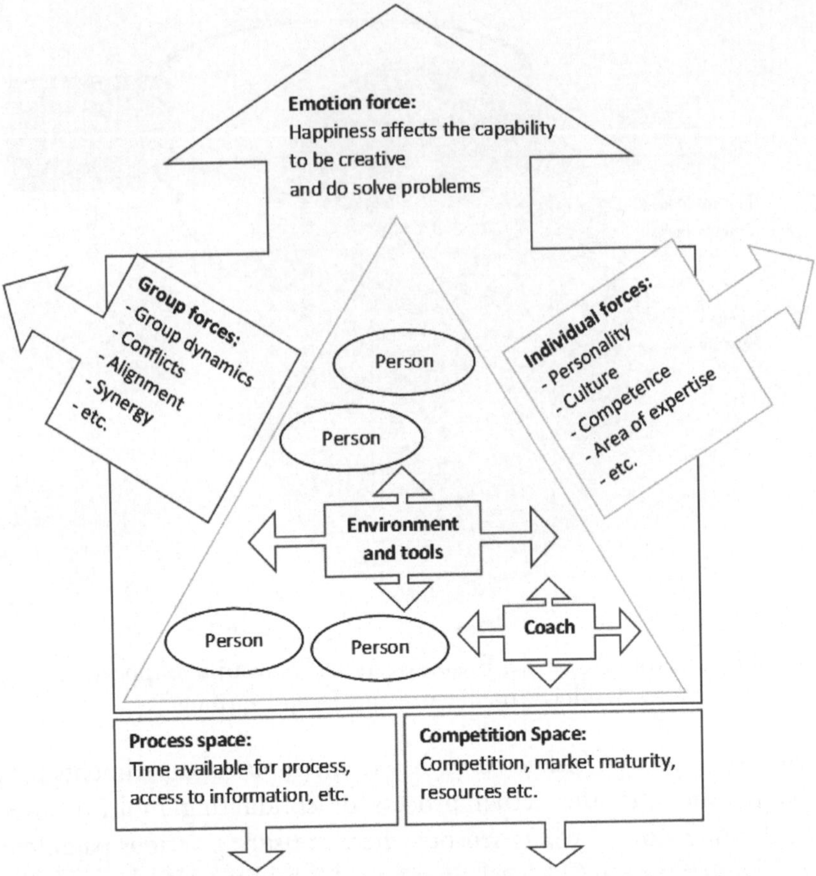

Fig. 2: Figure from—Valter's Seven Forces; a model for analyzing the forces affecting the business model innovation process[6]

3. E-BUSINESS, OMNICHANNEL AND ARTIFICIAL INTELLIGENCE

In this section of this article the focus is shifted firstly towards e-business, omnichannel and secondly towards possible usage of artificial intelligence in combination with e-business, omnichannel and multi-business model innovation. E-business, omnichannel and artificial intelligence are all very large and broad concepts that already have been researched and written many research articles about, this article will as an example narrow its focus into examined the how multi-business model innovation could be used to facilitate improve or even generate new omnichannel delivery business models, also we adopt the terminology from the article omnichannel fulfillment strategies: defining the concept and building an agenda for future inquiry[7] see Figure 3 with the division into omnichannel demand-side, omnichannel fulfilment strategies and omnichannel delivery.

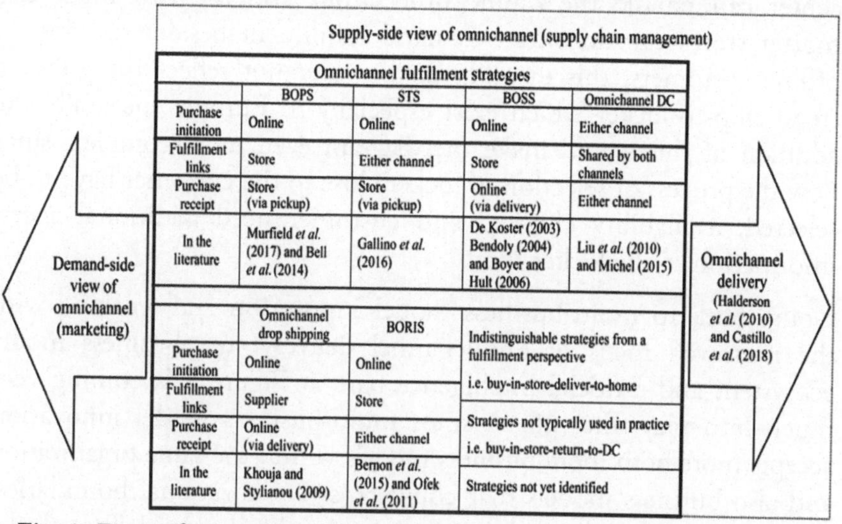

Fig. 3: Figure from—Omnichannel Fulfillment Strategies: Defining the Concept and Building an Agenda for Future Inquiry[7]

With the focus narrowed into the delivery part of the omnichannel, the resent published article multi-period price optimization problem for omnichannel retailers accounting for customer heterogeneity,[8] shows a diagram, see Figure 4, that shows some of the complexity

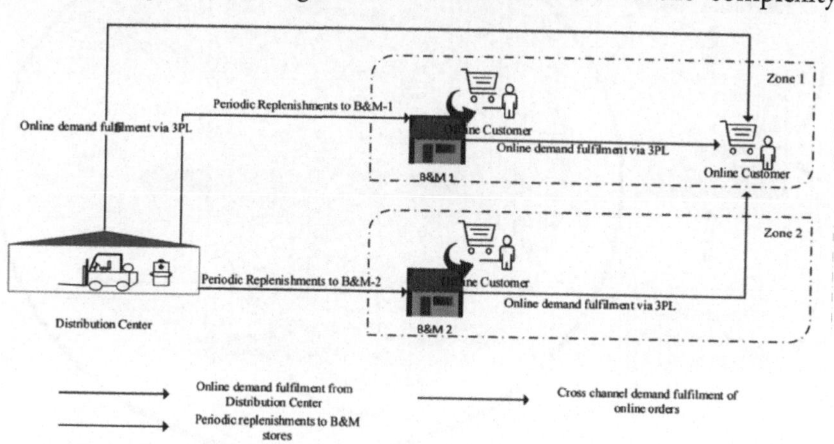

Fig. 4: Figure from—Multi-Period Price Optimization Problem for Omnichannel Retailers Accounting for Customer Heterogeneity[8]

B&Ms have delivering product to their customers, the diagram shows a distribution center that periodically do replenishment to two brick and mortar stores in different zones, furthermore, the distribution center can handle the online orders, but also the two brick and mortar stores can do online demand fulfillment besides severing its offline customers, this diagram do however not reflect the growing trend ship-to-locker which exist especially in Europe[7] naturally the addition of this would make the diagram even more complex, since now the process of selection of locker close to the customer have to be selected, availability checked and customer need additional access information to the locker.

Going back to multi-business model innovation and working with the narrowed focus of omnichannel delivery, the business model ecosystem and artificial intelligence part of Figure 5 is coming very much into play, first of all, since multi-business model innovation accepts more both more business models within the same organization and also business models that could cross organizational boundaries, it would be possible to be more creative in the modeling of the business model ecosystem, let for example think of other business

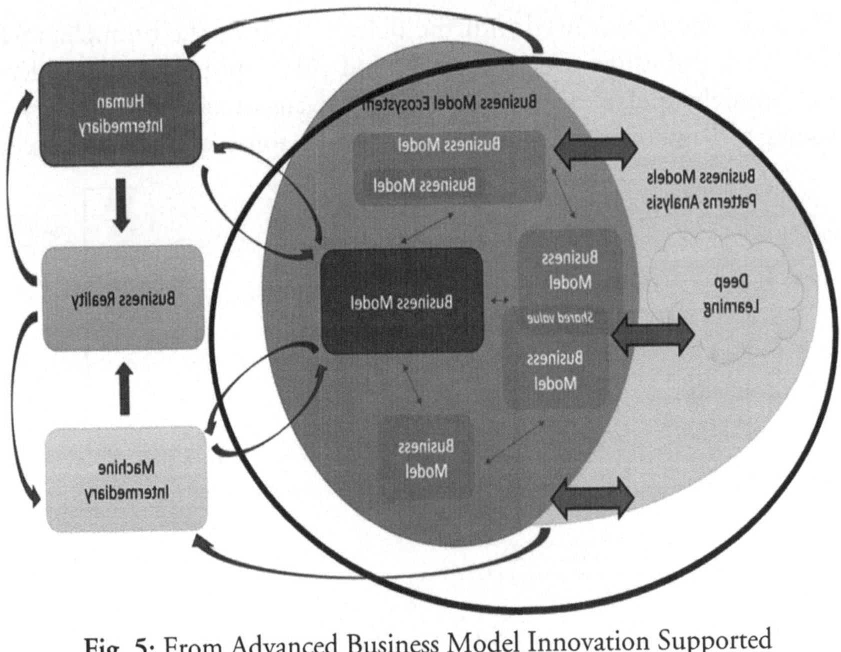

Fig. 5: From Advanced Business Model Innovation Supported by Artificial Intelligence and Deep Learning[3]

models for delivering products to customers, the business model pattern analysis might after having realized that other successful business model for transporting persons, let's say uber, suggest another distributive business model for delivery of packages where people could sign up and deliver package on their normal routes of driving and this way earn some extra money for a trip they would have done anyway and also save the environment for some CO_2 since now another vehicle doesn't need to drive those kilometers, another example could also be to create pick up point at your personal home and receive money for having a location that many people would pass by during their day, when the boundaries between organizations, industries and even private persons themselves are removed, many possibilities, combinations and synergies are emerging. Of course, not all the possible combination of synergies would be possible for all organizations to capture, since some might require heavy investments to fulfill, but without looking they would never know.

4. CONCLUSIONS AND FUTURE SCOPE

- Firstly, we examined the multi-business model innovation phenomena, where we discussed the model advanced business model innovation supported by artificial intelligence and deep learning.
- Secondly, we examined examine the multi-business model innovation process, where we discussed the model Valter's Seven Forces.
- Thirdly, we examined the concepts of e-business, omnichannel, where we discussed the categorization used in previous published omnichannel fulfillment strategies.
- Fourthly we narrowed or focus to omnichannel delivery and multi-business model innovation.
- Finally, we discussed the possible use of multi-business model innovation in omnichannel delivery context with examples.
- Within the topic of multi-business model innovation in e-business, omnichannel with artificial intelligence, there research has just begun and as such many research paths exist from here, one suggested path could be to empirical test to what extent the multi-business model innovation process is able to make brake down the barriers between organizations, industries and even private persons themselves to create true value for the ecosystems as a whole.

REFERENCES

[1] Valter, P., Lindgren, P. and Prasad, R. (2017). Artificial intelligence and deep learning in a world of humans and persuasive business models. 2017 *Global Wireless Summit (GWS)*, Cape Town, 2017, pp. 209–214.

[2] Valter, P., Lindgren, P. and Prasad, R. (2018). "The consequences of artificial intelligence and deep learning in a world of persuasive business models," in *IEEE Aerospace and Electronic Systems Magazine*, Vol. 33, No. 5–6, pp. 80–88, May–June 2018.

[3] Valter, P., Lindgren, P. and Prasad, R. (2018, April). Advanced Business Model Innovation Supported by Artificial Intelligence and Deep Learning. *Wireless Personal Communications,* 100, 1, s. 97–111.

[4] Lindgren, P., Valter, P. and Kingo, G. (2018). Sensing Multi Business Model Innovation via advanced sensor technology. *Nordic and Baltic Journal of Information and Communications Technologies.*

[5] Lindgren, P., Valter, P., Tonchev, K., Manolova, A., Neshov, N., Poulkov, V. (2018). Digitizing Human Behavior with wireless sensors in Biogas 2020. *Technological Business Model Innovation challenges.* In press; Wireless Personal Communications.

[6] Valter, P., Lindgren, P. and Prasad, R. (2018). Valter's Seven Forces; a model for analyzing the forces affecting the business model innovation process. *Nordic and Baltic Journal of Information and Communications Technologies.*

[7] Taylor, D., Brockhaus, S., Knemeyer, A. and Murphy, P. (2019). "Omnichannel fulfillment strategies: defining the concept and building an agenda for future inquiry", *International Journal of Logistics Management*, Vol. 30 No. 3, pp. 863–891. https://doi.org/10.1108/IJLM-09-2018-0223.

[8] Gupta, Vishal Kumar, Ting, Q.U. and Tiwari, Manoj Kumar (2019). Multi-period price optimization problem for omnichannel retailers accounting for customer heterogeneity, *International Journal of Production Economics*, Vol. 212, pp. 155–167, ISSN 0925-5273, https://doi.org/10.1016/j.ijpe.2019.02.016.

Online to Offline Commerce: An Analysis of Online to Offline Business Model w.s.r. Rural E-Commerce

B.B. Tiwari[1] and Bobby W. Lyall[1]

ABSTRACT: Customers' offline experiences and perceptions affect their online perceptions, which in turn affect their online purchase intentions. However, customers' experiences on an online platform also affect their offline behavior. With the improvement of the Internet, the combination of on the web and offline channels for organizations has received expanding consideration. Growing number of quantities of enterprises are selling their goods and services through both on the online and offline channels. For instance, the retailing and banking ventures have expanded their organizations with online channels and energized their clients to utilize online services by improving clients' offline encounters. Thus, offline channels can increase the usage of online channels. This effective mode is known as Online to Offline (O2O) business. Be that as it may, not all ventures can create practical online channels to pull in clients' consideration. In this way, numerous conventional offline undertakings depend vigorously on well known on the web offices to sell items or administrations. We concentrate on the online-to-offline (O2O) aspect of the business that differentiates it from other e-commerce platforms—its strong connection to local markets. We focus on travel cost and store density, the key local characteristics that affect consumer deal demand and merchant deal offering.

***Keywords:** Online to Offline Commerce, Internet & Mobile Association of India (IAMAI), Rural E-Commerce.*

1. BACKGROUND

E-commerce sector was focusing urban market rather than rural areas, but now the trend is changing and they are shifting their focus on the rural areas. Rural commerce means the commercialization of e business in rural areas including semi-urban areas including tier

[1]Professor, Shri Ramswaroop Memorial Group of Professional Colleges, Lucknow.

IV & V cities which are small towns, kasbas or rural local markets in deep rural areas. These urban market were consisting of tier-I, II & III cities which were generally the big cities including metro-cities. Quite a number of times, the items are manufactured locally in deep rural villages or kasbas or small towns and is shipped to big cities for sale again they are again reshipped to local towns for sale with a big tag or big brand name to final destination, but now this tradition is somewhat changing. Some of e commerce companies are trying to provide these products to local customer through local venders and manufacturers through the stores like storeking, bakarangi Kendra etc. Some times in the deep rural areas or towns major difficulties are faced by the consumers' of not getting the products in the local market. They have to travel 30 to 40 km for the product for which the travelling cost is more than its price. If e-commerce companies will start such kind of facility or online store with rural delivery with the facility of cash on delivery, it will not only improve the local education level but also will lead a future perspective market for the e-commerce companies. For this kind of change the companies can take the initiative of localizing their websites in rural language like snapdeal to focus the local market. The companies who are reaching the rural market they are also helping the government of India in taking a step forward towards digitalization. This will also help the rural youth getting the job through delivery services, third parties or logistics support to the companies. In India only postal department has enough power to connect the whole country in one go. It has its presence even in the deepest remote areas of the country. With the emergence of computer and email and development of information technology this department had been facing the losses for last many years and was facing a existence problem, but with the emergence of rural e-commerce this department has witnessed a dramatic growth in last few years by collaborating more than 400 small and big e commerce companies a logistic partner.

2. INTRODUCTION

The fast advancement of data innovation empowers an expanding number of customers to look and book items/administrations online first and afterward to devour them in physical stores. This new web based business model is called online to offline (O2O) online business and has gotten significant administrative and scholarly consideration.

With the improvement of the Internet, the combination of on the web and offline channels for organizations has received expanding consideration. Growing number of quantities of enterprises are selling their goods and services through both on the online and offline channels. For instance, the retailing and banking ventures have expanded their organizations with online channels and energized their clients to utilize online services by improving clients' offline encounters. Thus, offline channels can increase the usage of online channels. This mode of offline-online integration has been widely applied in the multichannel context (Bock *et al.*, 2012; Jin *et al.*, 2010; Yang *et al.*, 2013).

By joining on the web deals channels, conventional offline endeavors can likewise flexibly assorted kinds of administrations (Cassab and MacLachlan, 2006). Clients can peruse lists, check the value data and accessibility of items on the web, and even spot arranges previously visiting offline stores. Subsequently, online channels can expand the deals of offline channels. This effective mode is known as online to offline (O2O) business. Be that as it may, not all ventures can create practical online channels to pull in clients' consideration. In this way, numerous conventional offline undertakings depend vigorously on well known on the web offices to sell items or administrations. For instance, numerous inns work with online travel offices (OTAs, for example, Trivago and Ctrip, to advance and sell their rooms). Customers' offline experiences and perceptions affect their online perceptions, which in turn affect their online purchase intentions. Kwon and Lennon (2009) investigated consumers' online loyalty in the multichannel retailing context. The results revealed that a positive offline brand image of a retailer increases the retailer's online brand image. Bock *et al.* (2012) found that offline trust influences online trust in multichannel retailers' online operations. In the e-commerce context, customers' perceived offline service quality also influences their perceived online service quality (Yang *et al.*, 2011; Verhagen and Dolen, 2009).

However, customers' experiences on an online platform also affect their offline behavior. Xiang and Stanley (2017) reported that patient and doctor interactions on an online platform affect patients' intentions to visit doctors in brick and mortar hospitals. The interaction can even improve the quality of offline patient service. Gallino and Moreno (2014) confirmed that presenting the inventory information for physical retail stores increases customers' intentions to shop at physical stores. Phang *et al.* (2014) found that product promotion on a social media website affects offline sales in retail businesses.

Based on prior research (Jin *et al.*, 2010; Kwon and Lennon, 2009; Yang *et al.*, 2013), the integration of online and offline channels can be explained by the halo effect. The halo effect refers to a cognitive bias in which an observer's overall impression of a person, company, brand, or product influences his/her perception of the characteristics of the entity. If an observer likes one characteristic of the entity, then he/she will have a positive perception toward other characteristics. If an observer dislikes one characteristic of the entity, then he/she will have a negative perception toward other characteristics (Thorndike, 1920). Therefore, this study uses the halo effect to explain how online and offline satisfaction increase behavioral intentions toward online and offline channels

3. LITERATURE REVIEW

Customers' offline experiences and perceptions affect their online perceptions, which in turn affect their online purchase intentions. Kwon and Lennon (2009) investigated consumers' online loyalty in the multichannel retailing context. The results revealed that a positive offline brand image of a retailer increases the retailer's online brand image. Bock *et al.* (2012) found that offline trust influences online trust in multichannel retailers' online operations. In the e-commerce context, customers' perceived offline service quality also influences their perceived online service quality (Yang *et al.*, 2011; Verhagen and Dolen, 2009).

However, customers' experiences on an online platform also affect their offline behavior. Xiang and Stanley (2017) reported that patient and doctor interactions on an online platform affect patients' intentions to visit doctors in brick and mortar hospitals. The interaction can even improve the quality of offline patient service. Gallino and Moreno (2014) confirmed that presenting the inventory information for physical retail stores increases customers' intentions to shop at physical stores. Phang *et al.* (2014) found that product promotion on a social media website affects offline sales in retail businesses.

Based on prior research (Jin *et al.*, 2010; Kwon and Lennon, 2009; Yang *et al.*, 2013), the integration of online and offline channels can be explained by the halo effect. The halo effect refers to a cognitive bias in which an observer's overall impression of a person, company, brand, or product influences his/her perception of the characteristics of the entity. If an observer likes one characteristic of the entity, then he/she will have a positive perception toward other characteristics. If an observer dislikes one characteristic of the entity, then he/she will have a negative perception toward other characteristics (Thorndike, 1920). Therefore, this study uses the halo effect to explain how online and offline satisfaction increase behavioral intentions toward online and offline channels.

4. OBJECTIVE OF THE STUDY

We have the following objective to analyse in this paper.

- In this paper we want to find out the problem and prospects for e-commerce companies in rural areas (offline market as well) by examining the penetration level of internet education level required to use the online platform.
- For this kind of business (Online and Offline) and growth prospects for e-commerce companies in rural areas.
- We would also analyse the rural economy in form of education, employment, living standard and consumption pattern.
- The scope and analysis of reputation management business model in rural areas.

5. URBAN-RURAL DIFFERENCES IN INTERNET USAGE

The latest report by the Internet & Mobile Association of India (IAMAI) and Nielsen showed rural India had 227 million active internet users 10% more than urban India's about 205 million, as of November 2019 (TOI, May 6, 2020). There are around 71 million kids, aged 5–11 years, who go online using devices of family members. With this, India surpassed another milestone of having 504 million active internet users who are 5 years old or above—53 million more than 451 million in March 2019. Active internet users are defined as those who use the internet at least once a month (TOI, May 6, 2020).

With 265 million internet users, rural India is not only catching up with cities in terms of the sheer number of netizens, it is also mirroring the time spent, frequency, share of female users and mode of access with its urban cousin. And, while internet usage might look similar on the surface, the activities which urban and rural users engage in online are different, according to data and insights by leading research firm Kantar (TOI June 11, 2020).

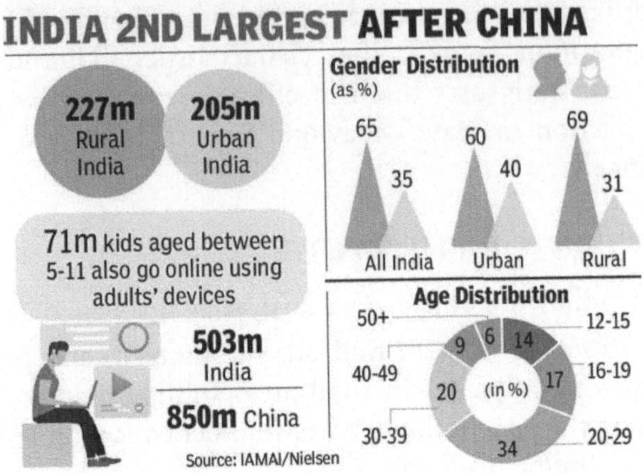

Fig. 1

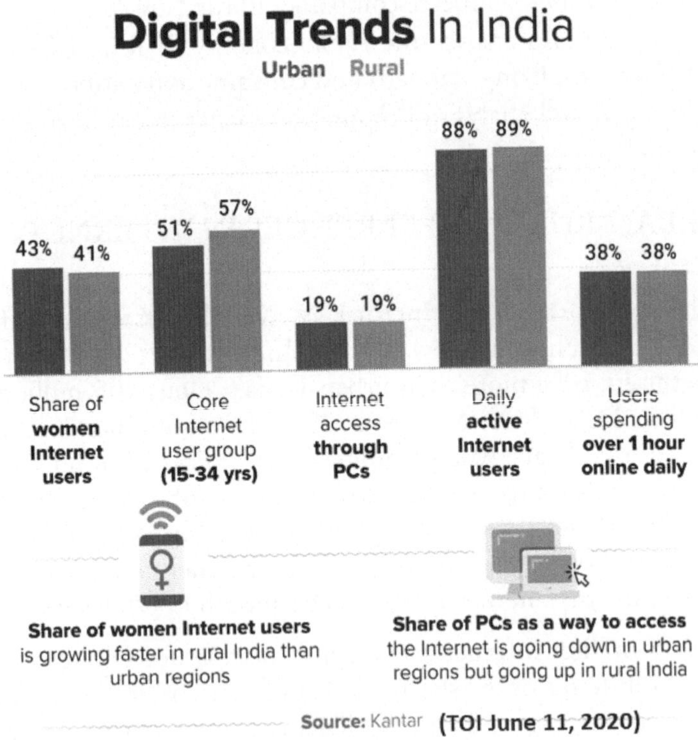

Fig. 2

Moreover, while urban India is close to reaching saturation levels with around 60% of the population having access to the internet; the headroom for growth in rural areas remains massive. The number of daily active users in rural India is 89%, versus 88% for cities and towns, with close to 40% of users in both regions spending over one hour accessing the internet daily. There is not much difference in the demographic or the overall usage and duration as well. But the moment we look at the usages, there's a significant difference. So, basically what this means is that, there are fewer activities that rural users are doing, but they're doing it for a longer period of time (TOI June 11, 2020).

6. REPUTATION MANAGEMENT MODEL IN O2O (OFFLINE TO ONLINE) BUSINESS

It's not stunning news that everybody utilizes the web to access and offer data. Individuals request items and administrations through sites and portable applications, and so on. You get the point. So it's critical to take note of that in the event that you sell any item or administration, individuals are going to search for audits, and do their due intensity before they buy. Many people first search for an item, organization, brand or expert through an internet searcher. Notwithstanding, the ascent of Youtube and other online media influencers likewise is a marker that surveys do make a difference and what individuals state about your item, administrations, brand, does as well.

To begin with, in the O2O (offline to online) internet business market, notoriety the executives needs to address members from both on the web and offline settings (e.g., online purchasers and physical eateries on Yelp). To give exact notoriety evaluation results, the notoriety the executives in this situation needs to gather both on the web and offline crude notoriety related data, while surviving notoriety the board frameworks/models mostly center around the data gathered from either an on the web or offline setting alone. Second, notoriety the executives in O2O web based business needs to take the change request data and offline dealers' genuine assistance capacities into account while assessing their notorieties. Not quite the same as these conventional web based business models, clients in the O2O web based business market expend the online-held items/administrations in physical stores. Each offline dealer has restricted help limit; if the quantity of customers who visit a trader surpasses its most extreme limit in a specific timeframe, its item/administration quality might be influenced. This infers an offline shipper will most likely be unable to give purchasers items/benefits that are predictable with those asserted on the web. Therefore, to check offline dealers' over-burden activity conduct, notoriety the board in the O2O web based business ought to consider their variance requests and their genuine assistance limits. Third, the prescient notoriety data about offline shippers can enable online shoppers to pick proper item/specialist organizations and decide their utilization time ahead of time. The extraction of prescient notoriety data, while achievable in the O2O situation, isn't considered by the surviving notoriety the executives frameworks.

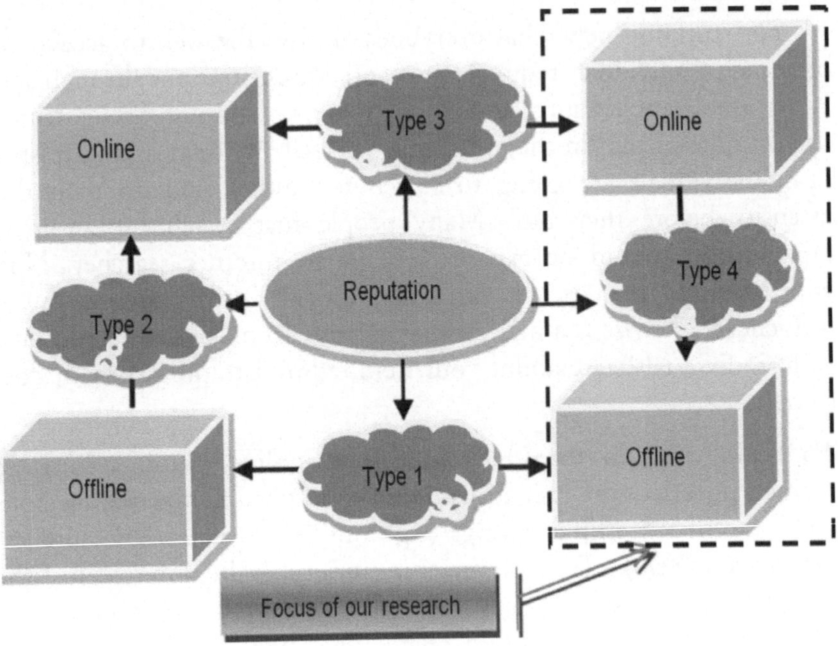

Fig. 3: Four Types of Reputation Management Research

For example, in order to provide precise reputation evaluation results for restaurants on Yelp, reputation information managers should use not only the online information such as online reviews but also some offline information about brick-and-mortar restaurants (e.g., the restaurants' reputation-related records such as real regulatory compliance records, industry standard compliance records and health inspection records).

7. HOW DOES ONLINE REPUTATION MANAGEMENT IMPACT BUSINESS?

The most exceedingly terrible thing you can say is that you are the main items or administrations out there in the market. There are 1,673,535,333 sites on the web as per Netcraft's October 2018 Web Server Survey and around 380 new sites are made each moment. This means at every second, somebody may make a fresh out of the brand new organization (simply like yours) and make a superior showing. So to stand apart you must be incredible for what it's worth. Your online notoriety ought to mirror this through surveys and verbal. You may endure weighty misfortunes in your business if negative substance or a terrible client experience becomes a web sensation. It might be just an infrequent irregular occurrence yet in the event that you don't counter these reports appropriately, you will have a major issue in your grasp. Individuals will accept the majority of your items are terrible or you may get known for helpless assistance.

8. CONCLUSION

From the perspective of online to offline channels, customer online satisfaction and intentions to book hotels via OTA websites affects the intention to visit hotels. From the perspective of offline to online channels, customer offline satisfaction affects the intention to book hotels. Thus, these findings demonstrate that customers tend to visit hotels when hotels and OTAs have better cooperation with each other.

Additionally, this paper posits and confirms the factors that increase online and offline satisfaction. System quality, information quality, and service quality are found to affect online satisfaction, and emotional value and social value are found to affect offline satisfaction. These findings can help hotels and OTAs to improve customer satisfaction, which in turn increases customers' behavioral intentions toward online and offline channels. Because satisfaction is the most important predictor of customer intentions to visit hotels, OTAs should cooperate with hotels that satisfy customers, and hotels should cooperate with OTAs that satisfy customers.

REFERENCES

[1] Doney, P.M. and Cannon, J.P., "An examination of the nature of trust in buyer–seller relationships", *The Journal of Marketing*, 61(2), (1997), 35–51.

[2] Golbeck, J.K. and Ramachandran, D., Computing with social trust, in: M. wan (Ed.), Trust and Online Reputation Systems, Springer, London 2009, pp. 287–311.

[3] Jin, B., Park, J.Y. and Kim, J. (2010). "Joint influence of online store attributes and offline operations on performance of multichannel retailers", *Behaviour and Information Technology*, Vol. 29, No. 1, pp. 85–96.

[4] Jin, B., Park, J.Y. and Kim, J. (2010). "Joint influence of online store attributes and offline operations on performance of multichannel retailers", *Behaviour and Information Technology*, Vol. 29, No. 1, pp. 85–96.

[5] Lee, K.C., Kang, I. and McKnight, D.H., Transfer from offline trust to key online percep- tions: an empirical study, *IEEE Transactions on Engineering* Management, 54 (4), (2007), 729–741.

[6] Rice, S.C., Reputation and uncertainty in online markets: An experimental study, Information Systems Research, 23(2), (2012), 436–452.

[7] Ruohomaa, S. and Kutvonen, L. "Trust management survey", Trust Management, 3477 (2005) 77–92.

[8] Sabater, J. and Sierra, C., "Review on computational trust and reputation models, Artificial Intelligence" Review, 24(1), (2005), 33–60.

[9] Stewart, K.J., Trust transfer on the world wide web, Organization Science, 14(1), (2003), 5–17.

[10] Times of India, June 11, 2020-https://tech.economictimes.indiatimes.com/news/internet/bharat-is-keeping-step-with-india-on-internet-usage-and-patterns/76310260

[11] Times of India, May 6, 2020, http://timesofindia.indiatimes.com/articleshow/75566025.cms?utm_source=contentofinterest&utm_medium=text&utm_campaign=cppst

[12] Wang, Y. and Vassileva, J., "Toward trust and reputation based web service selection: a survey, International Transactions on Systems Science and Applications", 3(2), (2007) 118–132.

[13] Yang, S., Lu, Y., Zhao, L. and Gupta, S. (2011). "Empirical investigation of customers' channel extension behavior: Perceptions shift toward the online channel", *Computers in Human Behavior*, Vol. 27, No. 5, pp. 1688–1696.

[14] Zhou, M., Dresner, M. and Windle, R.J., Online reputation systems: design and strategic practices, *Decision Support Systems*, 44(4), (2008), 785–797.

Analyzing the Ethical Role of Customer Towards Online Marketing

Priya*

ABSTRACT: Over the past two decades, online marketing has become a major channel for selling products and services around the globe. Online marketing get popularity due to their inevitable features. But this method of doing business has resulted in numerous conflicts between customer, sellers and vendors, as unexpected challenges and ethical problem have arisen. Authentic information about product, fast and accurate delivery of product, not sharing or misusing customer card number, personal information and purchase history, adequate and quick customer services drew attention towards ethical responsibilities of online business. But what about customer, are they adopted ethical approach while purchasing product online. The main objective of this paper is to examine the ethical role of customer towards online-marketing. To discover the facts or ways by which customer behave unethically and also suggest measures to resolve it. The research findings are based on the responses obtained with the help of self-structured questionnaire from the sample of 150 from Lucknow city only. Exploratory and descriptive research design has been used and data has been calculated with the help of descriptive statistic. Due to their small sample size and restricted research area the findings of this study cannot be generalized, so I would suggest further research on large sample to validate findings.

Keywords: *Online Marketing, Ethical Issues, Ethical Responsibility, Ethical Decision Making.*

1. INTRODUCTION

The internet, one of the greatest inventions of the 20th century, is being used in various fields of our everyday lives, as well as in contemporary business world. As a result of the global spread of the internet, a remarkable increase has been observed in the number of web-based retailers that provide certain advantages' such as more information, easier services and increased control for consumers

*Institute of Management Sciences, University of Lucknow, Lucknow, Uttar Pradesh, India. E-mail: drpriya.ims@gmail.com; priya_16_04@yahoo.co.in

(Liu and Goodhue 2008, Tsai *et al.,* 2006). According to the statistics, the number of internet users has reached 3 billion worldwide and among the top 20 internet user countries in 2019, India is on second position with 568 million internet users.

Slow internet connections, intangibility of product (not to touch), electronic methods of payment and lack of trust are the few drawbacks of online marketing. Regardless of these problems, there has been an increase in online shopping expenditures of people (Wolfinbarger and Gilly 2003) and consumers have begun to adapt to into online retailing (hereafter e-retailing) practices (Lohse *et al.,* 2000). Online marketing is today seen by many practitioners as the new arena for market communication and on top of the list of users of the different mediums is Facebook, Blogs, Twitter, YouTube and LinkedIn. These trends indicate that electronic retailing has become an important alternative to conventional shopping channels (Pavlou and Gefen 2004). Speed and capability to adopt new things very easily are the most important features of online market. Especially quickly changing environment is online market because the popularity of e-shopping is growing every day.

Perceived risk by consumers is one of the primary factors that makes them refrain from online shopping and prevents the establishment of customer loyalty (Rust *et al.,* 2002). Therefore, creating trust and transferring it to customers are very crucial points for turning visitors of e-retailers into loyal customers (Schlosser *et al.,* 2006). Now marketer is more focused on ethical issues which may emerged in online mode. It is the ethical responsibility of marketer that they provide proper information about product, their uses, expiry date, manufacturing details, quality product, customer data should be kept confidential like card number, online banking details, contact address and number. It means marketers should adopt ethical practices but question is that what ethics is? Ethics seeks an answer to the question "what is good" (Pires and Stanton 2002), it creates a line of discipline between what is desirable and undesirable, what is good and what is bad. Ethics of marketing is defined as ethical judgments applicable to decisions, applications and attitudes of marketing (Gaski 1999). E-retailing ethics is defined as the responsibility of e-retailers, including their trust-worthy, fair and honest behaviors towards customers and safeguarding the interests of their customers (Roman, 2007).

By this it is now clear that marketer ethical responsibilities will always influence customer preferences and success of online marketing. The main purpose of the present study is beyond this sphere and more focused on customer ethical behavior towards online marketing. If the marketer provides prompt and adequate services to the customer than it is also the responsibility of customer to behave ethically. Present study also tries to explore the various ways by which customer respond unethically and suggest some measures for both.

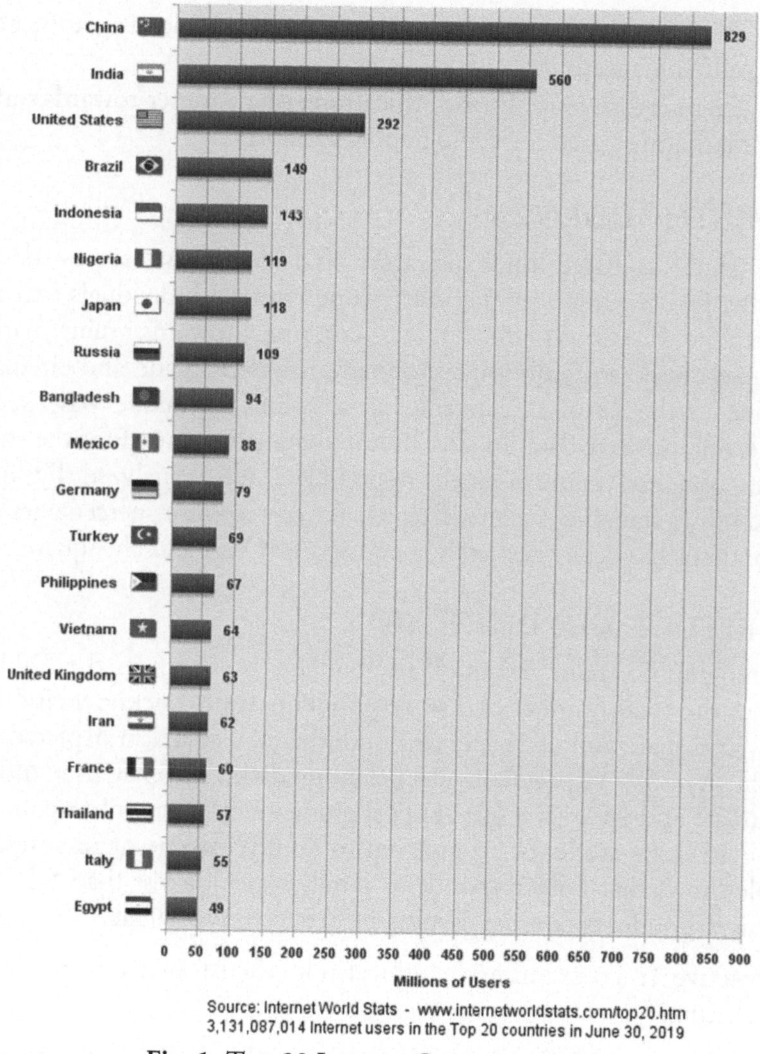

Fig. 1: Top 20 Internet Countries, 2019 with the Highest Number of Internet Users

2. OBJECTIVE OF STUDY

1. To examine the ethical role of customer towards online marketing.
2. To analyze the ethical role of customer towards online marketing based on demographic variables.
3. To explore the unethical means of customers towards online marketing.

3. HYPOTHESES OF STUDY

1. There is a significant relation between ethical role of customer and online marketing.
2. There is difference in the ethical role of customer towards online marketing based on demographic variables.

4. METHODOLOGY

The study is based on exploratory and descriptive survey design. Firstly, focused interview has been done with 10 individuals and tries to explore the various ethical role of customers towards online marketing. Secondly, structured questionnaire has been made and circulated online to the sample. Convenience sampling technique was used in collecting primary data. In all 150 respondents were used for the study. Data obtained from selected respondents were analyzed by using descriptive statistics such as frequencies of response, percentages and hypothesis has been checked by one-way ANOVA and chi-square.

5. RESULT AND DISCUSSION

Demographic characteristic of respondents is shown in the Table 1. From the total number of 150 respondents from Lucknow city there are 56% male and 44% female respondents. Table also depicted that 26% (n = 39) respondents are below graduation, 33% (n = 49) are graduate and 41% (n = 62) are post graduate. Majority of respondents (n = 132) are students. As concern to family income of respondents, table shows that 56% respondents families earning less than 5 lac and 28% respondents families earning in between 6 to 10 lac.

Objective 1: To examine the ethical role of customer towards online marketing.

H1: There is a significant relation between ethical role of customer and online marketing.

Table 1: Demographic Profile of Respondents

Characteristics		*Frequency*	*Percentage*
Gender	Male	84	56%
	Female	56	44%
Age	Below 20	51	34%
	21–25	87	58%
	26–30	8	5.3%
	31–35	2	1.3%
	36–40	1	0.6%
	Above 40	1	0.6%
Occupation	Businessmen	3	2%
	Service	10	6.6%
	Student	132	88%
	Other	5	3.4%
Academic Qualification	Below UG	39	26%
	UG	49	33%
	PG	62	41%
Family Income	Below 5 Lac	84	56%
	6–10 Lac	42	28%
	11–15 Lac	11	7.4%
	More than 15 Lac	13	8.6%

Outcome: At 5% level of significance, the critical (tabulated) value of $\chi2$ for degree of freedom (df) is (23) = 41.113 (As $\chi2$ calculated > $\chi2$ tabulated) Since the value of chi-square calculated is more than the tabulated chi-square (Table 2). Null hypothesis is rejected and alternative hypothesis is accepted. There is a significant relation between ethical role of customer and online marketing. It also analyzed that customers are always adopting ethical behavior while doing shopping online.

To determine the level of ethical role of customers towards online marketing percentage frequency distribution has been used. Figure 3 shows that more than half of the respondents are used to buy product online especially food items are not included in this categories,

Table 2: Chi-Square Table of Selected Respondents

Dimension	*Calculated Chi-Square Value*	*Degree of Freedom*	*Table Value (at 5%)*	*Null Hypothesis*	*Result*
Significant relation between ethical role of customer and online marketing	746.9	23	41.113	Rejected	Significant

otherwise it may raise to the 90%. While ordering items from online mode 63% never returned the used ones and 29% rarely done this. Almost 36% respondents are replacing some part of product with damaged parts and claim for new product from vendor and 41% respondents never involve in such unethical practices. Frequently cancelled product because of any reason also lies under the unethical practice, 45% respondents rarely do this and 36% usually or sometimes cancelled the product. If it is the responsibility of marketer to provide prompt and adequate product/services to the customers than customers also must show the sense of responsiveness. 5% of respondents usually and 25% sometime are not available for delivery person at schedule time along with 39% who rarely not available for the same.

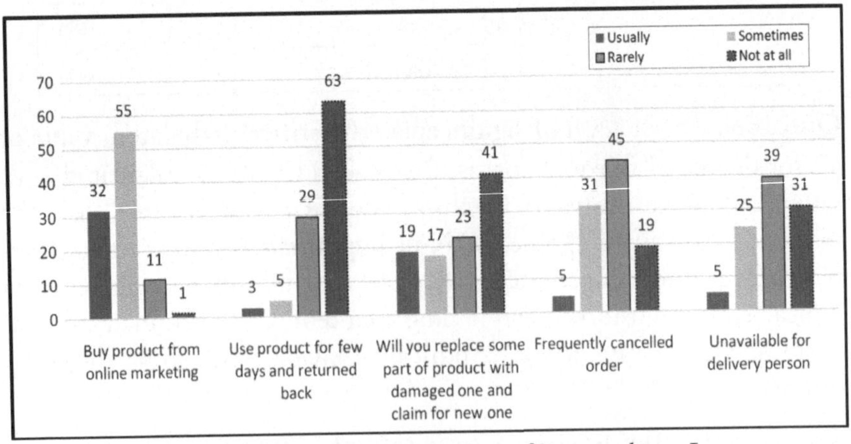

Fig. 2: Percentage Distribution of Respondents-I

While asking about the unavailability for delivery person due to non-availability of cash, 75% respondents says that they never do such practices. Figure 4 depicted that 86% respondent are not deliberately posting negative feedback or comment and trying to get benefits for the same. Majority of respondents were not deliberately provided their improper information details only for fun. Customers are sometimes order their product from more than one company and reject the other companies' product while they received product from anyone of them, 77% respondents show that they are not involve in such activities at all. 3% usually, 17% sometimes, 19% rarely and 61% not at all order multiple items through multiple companies and selecting the best one and returned back other items.

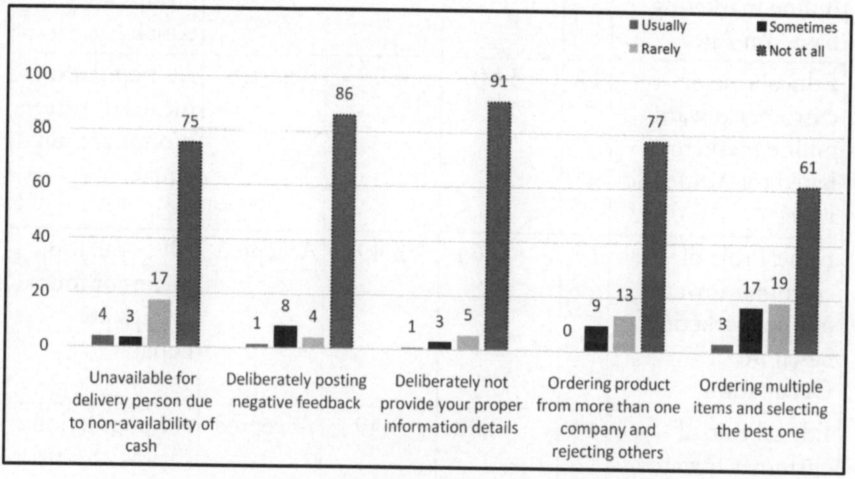

Fig. 3: Percentage Distribution of Respondents-II

Objective 2: To analyze the ethical role of customer towards online marketing based on demographic variables.

H2: There is difference in the ethical role of customer towards online marketing based on demographic variables.

Outcome: To determine whether any of the differences between the means of gender, age, academic level, occupation and family income are statistically significant, compare the p-value at significance level to assess the null hypothesis. The null hypothesis states that the population means are all equal. Usually, a significance level of 0.01 works well. A significance level of 0.01 indicates a 1% risk of concluding that a difference exists when there is no actual difference. Table 3 shows the difference in the ethical role of customer towards online marketing based on gender, age, academic level, occupation and family income.

Table 3: Difference in Ethical Role towards Online Marketing on Demographic Basis

Dimensions	*d.f.*	*F calculated*	*F tabulated*	*Null hypothesis*	*Result*
Ethical role of customer towards online marketing based on Gender	9	40.6	5.19	Rejected	All population means of two groups are not equal.
Ethical role of customer towards online marketing based on Age	15	1.71	3.49	Accepted	All population means of four groups are equal.
Ethical role of customer towards online marketing based on Academic Level	11	34.07	4.06	Rejected	All population means of three groups are not equal.
Ethical role of customer towards online marketing based on Occupation	15	0.64	3.49	Accepted	All population means of four groups are equal
Ethical role of customer towards online marketing based on Family Income	15	2.02	3.49	Accepted	All population means of four groups are equal

As concern to the ethical role of customer towards online marketing based on gender, the table value (5.19) is less than to the calculated value (40.6) so, null hypothesis is rejected and conclude that all of population means are not equal. It also indicates that ethical role of male may differ from female while they do online shopping. In the case of age, means of four groups are similar as null hypothesis is accepted. To assess the ethical role of customer on the bases of academic level it is found that below graduate, graduate and post graduate respondents shows different ethical role according to their academic level towards online marketing. The Table 3 shows that the calculated value of (occupation) F is 0.64 is less than the table value of 3.49 at 1% significance level. This analysis accepts the null-hypothesis of no difference in sample mean. Therefore, it concludes that the difference in ethical role towards online marketing due to occupation is not significant. The table also depicted that population means of family income groups are equal and there is no significant difference exists among these four groups towards online marketing.

Objective 3: To explore the unethical means of customers towards online marketing.

Outcome: Here is the list of unethical mode of customer towards online marketing:

- Use product for few days and returned back within the return back time period.
- Replace some part of product with damaged one and claim for new one.
- Frequently cancelled your order due to any reason.
- Unavailable for delivery person at schedule time.
- Unavailable for delivery person due to non-availability of cash at the time of delivery.
- Deliberately posting negative feedback or comment and trying to get benefits for the same.
- Deliberately not provide your proper information details only for fun.
- Ordering your product from more than one company and rejecting others while you received any of the one.
- Ordering multiple items and selecting the best one (may be influence of your family/friends/relatives) and returned back other items.

6. CONCLUSION AND RECOMMENDATION

With the advancements in technology, globalization of markets, globalization of production, and the rise of emerging markets, marketing ethics is becoming increasingly important. The study reveals that main reason for growing importance of online marketing is the increasing literacy about internet among people. They have identified that internet is truly advantageous through which they can serve their various purposes mainly social networking, online shopping and media sharing (photo, music, video). This efficacy of internet has increased their tendency of being online.

Based on the finding of the current study there is a significant relation exists between ethical role of customer and online marketing which means that customers are always adopting ethical behavior while doing shopping online. Majority of respondents reported that they never use unethical practices like frequently cancelled the order for better option, incorrect information, not available for cash on delivery, deliberately post the negative comment etc. while analyzing the ethical role of customer towards online marketing based on demographic variables, present study shows that male and female perceived the ethical role differently. Academic level of respondent also influences the ethical role regardless of age and occupation where there are no significant difference exists among these groups towards online marketing. Study also shows population means of family income groups are equal and there is no significant difference exists as it is a stereotype that family income may influence individual behavior and roles towards online marketing.

The current problem should be minimized by avoiding aforesaid unethical practices towards online marketing and this will only come from the individual customer inside. No one can bound them to behave ethically, but all the companies may prepare a code of conduct to the customer so that the particular problems have not emerged. Online marketer should opt the strategy of try and buy so that customer will first try and satisfied with their requirement and then only buy those products. Cash on delivery timing should be fixed by the customer and marketer and penalties should be imposed with non-adherence. For the promotion of products companies are providing facilities of free cancellation but if customers repeatedly cancel the product then companies should also impose certain penalties and this should be mandatory for all the companies so that this will not hamper their individual sales. Electronic goods should be only installed by concerned company so that customer will not change any part of it and this practices may also insure the proper installment of products. More recommendation should be included after the discussion in respective conference.

6.1 Limitations and Further Research

The study is confined to Lucknow city so the findings of this study cannot be generalized. Participants of the study are mostly young and educated people despite the fact that there has not been an intention towards this situation while sampling. This fact has become a factor complicating the process of comparison between groups while indicating that young individuals do online shopping more than other individuals. The study could be extended; so as to cover all the states of India as the researcher believes that ethical role of customer towards online marketing may be at the variance in different states.

REFERENCES

[1] Gaski, J.F. (1999). Does Marketing Ethics Really have anything to Say? A Critical Inventory of the Literature. *Journal Business Ethics,* 18, 315–334.

[2] Liu, B.Q. and Goodhue, D.L. (2008). An Exploration of the Hygiene and Motivator Aspects of Webqual Constructs in Predicting Website Reuse. *Proceedings of the 41st Hawaii International Conference on System Sciences.*

[3] Lohse, G.L., Bellman, S. and Johnson, E.J. (2000) Consumer Buying Behaviour on the Internet: Findings from Panel Data. *Journal of Interactive Marketing,* 14, 15– 29.

[4] Pavlou, P.A. and Gefen, D. (2004). Building Effective Online Marketplaces with Institution Based Trust. *Information System Research,* 15, 37–59.

[5] Pires, G.D. and Stanton, J. (2002). Ethnic Marketing Ethics. *Journal of Business Ethics,* 36, 111–118.

[6] Roman, S. (2007). The Ethics of Online Retailing: A Scale Development and Validation from the Consumers' Perspective. *Journal of Business Ethics,* 72, 131–148.

[7] Rust, R., Kannan, P.K. and Peng, N. (2002). The Customer Economics of Internet Privacy. *Journal of the Academy of Marketing Science,* 30, 455–64.

[8] Schlosser, A.E., White, T.B. and Lloyd, S.M. (2006). Converting Web Site Visitors into Buyers: How Web Site Investment Increases Consumer Trusting Beliefs and Online Purchase Intentions. *Journal of Marketing,* 70, 133–148.

[9] Top 20 Internet Countries-2019 with the Highest Number of Internet Users, www.internetworldstats.com retrieved on 10/02/2019.

[10] Tsai, H., Huang, H., Jaw, Y. and Chen, W. (2006). Why Online Customers Remain with a Particular E-Retailer: An Integrative Model and Empirical Evidence. Psychology and Marketing, 23, 447–464.

[11] Wolfinbarger, M. and Gilly, M.C. (2003). Etailq: Dimensionalizing, Measuring and Predicting Etail Quality. *Journal of Retailing,* 79, 183–198.

Modern Advertising Strategies and Consumer Buying Behavior

Surendra Kumar*

ABSTRACT: Expeditious changes in technology have a multifarious influence on human behavior. Behavior is most sensitive and dynamic character of human being which influenced by varying factors. Modern advertising aid and strategies have influenced advertisers and have a deep impact on consumer buying behavior. Expeditious changes in product offering by companies are trying to reach maximum number of buyers within a short span of time. Bounteous information, varying product and services have given buyer options to take decision of his choice. But as the variety of offering increases purchase dilemma also increases. In such circumstances, the buyer tries to find out relevant information from different sources. Advertisement is the medium which help buyers in decision making by reducing cognitive dissonance.

This study is an effort to explore modern advertising tools, advertiser strategies and its influence on consumer buying behavior. The research is designed in such a way so that various aspects can be explored including personal, social and technological. Identification of these factors will help advertiser as well as consumer in better decision making.

Keywords: *Advertising, Advertising Models, Advertising Strategies, Consumer, Buying Behavior, Cognitive Dissonance.*

1. THE CONCEPT OF ADVERTISING

As human being we are affected by our sensation. Sensations get a stimulus from the environment. In the environment, various types of stimulus come—different form of information i.e. visual, auditory, and tactile, taste and smell. Auditory and visual information is crucial and important to marketers to influence customer's behavior by influencing their emotions through advertisement. Visual and auditory forms of advertisement cannot be controlled by customers because the information will come to us through these means whether

*Assistant Professor, Rajkiya Engineering College Banda.

one is willing to accept it or not. Once the information receives the customer has the choice to make a purchase decision.

Advertising gives businesses the tools they need to create consumer awareness for their products and services and ultimately to increase sales. Advertising is all about mass publicity of products. Advertising involves creating awareness of product's uses and their benefits to consumers. By doing this, it makes a product to be available to those who want it and this satisfies the needs of the advertiser in form of increasing sales. According to Cohen, advertising is a business activity that employs creative techniques to design persuasive communication in mass media that promote ideas, goods, and services in a manner consistent with the achievement of the advertiser's objective, the delivery of consumer satisfaction and the development of social and economic welfare. (Cohen, 1988)

From Cohen's definition, it can be found that advertising satisfies three objectives; to increase sales of the firms, to guarantee consumers a great deal of service and finally to ensure the social and economic welfare of society. Advertising can be done through various media such as; radio and television, billboards, magazines and newspapers and websites. (Cohen, 1988)

With growth competition and marketing functions in business advertising emerges as major area of business functions. According to (Roberts, J. 1987) in 19th century, economist were busy trying to develop the theory of perfect competitive markets, this theory assumed that, there was perfect information in the market and that, consumers had fixed preference for their products which were homogenous in nature. It was considered as wastage of resources on advertising because consumers were not in any way going to respond to that. The advancement in transportation and technology, made producers rethink their decision to improve their capacity and thus, ensure publicity of their products. (Roberts, J. 1987)

Chamberlin (1933) in his work "The Theory of Monopolistic Competition" came up with new ways of looking at advertising. He modeled the expenditure of a firm as a "selling cost" that expands a firm's demand for a differentiated product. In his work, he describes a market structure in which there are many firms producing and selling similar but not identical products.

An early reflection was given by (Alfred Marshall 1890, 1919). In his works, "Principles of Economics" and "Industry and Trade". He marks out two roles played by advertising. To him, advertising might be useful in providing information to consumers which will help them satisfy their wants.

Objectives of the Study: The study was guided by the following specific objectives:

1. To understand the basic concept of advertisement.
2. To identify the changing pattern of advertisement.
3. To know different advertisement models.
4. To determine ways in which advertisement influence purchasing behavior.
5. To explore the future of advertisement.

2. ROLES OF ADVERTISING

Marketing Role: Marketing is the process a business uses to satisfy consumer needs and wants through goods and services.

Communication Role: Advertising is a form of mass communication by which advertiser disseminates desire information to target customers.

Economic Role: Two main views about advertising, either the market power model or the economics of information theory by which a businessman get insight of future demand of product or services.

Societal Role: Informs us about new and improved products, teaches us how to use these innovations, etc.

3. ADVERTISING COMMUNICATION PROCESS

The concept of advertising can be explained in five steps sender, encoding, message, decoding and receiver. This process explains the different stages through which message is formed and traveled to the audience. Advertising message is not just a message; it is a bundle of representation of the product and the company. The advertising process starts from sender and end up to receiver (Schramn, 1995).

Elements in Advertising Communication Process: The different elements of advertising communication process are shown in following Figure 1.

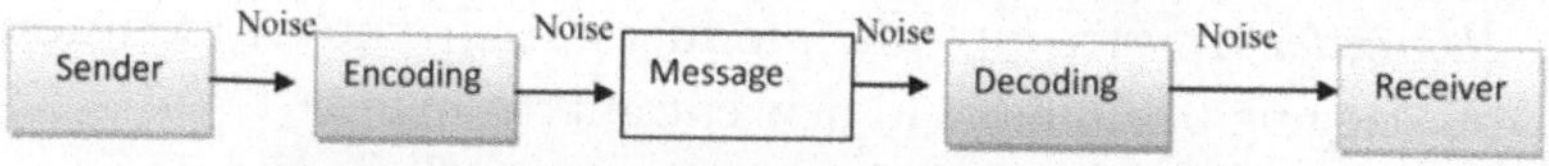

Fig. 1: Advertising Communication Process

4. ADVERTISINGS MODELS

The Figure 2 below describes various models of advertising. In this study the researcher used the AIDA Model as described below:

Stage	**AIDA Model**	**Hierarchy of effects Model**	**Innovation-Adoption Model**	**Hierarchy or needs Model**
Cognitive Stage	Attention ↓	Awareness ↓ Knowledge ↓	Awareness ↓	Exposure ↓ Reception ↓ Cognitive response ↓
Affective	Interest ↓ Desire ↓	Liking ↓ Preference ↓	Interest ↓ Evaluation ↓	Attitude ↓ Intention ↓
stage		Conviction		
Behavior stage	↓ Action	↓ Purchase	Trial ↓ Adoption	↓ Behavior

Fig. 2: Various Models of Advertising

Source: (Schramn, 1995).

5. PURPOSE OF ADVERTISING

Advertisement fulfill following purpose of advertiser:

1. ***Informative Advertising:*** The advertisement in the initial phase of product life to disseminate information about presence of product is known as informative advertisement.
2. ***Persuasive Advertising:*** To influence consumers mind set to purchase product or services which are known to them and have hidden desire or inclination for the products and services. Such advertisement done in growth phase of product to increase sales volume.

3. *Reminder Advertising:* The product already known to customers but lagging behind due to new entrants in market.

The advertisers try to influence customers by reminding them about product and services.

6. TYPES OF ADVERTISING

Businesses have the opportunity to choose from several advertising types, including print advertising, broadcast advertising, digital advertising and outdoor advertising etc. While each of these types presents its own pros, and cons. Advertiser chooses the one type or combination of types that best suits the company's product, target consumers and advertising budget.

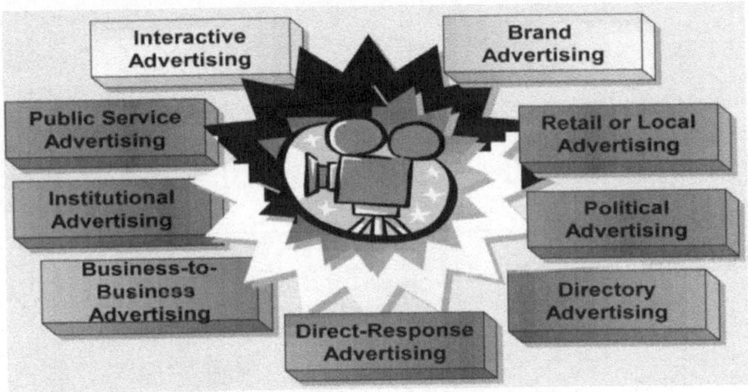

Fig. 3: Types of Advertising

1. *Electronic Advertising:* Electronic advertising includes advertising on radio and television. Businesses buy local or national ad spots on their preferred stations for advertisement communication, which are aired to viewers and listeners. Audience measurement metrics for TV and radio are readily available, meaning businesses can determine the station with the highest number of viewers or listeners, as well as estimate ad effectiveness. Although the establishment of many TV and radio stations has led to audience fragmentation, broadcast advertising mediums still have a wider reach than print advertising mediums.
2. *Print Advertising:* Advertisements placed in newspapers, magazines and newsletters covers under print advertising. The print ads can be published as display ads or as classified listings. Although the number of customers who regularly read a newspaper is in

decline, businesses can buy ads in papers with either national or local circulation to achieve the desired results. Magazines and newsletters have a longer life than newspapers; they typically lie around for months where they can be seen. With increasing use of IT numbers of hard print readers are declining.

3. ***Outdoor Advertising:*** To capture area specific region customers' businessmen select this medium of advertisement. It is a cheaper and long lasting way of advertisement. Outdoor advertising involves putting ads on billboards erected strategically along highways, mounted to buildings, or placed on the exteriors and interiors of business vehicles such as taxis, auto and buses etc. Outdoor advertising suits businesses targeting consumers in specific geographic regions. Compared to television advertising, outdoor advertising is inexpensive, making it particularly suitable for small businesses with limited advertising budgets. It is popular in along with highways and nearby railway tracks.

7. DIGITAL/SOCIAL MEDIA ADVERTISING

Advertisement uses Internet technologies such as social media sites, email and search engines to deliver promotional messages to targeted customers come under Digital, Internet or online advertisement. Such form of advertisement is rapidly growing in worldwide including India.

Social Media

Fig. 4: Social Advertising

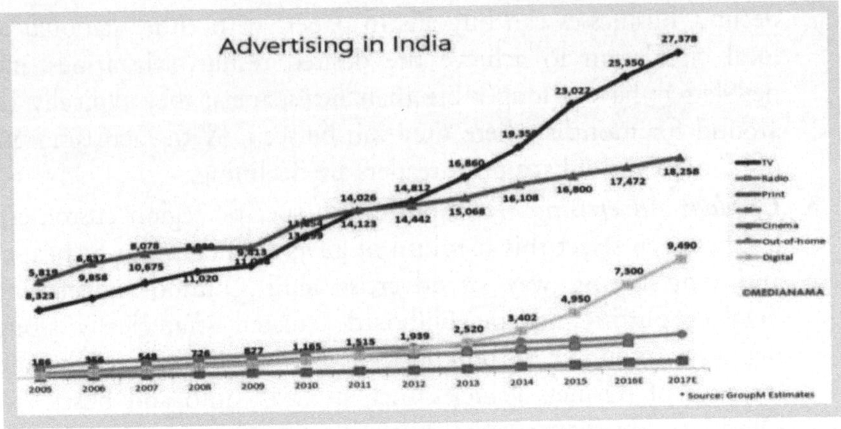

Fig. 5: Advertising Trends in India

8. OTHER TYPES OF ADVERTISEMENT

Besides print, electronic and digital advertisement some other form of advertisement are there which are becoming very popular among businessman like sponsorship of event, logo of company on uniform Product placement and telemarketing are alternative advertising techniques that businesses can employ. Product placement involves promoting a product though appearances in film or television. For example, a soft drink manufacturer can strike a deal with a film company so that actors are filmed drinking his product instead of that of a competitor in an upcoming movie. This type of product placement is beneficial to businesses that sell luxury goods. Displaying a company's logo on the uniforms of a neighborhood baseball team is a low-cost and affordable branding approach that works for local businesses.

Telemarketing involves having sales agents make direct calls to existing and prospective customers to inform them about a company's products or services. Because telemarketing is interactive, businesses can use it to develop a rapport with customers.

9. MODERN ADVERTISING ISSUES

A. **Promotional Strategies:** Small businesses these days have many choices when it comes to promoting their products and services. Regardless of what your company sells or does, it's important to learn about who your consumer is so you can effectively target them with your promotion strategy.

Fig. 5: Modern Advertising Issues

1. ***Developing a Promotion Strategy:*** To promote a brand it is critical to gain a good understanding of what makes a product or service unique. Find out where the brand stands in the competitive landscape and pinpoint what it is about that truly different from the others. This will help a advertiser to figure out how to promote brand.
2. ***Reach to Customers with Traditional and Online Advertising:*** Advertising is all about to reach maximum numbers of targeted customers. It allows you to promote your business to a large number of people. Traditional advertising include television, radio, newspapers, magazines and billboards. Online advertising includes social media marketing, text and search ads and remarketing. Businesses use advertising to create a brand image for their company and reach both new and existing customers.
3. ***Cultivate Relationships with Customers by Personnel Selling and Direct Marketing:*** Personal selling is one of the most expensive forms of promotion but it is also one of the most effective because it focuses on relationships. Personal selling involves reaching out to your consumers' one on one, either in person, on the phone or over email. Businesses use personal selling to cultivate long-term relationships and establish partnerships.

   Advertising is about reaching a large number of people while direct marketing focuses on reaching a select, small group. Direct marketing can be done through email, postal mail or social media messages
4. ***Brand Image Building with Public:*** One of the best promotion techniques is public relations, which refers to developing a positive

brand image in the media. Image building is a way to connect with target audience by sharing favorable information about business. Advertisers conduct public relations efforts through press conferences, press releases and media interviews. Sometimes advertisers also use sponsorships as a public relations method to establish a positive image for their organization. Small businesses can sponsor local fairs or markets in addition to local sports teams fun activities, events etc.

5. *Sales Promotions to Increase Revenue:* Sales promotion involves discounts, coupons, contests, prizes, loyalty programs and other incentives designed to entice customers to purchase products immediately. This is a good way to inform new customers about the products and services offer and remind existing customers about business to get instant and quick result.

B. **Consumers Buying Behavior:** Consumers buying behavior is focusing on how individuals make decisions to spend valuable resources like time, money and effort on consumption of related items. This includes what they buy, why they buy it, when they buy it, where they buy it, how often they buy it, how often they use it, how to evaluate it after the purchase and the impact of such evaluation in future and how they dispose of it.

According to (Proctor *et al.*, 2002), the principle aim of consumer buying behavior analysis is to explain why consumers act in a particular way under certain circumstances. Other author argues that, it's important to marketers to recognize why and how individuals make their purchase decision. With this information, marketers are able to determine better strategic marketing decisions.

C. **Types of Consumer Behavior:** There are different types of consumer behavior namely; dissonance reducing, habitual, variety seeking and complex buying behavior as described below:

1. *Dissonance Reducing Buying Behaviour:* When the customer finds it difficult to differentiate among the brands then dissonance reducing buying behavior occurs. As a result, consumers may respond primarily to a relatively better price. After the purchase consumer might experience post purchase dissonance (after sales discomfort). This is the consumer behavior displayed mostly by uninformed consumers (Kotler and Keller, 2006).

2. ***Habitual Buying Behavior:*** Habitual buying behavior is a consumer purchase decision where by the consumers' level of involvement is low. This means that consumers don't search much information among the available brands and they don't find significant differences among the brands and buy the product without a high level of involvement. If the consumers keep buying the same brand over and over again, it becomes their habit (Kotler and Keller, 2006).
3. ***Variety Seeking Buying Behavior:*** This purchase decision is common among consumers who want to stay ahead of the latest fashion trends. In case of variety seeking buying behavior the level of consumer involvement is low, but consumers perceive significant differences among the brands. In variety seeking buying behavior, consumers very often switch from one brand to another (Kotler and Keller, 2006).
4. ***Complex Buying Behavior:*** Complex buying behavior can be defined when consumers are highly involved for making a purchase decision. Complex buying behavior calls for high level of involvement on the part of the consumer. In case of high involvement, consumers distinguish salient differences among the competing brands. Consumers' are highly involved in case of expensive and highly self-expressive products (Kotler and Keller, 2009).

10. FACTORS AFFECTING CONSUMER PURCHASE DECISION

1. ***Cultural Factors:*** Cultural factors exert a broad and deep influence on consumer behavior which including the roles of buyers' culture, subculture and social class. Each culture contains smaller subcultures, or groups of people with shared value systems based on common life experiences and situations. Subcultures include nationalities, religions, racial groups, and geographic regions (Kotler and Armstrong 2008).
2. ***Social Factors:*** A consumer's behavior also is influenced by social factors, such as the consumer's small groups, family, and social roles and status. Social class is an invisible stratification of the inhabitants of the society into different groups based on some traits of the people. Inhabitants in a society can be divided into different social classes according to their income level, occupation,

education and so forth (Kotler and Armstrong 2008). A person's social class can be defined by what he or she does with money. The consumption choice of a person also determines the person's position in society. Every social class varies from each other because of having its own traits that set it apart from other class. Social classes vary in costumes, language patterns and many other activities and preferences (Kotler and Armstrong, 2008).

3. ***Personal Factors:*** A buyer's decisions also are influenced by personal characteristics such as the buyers' age and life-cycle stage, occupation, economic situation, lifestyle, and personality and self-concept. People change the goods and services they buy over their lifetimes. A person's occupation affects the goods and services bought. Similarly, a person's economic situation affects product choice (Kotler and Armstrong, 2008).
4. ***Psychological Factors:*** Buyers choices are further influenced by major psychological factors like motivation, perception and attitudes. Motivation is the driving force within individuals that impels them to action. Perception is the process by which people select, organize, and interpret information to form a meaningful picture of the world (Kotler and Armstrong, 2008). Attitude describes a person's relatively consistent evaluations, feelings, and tendencies toward an object or idea. Attitudes put people into a frame of mind of liking or disliking things, of moving toward or away from them. Attitudes are of considerable importance in understanding the role of attitudes in consumer behavior is an appreciation of the structure and composition of an attitude.

11. CONCLUSION

As for advertising is concerned with consumer buying behavior, the paper finds that with the increasing influence of social media and other means of information communication. The challenges of advertisers are also rapidly increasing. Now an advertiser has choices and selects the option to disseminate information to those who really in need and in search of information. The advertisement can be customized as per customer need and his/her buying behavior. There is a new model of advertising that is also emerging as forced advertising where a customer forced to write or select customized information from a given database. Such information is in the form of captcha while logging into a computer or website. Another way of following customer preferences is through its search history, in this way companies try to follow and remind a customer on his browsing page and emails. By observation of current advertising trends, it seems that the future will be for customized advertising and a successful advertiser will be one who has a better-customized database.

REFERENCES

[1] Khan and Martin (2003). Sales and Distribution (1 Edition) Anurag jain Publishing company, New Delhi.

[2] Saxena, Rajan (2003). Marketing Management (II Edition), Tata McGraw-Hill Publishing Company Ltd., New Delhi.

[3] Tiwari, A. and Roy, D. (2012). Measuring Brand Strength: Concept and Mobile Handset Study. *International Journal of Mobile Marketing*, 7(3), 38–55.

[4] https://bizfluent.com/how-4719561-internet-advertising.html

[5] https://www.thebalancesmb.com/thmb/SL6721KU0ANXz3uFP93c9KIDcZk=/950x0/filters:format(webp)/different-types-of-advertising-methods-38548_FINAL-5b8804db46e0fb0050115a14.png

[6] https://www.thebalancesmb.com/different-types-of-advertising-methods-38548http://www.knowonlineadvertising.com/facts-about-online-advertising/mode-of-advertising

[7] https://simplicable.com/new/advertising-strategy

Issues and Policy Options for E-Commerce Growth in India

B.M. Jani*

ABSTRACT: Economic reforms in India provided a vital boost to digital economy in general and e-commerce development in particular. The e-commerce industry is on rise and has created huge demand for analytic resources in the Indian market. They face intense competition, short time to market and challenging customers, all of which push up the cost of acquisition and retention. Smart phones, 5G network and growth of fintech firms have provided huge market for e-commerce in India. The impending growth of digital assets will present India with many unique opportunities to leapfrog its traditional deficit in physical Infrastructure. E-commerce has become a new digital highway in India. E-marketing strategy has achieved many Everest of Indian globalizations. 19th Century globalization was prone to labour movement, 20th Century of capital mobility, whereas, 21st Century confined to digital revolution in general and e-commerce growth in particular.

This paper is divided into three parts: the first one shows growth of e-commerce in India and benefits of e-commerce in India, the second one expresses issues and challenges of e-commerce in India, whereas, the third one offers policy options for sustainable growth of e-commerce in various sectors of India.

Keywords: *Degree and Extent of e-Commerce, Digital Revolution, On-line Transactions, e-Payments.*

1. INTRODUCTION

Economic reforms in India provided a vital boost to digital economy in general and e-commerce development in particular. The e-commerce industry is on rise and has created huge demand for analytic resources in the Indian market. They face intense competition, short time to market and challenging customers, all of which push up the cost of acquisition and retention. Smart phones, 5G network and

*Rtd. Director, Grow More Institute of Management, Himatnagar, Gujarat, India. E-mail: bmj1947@yahoo.com

growth of fintech firms have provided huge market for e-commerce in India and all over the World. The impending growth of digital assets will present India with many unique opportunities to leapfrog its traditional deficit in physical Infrastructure. E-commerce has become a new digital highway in India. E-marketing strategy has achieved many Everest of Indian globalizations. 19th Century globalization was prone to labour movement, 20th Century of capital mobility, whereas, 21st Century confined to digital revolution in general and e-commerce growth in particular.

The aim of this paper is to focus policy towards digital growth and paperless transaction for trade and commerce. This paper is divided into three parts: the first one shows growth of e-commerce in India and benefits of e-commerce in India, the second one expresses issues and challenges of e-commerce in India, whereas, the third one offers policy options for sustainable growth of e-commerce in India.

2. DEGREE AND EXTENT OF E-COMMERCE GROWTH

The growth of e-commerce has radically altered the way the World does business in every conceivable facet. The e-commerce market has currently in the size of \$ 3.1 billion and it is likely to grow \$ 226 billion in the next five years in India. And also expected investment worth of \$ one million to fetch \$ 750 million return and likely to increase \$ billion value addition in Indian economy.

In all, 53 e-commerce companies working in India has secured finance \$ 853 million in venture capital. The market share of e-commerce companies is on the rise. The retailers will require most cutomerization to stay competitive and e-commerce has relevance in the coming years. However, consulting firms provide opportunities over e-commerce firms to work with multiple clients and at all levels. As there is an expansion of digital world trade, e-commerce website application is found to be very smart and more useful to the sellers and buyers.

Every one welcomed administration of internet with the US companies. E-commerce growth in BRICs nation is very fast, which has been evidenced by rising business of the companies. An attempt is made here to show percentage share of e-commerce in overall business in some the countries.

Table 1

S.No.	Name of the Country	% age Share of e-Commerce
1.	Australia	5.7
2.	Brazil	19.1
3.	Canada	14.0
4.	US	11.4
5.	UK	12.2
6.	China	63.8
7.	India	31.8
8.	Russia	17.1
9.	South Korea	7.4
10.	Japan	7.1

Source: The Economic Times, Ahmadabad, 25th Sept 2015, p. 12.

E-shopping World is quite different than normal buying and selling in cash and manually. Here brand-managers, top level marketing traders associated in e-commerce. By and large, e-shopping appears as Grambling business as over stock by the e-shopping companies became owners of crore of Rupees in spite of goods are held up in godowns. In this regard, British Postal System is making maximum scientific use of e-shopping. Many new startup companies have entered in e-marketing and hence marketing has become more competitive.

In commodity market present stock of a commodity is sold in ₹ 23,800, the same product will be available and offered by e-commerce in ₹ 18,200. Sometimes, customers do not know the difference between both the prices and also reasons behind it. It appears as magic of e-commerce. It is necessary to know funding used and e-commerce value by leading e-commerce companies in India.

Table 2

S. No.	Name of the Company	Funding in Rs. in crore	e-Business Rs. in crore	Received Orders per day
1.	BigBasket	392	1510	10,000
2.	LocalBanaya	129	1100	1000
3.	ZopNow	63	319	1000
4.	Grofers	288	728	500 to 800
5.	Flipkart	–	–	–
6.	Amazon	NA	NA	NA
7.	Oi	NA	NA	NA
8.	Walmart	NA	NA	NA

The above table provides a clue that there are e-commerce companies, having higher funding with higher business with higher number of customers, whereas, we have the last company having higher e-commerce with less number of customers. However, it is maintained that e-commerce is very useful for large transaction in quantity and in value of goods and services. Walmart company has more than 10,000 Mega Malls in 21 countries. All are dealing with e-commerce. Walmart Company had given bribes to American members of Parliament worth of $ 40,00,000 for lobbying in order to enter Indian markets. Walmart has stake in Chena e-commerce group. The Group like Shoppers Stop, Wills Lifestyle, Spice hotspot and Ezone are trying to capture Indian's Next Big Growth Epicentre like small towns and cities. All retailers embark on new destination.

3. BENEFITS OF E-COMMERCE

1. Life style is growing in double digit even after growth of e-commerce.
2. E-business has become from zero to Hero largely due to skilled-based e-business having application of all new technologies pertaining to e-commerce growth.
3. E-commerce volume growth was 60% in 2014 over year 2013 in India. Estimated advertisement spending by e-commerce players reached to ₹ 3430 crore, which constitute 7% of the total spending by them. Thus, their advertisement spending recorded 50% rate of growth year to year. Digital advertising account for 9.51% of ad-spent in 2015, whereas, TV to stay dominant medium with a 45.1% share in India (E/T 22/4/2016).
4. US-based Amazon e-commerce company is engaged in Fast Moving Consumer Goods (FMCG) having sales worth of 1.9 million FMCG products sold by the company. It has online retail business with doorstep deliveries of fresh food, fruits and vegetable. After getting approval of FDI, the company Amazon India can expand e-business in Indian expanding e-market with on discount and low margin categories such as FMCG.
5. ALIBABA-backed (Chinese) company Paytm e-commerce company has high standards for merchants as sellers looking to qualify for Paytm Mall as customers have stringent requirement of supply inventory and logistics. It is a new landmark in marketing of

consumer movement by the company. An entry of this company in e-commerce of India means an entry of China in e-commerce business of India. E-tailing is tripled to $13 billion. The company is facing funding to compete with global rival Amazon. ALIBABA is going to put in $177 million to boost e-business of Paytm. Thus, e-commerce is part and parcel of globalization process and the WTO.

6. In order to develop business in India, e-commerce company like Flipkart has cut done merchant fees, and other charges. It has lowering collection charges for cash on Delivery orders at least 40%, depend upon category of product and seller's marketplace. The reduction in charges will bring down overall cost of doing business through the site by about ₹ 30 per unit an average.
7. The Goods and Service Tax (GST) council has reduced the tax the e-commerce firms are mandated to collect at source (TCS) from the sales of their platform all the down to 1%. The proposal is still flawed and must be scrapped. As such Amazon, Flipkart etc. are barred by policy from selling their own stuff and work as a marketplace. Levying a service tax, they charge for providing service is rational.
8. E-commerce has provided facilities to the customers 'Cash on Delivery', which has increased confidence of people. This has resulted e-commerce sights ready for sales during Diwali and Christmas. Digit-wise e-commerce companies break their back to their market front.
9. Many producing companies to sell their goods in bulk and they are trying to link with e-commerce companies for bargaining. There are several entrepreneurs, those who are trading with small profit margin with large amount of trade. Thus, e-commerce has different mathematics/accounting to face national and global level competition.
10. Brand-managers, group of IITs engineers and owners of startup companies are trying to increase image-building of producing companies and they became millioners over a night in India.
11. The Hyper Business Local Model is lauded for not only saving of time but also to save capital by e-business companies in India as India has remained as overweight market and while, it may not be cheapest market as India has high quality e-commerce companies.

12. There are experts in e-commerce those who provided new innovative ideas of operation and preparing Mega plan to boost e-business in India. These include, Kunal Bahl, Vijay Shekhar, Pranay Chulet, Sanjeev Juneja, Bhavish Aggarwal, Nitin Kamath, VSS Mani and Arvind Bansal. These experts are busy to improve ecosystem of e-commerce.

4. ISSUES AND CHALLENGES OF E-COMMERCE

1. A leading company of e-commerce in India has only 5% market share, whereas, ALIBABA of china has achieved 80% of total market share. Thus, self standing by e-commerce companies in India has big challenges.
2. Looking to the wider use of internet in India and all over the World, a little desired change may bring long term disadvantage in e-commerce functioning.
3. E-commerce market is not perfect market considering prevailing of uniform price on all websites for sales. It is feared that uneducated customers in urban and rural areas can be cheated, e-transaction.
4. Hackers' gang is smarter than Software engineers and e-staff. The know or identify psychology, who are going to surfing and mentality to earn more. The hackers will take such people in trap by attractive offers so as to catch the customers. Malpractices of e-commerce draw attention of all researchers in electronics media, which is big challenge to e-commerce and customers. There are several ways of cheating bi e-commerce, which include, internet, e-mail, Whatsapp, Social networking sites are free without regulation. They are without code of conduct. Privacy and leakage of password in internet appear common. Mobile payment wallets are a threat to banks.
5. Combination of e-commerce and mobility is big game. New players will expand their market share. The competition in e-commerce may expand Indian markets. But in no case should adversely affect the customers.
6. Rising e-commerce posed a challenge before making industry for quick e-payment in the accounts of the company. There is a space for 10 new opening of payments banks in India.
7. Internet should remain free from restriction as e-commerce encourages branded items, which can be purchased from the any

corner of the World. E-commerce can only be successful, when internet speed may increase and quality of internet services can be improved.

8. E-commerce firms can crack down serial returners by rating, blacklisting as they feel that retune policy is misused and e-tailer can change policy to dry up Deluge of returns.
9. Insurance sector is neglected by e-commerce in India compared with other countries as there is no digitization in the industry, which has not made e-transaction and e-policy possible.
10. There are no educative programmes from e-commerce companies or e-bankers or from the government in India to educate people with the process.

5. POLICY OPTIONS FOR FURTHER GROWTH

1. There is no clear definition of e-commerce, which has led to confusion. The Government must have clear policy, which will contain definition of e-commerce units, classify them by size, and set norms for workforce and procedure to set up shops in other countries.
2. The government of India and other regulatory agencies of e-commerce go in for stringent rules to monitor e-commerce in general and e-transactions and e-payments in particular. Internet users must be facilitated by compensation or clear rights of customers and they should not suffer from loss of money or information.
3. Doing Business Report 2016 of the World bank has made ranking of the countries to come top. In order to improve ranking of India, it is necessary to have co-ordination between States and Local Corporation in India.
4. Indian companies will have to go in for e-commerce so as to transform business to crate sustainable value in local and global markets. The will have to identify opportunities, ready to take risk and challenges.
5. Due to cyber crime, World is facing $445 billion losses, which stands around ₹ 31000 crore. There is an increase in cyber crime number in India, which has remained 1822 crimes in 2010, 2211 in 2013 and 34 77 in 2015. These are crimes with filing of FIR and actions are taken by the court of Law criminals are punished.

6. More merger and acquisitions are necessary of small e-company with large one so as to build capacity in e-markets. This process may increase economic viability and technical feasibility of e-companies in e-market in emerging market economy like India. Off-line Gourmet retailer Godrej Nature Basket e-company acquired Ekstop.com as a part of on-line strategy. Similarly, Snapdeal and Amazon to bring to its offering online. This may help to national or regional player within technological age enter a smaller city as they can buy out local players and get ready to widen customers base.
7. There is Patent War between Apple of USA and Samsung of South Korea. Violator of the Patent is ready to pay $ 5480 lakh dollars. In this regard, outside settlement is desirable. Still, however, there is need code of conduction for e-commerce companies working at multinational level.
8. Dynamic pricing appear to be constant for e-commerce companies as reduced price by sellers are incentivized by marketplaces. There will be higher pricing when they are out of stock for certain product or a period or catalogue is not complete. Apart from demand and supply of the product, merchants and retailers are updating prices constantly to tackle demand and supply in e-market. At a time, when everyone is operating online stores, selling fashions were to gizmo, some e-commerce firms are operating physically stores to win customers of large size. This may not affect national price as per price policy.
9. E-cheating has increased due to rise in e-commerce and e-payment. Those consumers are cheated, who have their own website. It appears that Government of India should help to fund website preparation to the enterprises of startups. This so as IT business is like to increase from $ 132 billion in 2015 to $ 355 billion in 2015 in India. Earning from service tax may enable government to fund partly by providing financial incentives to e-commerce companies.
10. Management and commerce education will have to teach e-commerce on internet and smart phone and e-payment would efficient mean of payment. With tablet, Laptop, and e-learning horizon of e-commerce will be expanded in India. Digital is no panacea as students will have to eat digital cake in lieu of

unavailable basic bread. Digital smart board will be replaced by TV screen.

11. For Network Neutrality, there is need to have separate law to push smart data pricing in the interest of large class of e-customers. Sate and security of data must be maintained by the government.
12. Why e-commerce companies are go in for offline advertisement? As such, efficient advertising and expansion of e-business their advertisement should be only through online advertisements are useful to the web-accessory.

6. CONCLUSION

An analysis contained in this paper, the present researcher is of a view that e-commerce expansion in India has very vast scope. Honesty, integrity and faithfulness on the part of e-commerce companies, e-retailers, e-payment operators and on the part of other stakeholders appear absolutely necessary. This may repose sound confidence among e-customers, which may flourish e-commerce at high level in India. The association of e-commerce and the government will have to plan for better functioning of e-commerce in Indian situation. The success story of e-commerce of China reveals growth 88% of total market and rising e-business worth of $ 439 million in 2014 as 594 million people in China have an access of the internet. In Indian case, e-commerce growth may prove as a provider of new job opportunities and it has become hotspot for several career opportunities for electronics engineers. At present, e-commerce utility is very low in India but it can spread like fire, because connectivity has largely expanded with a new class of cyber entrepreneurs in India. It is surprising to know that Home Appliances and readymade Garments market as a whole transferred from physical business to e-commerce in India. In short, e-commerce growth depends upon, the priorities of the business are mind share, market share, and profit share. The investment in each phase has to be justified. The next generation of e-commerce is hyper local mobile commerce for frequent use cases, such as groceries and food. In two cities of America, Use of 5G network has started by vary-zone in this April. This shows amazing growth and speed of e-commerce all over the world. At present 5G network is superior to 4G as internet will run 20 time fast. This means high quality film of 2 and half hour will be down loaded within a second and hence to enjoy live games may be double by the 5G. Thus, South Korea is ahead in internet technology over China and the US. E-commerce would be possible on smart phone.

REFERENCES

[1] Agrawal, Yogi (2017). "AS Digital India Grows, your data at huge risk", Deccan Chronical, 9th Jan., p. 8.

[2] Alwadhi, Neha (2014). "Cyber Security Policy Must be Practical", The Economic Times 22nd Oct., p. 5.

[3] Bansal, Suchi (2016). Why e-commerce firms Advertise offline?, The Economic Times, 5th Nov., p. 7.

[4] Bhatt, Shefali (2016). How Tech Disrupted Banking" The Economic Times, 5th May, p. 1 to 4 supplement.

[5] Evelyn, Fok and Shrivasatava, Aditi (2015). "Racing to Deliver", The Economic Times, 24 April, p. 12.

[6] Ganguly, Payal (2016). The Big Leap: e-commerce, The Economic Times, 28th Oct., p. 13.

[7] Ghosh, Sugata (2015). "Why India inc needs to Wake up to the Cyber Crime Red Alert", 23rd April, p. 12.

[8] Ibid (2015). "Dynamic Pricing is the only constant for e-commerce companies", The Economic Times, 11th Nov., p. 5.

[9] Ibid (2016). E-commerce firms Brace for Life without Disconnects", The Economic Times, 12th July.

[10] Puri, Aditya (2017). Going Digital only Way to End Corruption", The Economic Times, 6th March, p. 14.

[11] Report (2015). "China overtake us in e-commerce", The Economic Times, 31st Oct., p. 11.

[12] Singh, Shelley (2016). "For e-commerce Companies Alogrithmisk King", The economic Times, 21st April.

[13] Team, B.E. (2017). "To Learn Unlearn", The Economic Times, Brand Equity Supplement, 7th Sept.

[14] Vignesh, J. (2017). "Intellegent Commerce", The Economic Times, Ahmadabad, 10th March, p. 1.

[15] Vittal, Irin (2014). "Follow the online Herd", The Economic Times, 24 Nov. p. 10.

[16] Websites of leading e-commerce companies working in India.

E-Commerce: Empowering Citizens in Rapid Globalization and Techno Superior Culture with the Inclusion of Digital India

Ajay Kumar Yadav[1], Anshul Pandey[2] and
Rohit Kumar Vishwakarma[3]

ABSTRACT: The e-commerce has transformed the style of business not only in overseas country but also in the world's one of the most prospective trading country i.e. India. The ongoing digital transformation is expected to increase total internet user base by 2021 in our country. The Digital India programme, initiative taken by the Government of India envisages a complete digital transformation of society and the development of a knowledge economy. It is also an effect of this program that many innovations and technological advancements have taken place to bring digital revolution.

Through the improved digital infrastructure along with high speed internet connectivity, it is tried to refashioning India into a digitally empowered society. Insuring the availability of government services to citizens electronically, has also cleared the prospects of the electronic commerce companies to accelerate the pace of online trading in India. It is happening because of the curiosity of knowing the things on the personal smart devices.

This paper highlights the swiftness of ecommerce with the digital India campaign jointly for users and service providers to make a significant impact in governance as well as the advancement of citizen's lifestyle.

Keywords: *Digital India, Smart Devices, Digital Revolution etc.*

---

[1]Assistant Professor, Department of Computer Application, United Institute of Management, Naini, Prayagraj (U.P.). E-mail: ajaykumar.uim@gmail.com
[2]Assistant Professor, Department of Business Administration, United Institute of Management, Naini, Prayagraj (U.P.). E-mail: pandeyanshul3@gmail.com
[3]PhD Research Scholar, Ravindra Nath Tagore University, Bhopal (M.P.). E-mail: rohitvish24@gmail.com

1. INTRODUCTION

In current scenario world has transformed from knowledge centric to techno centric. The efficient way to communicate with the citizens of the world's largest democracy with a population of 1.36 billion is only possible by communicating with everyone on a digital platform.

Ecommerce or electronic commerce, deals with the buying and selling of goods and services, or transmitting of funds/data, over an electronic platform, mainly the internet. These business transactions are categorised into either business-to-business (B2B), business-to-consumer (B2C), consumer-to-consumer (C2C), consumer-to-business (C2B) or the recently evolved business-to-business-to-consumer (B2B2C).

Ecommerce processes are conducted using applications, such as email, fax, online catalogues and shopping carts, electronic data interchange (EDI), file transfer protocol and web services and e-newsletters to subscribers. E-travel is the most popular form of ecommerce, followed by eTail which essentially means selling of retail goods on the internet conducted by the B2C category.

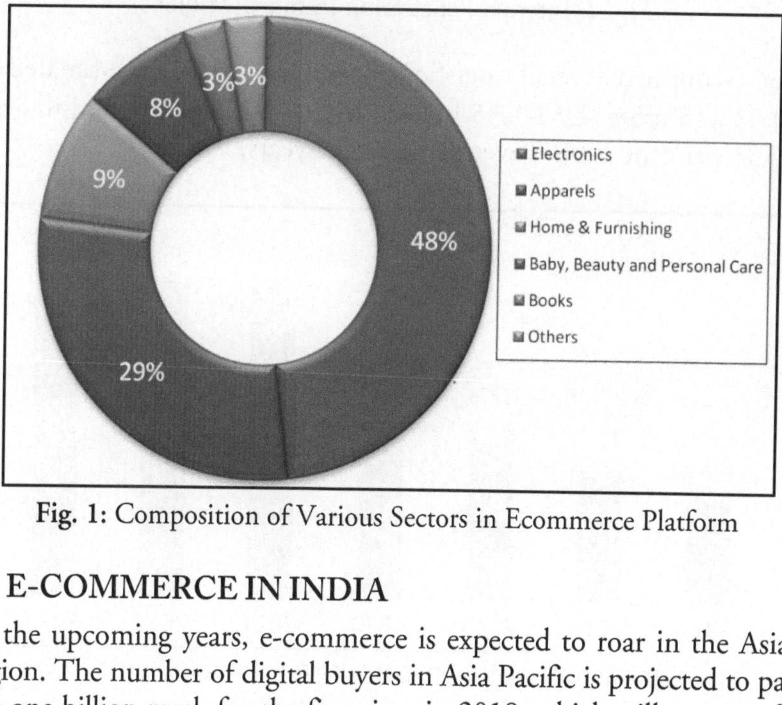

Fig. 1: Composition of Various Sectors in Ecommerce Platform

2. E-COMMERCE IN INDIA

In the upcoming years, e-commerce is expected to roar in the Asian region. The number of digital buyers in Asia Pacific is projected to pass the one billion mark for the first time in 2018, which will account for

60 percent of all internet users in the region. In line with the regional growth, India, a fast-growing emerging Asian market, shows optimistic projections for the e-commerce industry.

Internet penetration in rural India is expected to grow as high as 45 per cent by 2021 compared to the current rate of 25.36 per cent.

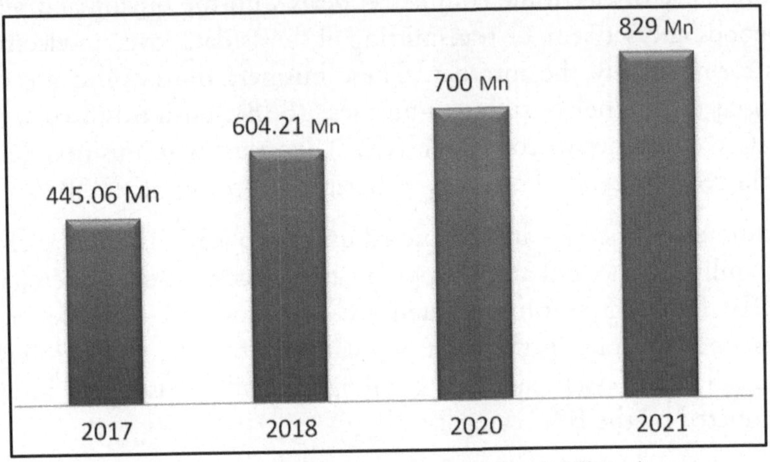

Fig. 2: Internet Penetration in India (Millions)

The e-commerce retail logistics market in India is estimated at ₹ 9,435.15 crore (US$ 1.35 billion) in 2018 and is expected to grow at a 36 per cent CAGR over the next five years.

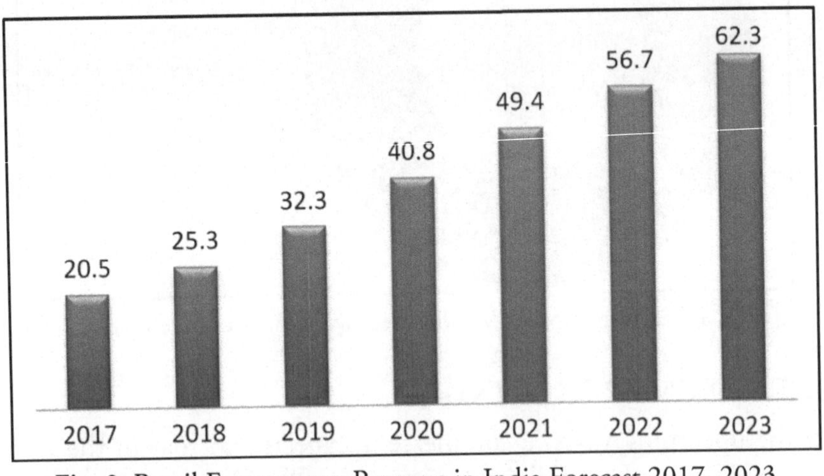

Fig. 3: Retail E-commerce Revenue in India Forecast 2017–2023 (in billion U.S. dollars)

3. MAJOR DEVELOPMENTS IN THE INDIAN E-COMMERCE SECTOR

Flipkart, after getting acquired by Walmart for US$ 16 billion, is expected to launch more offline retail stores in India to promote private labels in segments such as fashion and electronics. In September 2018, Flipkart acquired Israel based analytics start-up Upstream Commerce that will help the firm to price and position its products in an efficient way.

Paytm has launched its bank—Paytm Payment Bank. Paytm bank is India's first bank with zero charges on online transactions, no minimum balance requirement and free virtual debit card. Google is also planning to enter into the E-commerce space by November 2018. India is expected to be its first market.

Reliance retail is going to launch online retail. It has already launched its food and grocery app for beta testing among its employees.

Google and Tata Trust have collaborated for the project 'Internet Saathi' to improve internet penetration among rural women in India.

4. DRIVING ELEMENTS OF E-COMMERCE'S GROWTH IN INDIA

According to reports published by International Monetary Fund (IMF) and Central Statistics Office (CSO), India is among the fastest growing economies of the world. Among several factors, a conscious patronization of online commerce, and an emergence of retail as a dominant market segment have contributed to the unprecedented growth of ecommerce in India. Following are the major factors for the growth of E-commerce sector in India:

- Participation of niche companies
- Unmatched FDI
- Uniform GST
- Inclusion of food and grocery.

4.1 Participation of Niche Companies

With the increase in awareness about the benefits of online trading, there has been a significant rise in investment in ecommerce business. Hand in hand with offline trading, many established business houses have setup online transaction channels. Every other day a new company is being set in the online retail segment.

Specialization and customization are the underlining features of online trading. Ecommerce companies are specializing in exclusive items and have consciously moved away from the 'one for all' concept. Every new company is focusing on a definite item or targeting a particular demographic segment. So instead of addressing universally, it is better to concentrate on a single area and execute it to your best ability. Consumers prefer this kind of preferential treatment and personalized attention. India, being a land full of diversity offers ample scope for new companies to join in this ecommerce business tirade. Business opportunities are limitless considering the innumerable clothing, food, and cultural habits of Indian communities.

4.2 Unmatched FDI

Foreign direct investments (FDIs) till lately was not allowed in ecommerce for the single brand or multi-brand retail companies. It was only allowed for B2B businesses. Now, FDI is allowed in cases of wholesale trading or in cases where involvement is limited to use of technology platform. The ever-cxpanding Indian ecommerce market has attracted companies from Europe and United States who are joining as conglomerates. Though FDI has been successful in lending variety to online market of India, their full participation is limited by government laws.

4.3 Uniform GST

A uniform taxation structure, which GST (Goods and Services Tax) purports to achieve would contribute to the success of ecommerce business in India. Online business is carried out pan-India, and a uniform tax structure makes calculations easier and uniform. Same tax for same product or service across Indian Territory would certainly help in maintaining price uniformity. For online business operators, differential tax structure was a deterrent.

4.4 Inclusion of Food and Grocery

Earlier food and grocery were never thought of as items for online trading. However, with the change of working habits, and consumers opting for adaptability and convenience, there are now innumerable small and large ecommerce companies selling provisions and food items.

Indian ecommerce industry is in a position to sustain itself as a viable business opportunity not only for established names but even for start-ups.

5. PROSPECTIVE FACTORS FOR E-COMMERCE COMPANIES IN INDIA

Every day we wake up to the news of some of the other company foraying into e-commerce space in India. Earlier it was Google and now RIL is announcing its plans to enter into e-commerce through a hybrid model. These trends point out one thing for sure that ecommerce has a huge potential in India.

According to Goldman Sachs, India's e-commerce market will account for 2.5% of India's GDP by 2030 and is likely to touch $300 billion. As per Walmart, total retail will grow at a compounded annual growth rate (CAGR) of around 9% between financial years 2018–23, while e-commerce market in India will grow by around 36%.

5.1 Technology Revolution

Shopping as an experience has changed in India. In earlier days, shopping was a fun and free time activity enjoyed with family and friends. Today, it is a solo activity, digitally influenced and all about convenience. The concept of shopping anything-anywhere-anytime has given the boost to the e-commerce industry in India. *A report by the Boston Consulting Group says that by 2025, India is expected to have 850 million online users.* This exponential growth has made India one of the largest consumers base in the world.

5.2 Digital Wallets

Digital India campaign and Demonetization has spelt wonders for the e-commerce industry. For convenience and safety, regular buyers are parking a fixed amount of money in mobile wallets like PayTm, Ola Money, gpay, phonepe, Mobiwik, BHIM etc. and using it for quick payments. Even banks have come up with their online wallets.

5.3 Online Payments

There is also growing awareness about using net banking and debit/credit cards with the inclusion of digital India program. To capitalize on this popularity, mobile wallets and banks are also flooding users with cashback and discount offers.

5.4 Festive Seasons

Being a land of diverse religion and faiths, India has festive and wedding seasons generously spread across the year. We all know that festivals and weddings are the symbol of shopping. It is a boom time for retailers because people hardly head to malls these days, online selling is the best option. E-commerce is the now most preferred way of shopping for self and loved ones.

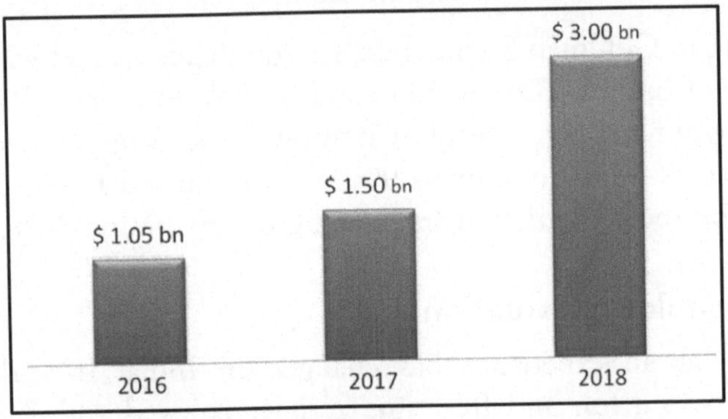

Fig. 4: Gross Merchandise Value of E-commerce Firms during Diwali across India

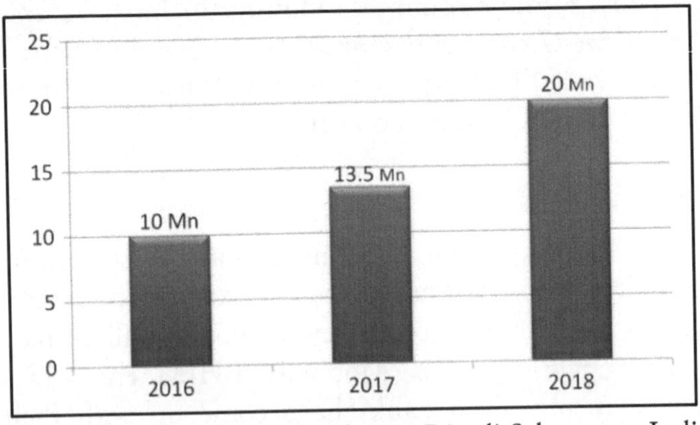

Fig. 5: Number of Shoppers during Diwali Sales across India

5.5 Sense of Discounts

No one can deny that Indians find a sense of achievement if they are able to strike a hard bargain or negotiate a good deal. Online shopping in India thrives on deals, discounts and cash backs. As per statistics from Cuponation, India ranks as the highest user of coupons leaving countries like Brazil, Spain, Australia and Singapore behind. Due to the growing access to a smartphone, 62% of Indians using coupons are on smartphones. This is again higher than Brazil (30%), Spain (22%), Australia (28%) and Singapore (37%).

5.6 Power of Small-Town Shoppers

India has a considerable population in small towns and villages. As per Red Seer, small-town Indians contribute around 41% of all online shoppers. With such a big share, there is a lot of scope and wide consumer base for e-commerce companies to grasp position. The leading players are already launching campaigns to tap the power of rural India. Amazon, under its Project Udaan, has partnered with small stores in rural India, wherein shopkeepers guide customers to shop on Amazon. *RedSeer also predicts that non-metro towns will account for 55% of all active online shoppers in 2020.*

6. GOVERNMENT INITIATIVES TO SUPPORT E-COMMERCE IN INDIA

Government of India has announced various initiatives namely, Digital India, Make in India, Start-up India, Skill India and Innovation Fund. The timely and effective implementation of such programs will likely support the e-commerce growth in the country. Some of the major initiatives taken by the government to promote the e-commerce sector in India are as follows:

- In order to increase the participation of foreign players in the e-commerce field, the Indian Government hiked the limit of foreign direct investment (FDI) in the E-commerce marketplace model for up to 100 per cent (in B2B models).
- The heavy investment of Government of India in rolling out the fiber network for 5G will help boost ecommerce in India.
- In the Union Budget of 2018–19, government has allocated ₹ 8,000 crore (US$ 1.24 billion) to BharatNet Project, to provide broadband services to 150,000 gram panchayats.

- As of August 2018, the government is working on the second draft of e-commerce policy, incorporating inputs from various industry stakeholders.
- Under the Digital India movement, government launched various initiatives like Udaan, Umang, Start-up India Portal etc. Udaan, a B2B online trade platform that connect small and medium size manufacturers and wholesalers with online retailers and also provide them logistics, payments and technology support, has sellers in over 80 cities of India and delivers to over 500 cities. The government introduced Bharat Interface for Money (BHIM), a simple mobile based platform for digital payments.

7. CONCLUSION

The Indian e-commerce industry has been on an upward growth trajectory and is expected to become the second largest e-commerce market in the world by 2034. Technology enabled innovations like digital payments, hyper-local logistics, analytics driven customer engagement and digital advertisements will likely support the growth in this sector. The growth in e-commerce sector will also boost employment, increase revenues from export, increase tax collection by ex-chequers, and provide better products and services to customers in the long-term. The launch of the Digital India programmes in the country is transforming the economies and governance with the power of technology.

REFERENCES

[1] Anooja, A., "Digital India with E-Commerce Revolution in Rural India: Transform India digitally and economically", *Engineering International,* Vol. 3(2), 2015, ISSN 2409-3629, pp. 57–64.

[2] Chinnu, Rajan, "Digital India", *International Journal of Emerging Research in Management & Technology,* Vol. 6(10), October 2017, ISSN: 2278-9359.

[3] Dashora, Jyoti, "Digital India: Limitations and opportunities", *IJARIIE,* Vol. 3(3), 2017, ISSN (O)-2395-4396, pp. 1592–1603.

[4] Dua, Seema, "Digital India: Opportunities & Challenges", *International Journal of Science Technology and management,* Vol. 6(3), March 2017, ISSN: 2393-1529, pp. 61–67.

[5] Giridhari, Mohanta; Sathya, Swaroop Debasish and Sudipta, Kishore Nanda, "A Study on Growth and Prospect of Digital India Campaign", *Saudi Journal of Business and Management Studies,* Jul, 2017 ISSN 2415-6663 (Print), Vol. 2(7), pp. 727–731.

[6] Khosla, Madhurima and Kumar, Harish, "Growth of E-commerce in India: An Analytical Review of Literature", *IOSR Journal of Business and Management,* June 2017, e-ISSN: 2278-487X, p-ISSN: 2319-7668. Vol. 19(6), pp. 91–95.

[7] Kumar, Anuj; Fahad, Fayaz and Kapoor, Namita, "Impact of E-commerce in Indian Economy", *IOSR Journal of Business and Management,* Vol. 20(5), May. 2018, e-ISSN: 2278-487X, p-ISSN: 2319-7668, pp. 59–71.

[8] Kumar, Tukesh; Prdhi, Shwati and Bisen, Abhay, "Role of Digital India in Rural Areas", *International Journal of Advance Engineering & Research Development,* March 2017, e-ISSN: 2348-4470, p-ISSN: 2348–6406.

[9] Luvy, "Impact of Digital India by 2019", *International Journal of Scientific & Engineering Research,* Vol. 9(4), April-2018, ISSN 2229-5518, pp. 1285–1288.

[10] Madan, Chandra Boro, "Digital India: Concepts and Implications", *International Journal of Creative Research Thoughts,* Vol. 5(4), November 2017 | ISSN: 2320-2882, pp. 923–927.

[11] Manjeet, Panwar, "Digital India: Scope and challenges", *International Journal of Academic Research and Development,* Vol. 2(3), May 2017, ISSN: 2455-4197, pp. 412–415.

[12] Omkar, Gurjar and Kunal, Bhattacharya, "E-commerce Trends in India in Global Perspective in Light of Digital India Initiatives", *Proceedings of the Seventeenth Asia-Pacific Conference on Global Business, Economics, Finance & Social Sciences (AP18 Hong Kong Conference),* ISBN: 978-1-943579-54-9 Hong Kong—SAR. January 19–20, 2018.

[13] Padhi, Priyadarshini, "Digital India: Issues and Challenges", *International Journal of Research in IT and Management (IJRIM),* Vol. 7(5), May 2017, ISSN(O): 2231-4334 | ISSN(P): 2349-6517, pp. 44–49.

[14] Sharma, Aditya; Trivesh, Sharma and Kavish, Sharma, "Digital India—A New change in Indian Economy", *EPRA International journal of Economic and Business review,* Vol. 3(12), ISSN: 2449-0187, pp. 154–159.

[15] Sharma, Jyoti, "Digital India and its Impact on the Society", *International Journal of Research in Humanities & Soc. Sciences,* Vol. 4(4), May–June: 2016, ISSN (P) 2347-5404, ISSN (O) 2320 771X.

[16] Shekhar, Srivastava, "Digital India-Major Initiatives and their Impact: A Critical Analysis", *ELK Asia Pacific Journal of Marketing and Retail Management,* Vol. 8(3), 2017, ISSN 2349-2317 (Online).

[17] Vijayan, Aiswarya, "Digital India—A Roadmap to Sustainability", *International Journal of Innovative Technology and Exploring Engineering,* Vol. 8(5), March, 2019, ISSN: 2278-3075, pp. 571– 576.

E-Commerce and Consumer Relationship Management

B.B. Tiwari[1], Vikrant Gahlaut[2] and Amit Pandey[3]

ABSTRACT: Customer Relationship Management (CRM) can be defined as a continuous process during which businesses come into contact with their customers. Customer Relationship Management (CRM) can be understood as a rotation process during which companies interact with their customers, generating, aggregating and analyzing customer data and utilizing results for service and marketing activities, the purpose of this document is to understand the influence of customer relationship management as a motivational factor for online shopping in the e-business environment. Both physics and e-commerce are made possible by special software applications that are used to collect, process and analyze customer data.

Increasing use of the Internet for commercial purposes has increased the growing influence of e-commerce in global business activities. Countries such as India, China, Brazil, and Southeast Asian countries have become the focal point of IT enabled services and provide the means to lead global electronic commerce smoothly. Therefore, with increasing com petition in the global e-market, attention is slowly shifting towards the customer.

The rapid development of Internet users has made it easy and improved online marketing in the global marketplace, the basis of the number of customers who buy online increases more than the number of customers who use the internet for other purposes, customer participation is the basis of every business success, because with the client, no activity can survive or adapt to the change that was brought by the new technology.

Keywords: *Customer Relationship Management, E-Commerce.*

---

[1]Professor, Shri Ramswaroop Memorial Group of Professional Colleges, Lucknow.
[2]Sr. Accounts Officer, Shri Ramswaroop Memorial Group of Professional Colleges, Lucknow.
[3]Shri Ramswaroop Memorial Group of Professional Colleges, Lucknow.

1. INTRODUCTION

E-commerce is rapidly transforming the way companies interact with each other, as well as with consumers and governments. As a result of changes in the ICT landscape, e-commerce is growing rapidly in several emerging markets and developing economies. Technologies designed to improve business transactions over the Internet have evolved so rapidly.

Electronic commerce has so many advantages in our lives because it makes it convenient in people's daily lives. Several explanations have been proposed for electronic commerce that most of them are based on past experiences in the use of electronic commerce. As with electronic commerce, electronic commerce also has a number of different definitions and is used in different contexts. One of the first to use the term was IBM, in October 1997, when it launched a campaign around electronic commerce. Today, large corporations are reconsidering their business in terms of the Internet and their new culture and capabilities, and this is what some see as e-business. Electronic commerce is a powerful concept and process that has fundamentally changed the current of human life. Electronic commerce is one of the main criteria of the revolution in information technology and communication in the field of economics. This style of negotiation due to the enormous benefits for humans has spread rapidly. It can certainly be said that electronic commerce cancels many of the limitations of traditional businesses. For example, the form and appearance of traditional businesses has fundamentally changed. These changes are the basis of any decision in the economy.

1.1 What is E-Commerce?

Electronic commerce, or e-commerce, is the buying and selling of goods and services on the Internet. Other than buying and selling, many people use Internet as a source of information to compare prices or look at the latest products on offer before making a purchase online or at a traditional store. E-business is sometimes used as another term for the same process. More often, though, it is used to define a broader process of how the Internet is changing the way companies do business, of the way they relate to their customers and suppliers, and of the way they think about such functions as marketing and logistics.

For the purpose of this study e-commerce is taken to mean doing business electronically. (Lindsay P., 2002)

1.2 Why E-Commerce?

With the increasing diffusion of ICTs, more specifically the Internet, the global business community's rapidly moving towards Business-to Business (B2B) e-Commerce. The buyers gain a clear advantage when the Internet gives them access to the global market, by which they can compare prices across regions, find out whether prices vary by order fragmentation and get awareness about substitute products. Due to transparency of the market, customer can compare the services of various e-commerce sites easily. For instant, in case of e-commerce the competitors are one click away from customer. If clients are not happy with the products, prices or services offered by a particular ecommerce site, they are able to change much more easily than in the physical. From the Sellers' point of view, they don't need to have physical existence of shop.

2. WHAT IS CUSTOMER RELATIONSHIP MANAGEMENT

CRM is a combination of policies, processes and strategies implemented by an organization to unify customer interactions and provide a means to keep track of customer information. It includes the use of technology in attracting new and profitable customers, forming strong links with existing ones. Customer Relationship Management is an emerging tool that allows marketing to maintain its presence in the dynamic marketing environment. Customer relationship management is high on the business agenda. Recent research conducted by Business Intelligence reveals that six out of ten companies have already begun in the CRM trip. CRM needs a deep understanding of customer expectations, attitudes and behaviors through a well-organized and maintained customer database and innovative customer strategies. CRM's goal is to ensure customer satisfaction and customer satisfaction at every interface level with the company.

3. REVIEW OF LITERATURE

Ramana Kumar, K.P.V. (2008) writes about the Customer Relationship Management or Relationship Marketing. He refers to all marketing activities directed towards establishing, developing and maintaining relational exchanges successfully. According to V. Ramanathan (2008), Customer Relationship Management is an emerging tool that enables retail marketers to maintain their presence in the dynamic market environment. In early days CRM was the tool preferred by the manufacturers in order to motivate and retain retailers. Now retailers are applying this very same tool in order to retain customers. Internet and e-commerce are closely wrapped towards developed countries. But they can achieve tremendous benefits to developing countries if it is applicable as an ideal business purpose. Ecommerce is a revolution in business practices (Ohidujjaman, *et al.*, 2013). The term commerce is viewed as transactions conducted between business partners. Electronic commerce is an emerging concept that describes the process of buying and selling or exchanging of products, services and information via computer networks including internet (Anupam-2011). Commercial transactions involve the exchange of value (e.g., money) across organizational or boundaries in return for products and services. Exchange of value is important for understanding the limits of e-commerce. Without an exchange of value, no commerce occurs (Laudon and Traver). E-business has changed processes within and between enterprises. Electronic Data Interface (EDI), widely introduced twenty five years ago on dedicated links between firms, showed how information could be directly passed from the operating systems of one enterprise into the order processing, production and logistics systems of another (Clayton and Criscuolo). If implemented properly, E-commerce technologies can result in business process improvements and increased efficiencies. Leveraging Ecommerce technologies should result in improvements to developing countries, but so far have not produced the desired results (Jeffrey S. Ray-2011).

4. OBJECTIVES OF THE STUDY

The main objectives of the study are as follows:

- To get a full acquaintance of the E-commerce.
- To identify the benefits of E-commerce.
- To know the challenges in E-commerce.
- To understand and identify the Customer Relationship Management Practices followed by the retail stores.
- To study the various CRM techniques adopted by organized retail firms and stores.

- To study the benefits of CRM to the retailers and customers.
- To provide the effectiveness of loyalty program adopted by retail stores.

5. RESEARCH METHODOLOGY

The paper has been written on the basis of secondary data. The secondary data were collected from published books, journals, research papers, magazines, daily newspaper, internet and official statistical documents. The study is qualitative in nature.

Distribution channel of e-commerce among the customers, workers, suppliers, distributors and competitors: E-commerce provides organization networks, wherein small firms depend on "partner" firms for supplies and product distribution to address customer demands highlly effectively. To manage the chain of networks linking customers, workers, suppliers, distributors, and even competitors, an integrated or extended supply chain management solution is needed.

Supply chain management (SCM) is defined as the supervision of materials, information, and finances as they move from supplier to manufacturer to wholesaler to retailer to consumer. It involves the coordination and integration of these flows both within and among companies. The goal of any effective supply chain management system is timely provision of goods or services to the next link in the chain (and ultimately, the reduction of inventory within each link).

There are three main flows in SCM, namely:

- The product flow, which includes the movement of goods from a supplier to a customer, as well as any customer returns or service needs.
- The information flow, which involves the transmission of orders and the update of the status of delivery.
- The finances flow, which consists of credit terms, payment schedules, and consignment and title ownership arrangements.

Some SCM applications are based on open data models that support the sharing of data both inside and outside the enterprise, called the extended enterprise, and includes key suppliers, manufacturers, and end customers of a specific company. Shared data resides in diverse database systems, or data warehouses, at several different sites and companies. Sharing this data "upstream" (with a company's suppliers) and "downstream" (with a company's clients) allows SCM applications to improve the time-to-market of products and reduce costs. It also allows all parties in the supply chain to better manage current resources and plan for future needs.

5.1 Forces are Influencing of E-commerce among the Consumers

1. ***Economic Forces:*** One of the most evident benefits of e-commerce is economic efficiency resulting from the reduction in communications costs, low-cost technological infrastructure, speedier and more economic electronic transactions with suppliers, lower global information sharing and advertising costs, and cheaper customer service alternatives.
2. ***Market Forces:*** Corporations are encouraged to use e-commerce in marketing and promotion to capture international markets, both big and small. The Internet is likewise used as a medium for enhanced customer service and support. It is a lot easier for companies to provide their target consumers with more detailed product and service information using the Internet.
3. ***Technology Forces:*** The development of ICT is a key factor in the growth of e-commerce. For instance, technological advances in digitizing content, compression and the promotion of open systems technology have paved the way for the convergence of communication services into one single platform. This in turn has made communication more efficient, faster, easier, and more economical as the need to set up separate networks for telephone services, television broadcast, cable television, and Internet access is eliminated. From the standpoint of firms/businesses and consumers, having only one information provider means lower communications costs.

6. TYPES OF ELECTRONIC COMMERCE

The following types of e-commerce:

1. ***B2B E-Commerce:*** Companies doing business with each other such as manufacturers selling to distributors and wholesalers selling to retailers. Pricing is based on quantity of order and is often negotiable.

2. *B2C E-Commerce:* Businesses selling to the general public typically through cataloes utilizing shopping cart software. By dollar volume, B2B takes the prize, however B2C is really what the average Joe has in mind with regards to ecommerce as a whole for example indiatimes.com.
3. *C2C E-Commerce:* There are many sites offering free classifieds, auctions, and forums where individuals can buy and sell thanks to online payment systems like PayPal where people can send and receive money online with ease. eBay's auction service is a great example of where customer-to customer transactions take place every day.
4. *Others:*
   - G2G (Government-to-Government)
   - G2E (Government-to-Employee)
   - G2B (Government-to-Business)
   - B2G (Business-to-Government).

7. WHAT IS E-COMMERCE CRM SYSTEM

E-commerce CRM may be a term that you have recently come across online. A CRM system is something that allows you to store manage and use customer relationship data to improve your business in specific ways. What you decide to use your systems for is entirely up to you, and the goals that you have laid out for your company. Let's explore the concept of ecommerce CRM and CRM text solutions—what they are what they look like and how you should use them.

8. CRM IN E-COMMERCE: THE BASICS FOR BEGINNERS

Investopedia describes CRM as "the principles, practices, and guidelines that an organization follows when interacting with its customers". The full report includes direct interactions such as sales and services, but also the ability to anticipate the trends and behaviors of customers that can possibly improve individual experiences with your business. A customer relationship management system is a central location or software that can be used to store customer, account, information, and potential customer information that can be used for future sales opportunities. Small and large businesses will benefit from some e-commerce CRM systems because they place customer data firmly in cloud, "which means that you can access it from many people, anywhere, anytime, from any number of mobile devices. For the mobile device developer who has invested time, energy and money by creating a mobile e-commerce website reactive, CRM is more important than ever. By using selected CRM practices and processes, sales on an integrated CRM e-commerce website will help you better understand the customers of the cross-channel channel and what they buy from you.

9. THE IMPACT OF E-COMMERCE ON CONSUMER BEHAVIOUR

In addition to helping organize customer information and keep track of current sales opportunities, CRM systems also improve collaboration between employees. Since most CRM platforms are cloud-based, they can be accessed from nearly any location as long as you have a secure Wi-Fi connection. Some systems even have apps for mobile device users, so they truly are accessible from any location.

As a result, more visible and organized data will help provide products and services your customers want. A CRM platform can benefit your online store in the following ways:

- Better develop an understanding of the customer
- Attract new customers
- Retain current customers
- Decrease customer management costs
- Integrate with an ecommerce platform.

From a business partnership perspective, working relationships are heightened because ecommerce companies with CRM platforms are able to more effectively provide quality customer service.

9.1 How does it Impact on the Customer?

CRM doesn't directly impact the customer because it's more of a business-facing tool. However, if you are able to understand and utilize CRM systems properly, your company - and its customers - will be the benefactors.

There are four aspects of CRM that benefit the customer-relationship lifecycle:

- *Marketing:* Your business can run campaigns and generate leads based on a current database of information, expanding on what you already have.
- *Sales:* Your business not only can track its opportunities, but it can also use CRM platforms to assign, qualify and convert leads into sales. CRM helps track where the customer is in the buying cycle.
- *Orders:* Inventory management integrates with your ecommerce platform so you can have greater visibility on who you deliver products to and when.
- *Support:* Provide high quality customer support service through case management and developing a deep knowledge base on what certain customers do and do not like.

10. BENEFITS OF ECOMMERCE AND CRM INTEGRATION

Few benefits of integrating e-commerce and CRM systems include.

10.1 Improve Customer Experience

E-commerce and CRM integration can help you improve customer experience in multiple ways:

- By helping you provide self-service portals to let your customers access the order status, track shipment, check inventory and more.
- By leveraging the information to provide your customers the omni-channel experience.

10.2 Targeted Marketing and Promotional Campaigns

With information centralized you can now run targeted and personalized marketing and promotional campaigns. These targeted and personalized campaigns are bound to be more effective and drive sales to your business.

10.3 Increase Sales by Empower Sales Team

Your sales/customer service representatives can now access information like customer order history, payment history, product inventory and more and take informed sales decisions. For example, they can use the order history or browsing history (products viewed) to better cross-sell and up-sell products to your customers. In a B2B scenario, with access to customers' payment history (YTD Sales, MTD Sales, A/R aging,

Credit hold flag, etc.) your sales representatives can now better negotiate terms with your customers.

10.4 Improved Demand Planning and Scheduling

Enables customer centric demand planning and scheduling across the company. The company can now better forecast the demand for their products and manage their inventory (sales, sourcing, manufacturing, etc.) better.

10.5 Integrated RMA Management

RMA requests often originate from a CRM support case. Your customer support representative equipped with all the information is now better placed to resolve the customer issue via phone or via remote diagnostics.

10.6 Improved After Sales Service

After sales service is one of the most critical aspects of a CRM. With all the necessary information available on their fingertips, your customer representatives can now provide better after sales service to your customers. They can now not only address customer concerns regarding customer orders, product information and inventory but also improve sales by recommending products to customers.

10.7 Reduced Costs and Losses due to Errors

The automated information sync eliminates the need of manual data transfers which are prone to errors and can lead to unhappy customers (ultimately costing your business).

10.8 Gain Competitive Advantage

The new found efficiency and benefits can be the key to differentiate you from the competition.

11. FIVE WAYS TO BUILD E-COMMERCE STRATEGY WITH CRM

11.1 Building Your E-commerce Strategy with CRM

In the digital economy of today, e-commerce has evolved to play a key role in sales for organizations, both big and small. Digital or click only malls, marketplaces and portals are increasingly popular and people are utilizing their purchasing power to buy things off the internet that you may perhaps not find anywhere else. We believe that e-Commerce strategy with CRM can help such companies to build and enhance their customer base, and perhaps improve their customer service outcomes as well.

11.2 Use CRM to Build Loyalty

Integrating your online portal or store to your CRM is perhaps now a no-brainer. But utilizing some of the unknown features of a typical CRM to enhance your customer base is perhaps the key to gaining a competitive advantage. Loyalty programs and gifting programs can be run from your portal or website if they are integrated with your CRM. Build key programs that cash in on customer purchases, to bring your customers back for more. Whether its points or its free or extra benefits, consumer psychology is such that they wouldn't want to say no. Hub spot has come up with some great ideas on how these programs can be built here.

11.3 Build Customer Profile Snapshots

Profile your customers. Collect data. Collate and then curate to build detailed customer snapshots. What they like, what they hate, what they purchase and what they save, items they review, and their demographic as well as psychographic details. This will help you analyze key trends as to what sells, what doesn't sell, whom to sell what, and then how to promote better. Personalized selling has become the order of the day, and for that, knowing the customer is key to better strategy. Customer knowledge can help you to stand out, understand your customer profile and therefore, sell better and more.

11.4 Analyze Buying Trends to Build Better Plans

Integrating CRM with e-Commerce brings about a horde of data that gives answers to questions that companies haven't been able to answer before. Evaluating customer patterns and purchasing patterns helps to understand the reasons and purpose behind purchases. The data captured through e-Commerce portals into CRM can help determine the various views of the customer and their purchasing patterns, including how demographics and psychographics impact buying patterns. This doesn't simply stop there. These trends help to decide what products, product features, services, upsells and cross-sells are possible; helping you to plan better.

11.5 Integrate Social Media to Feel Customer's Temperament

Amongst other things, today's millennial generation is using social media for practically everything in their lives, including commenting, commemorating, complaining and having interactions with other people. Knowing what people are talking about, and what they are complaining about, is perhaps the key to better customer relationships. CRM can entirely integrate with social media channels to tap in on specific keywords, target trends, hashtags, and words, allowing you to see what the average customer is talking about. This can be key towards better decisions in sales and marketing.

11.6 Integrate Complete Chain for Entire Customer Experience

Ever encountered an organization where you called to complain, and you kept getting routed and rerouted to different people, each person not knowing how to handle your call or complaint. This only happens when customer experiences are not well designed. With a seamless customer experience designed to handle the most difficult of customers, CRMs can be key in maintaining effective customer relationships and building customer delight.

12. CONCLUSIONS AND RECOMMENDATIONS

This paper addresses the conceptual knowledge of search engine marketing or ecommerce marketing, literature review, current and future aspects of e-commerce in the Indian context. This paper discussed the major motivating factors of online shopping. Current development would be a valuable addition to researchers and academics; and a useful theory for professionals, advertisers and entrepreneurs. Some of the disadvantages of e-Marketing are reliability in terms of technology, security, privacy issues, maintenance costs due to a constantly evolving environment, greater price transparency and greater competition on prices and global competition through globalization. Whilst considering the limitations mentioned above; Advertisers and end users can effectively use this modern platform to make life easier and faster. Over the next 3 or 5 years, India will have 30 to 70 million Internet users, which, if not more than, correspond to many of the developed countries. The Internet economy will make more sense in India. With the rapid expansion of the Internet, ecommerce will play a very important role in the 21st century, new opportunities that will be open will be accessible to both large companies and small businesses [Waghmare (2012)]. Karoor (2012) explained that e-commerce encapsulates many of the dynamics of the 21st century of India. The huge potential, ingenuity, and energy of entrepreneurs in the industry is impressive. Online commerce in India is expected to grow in both revenue and geographical terms. Additional search areas in e-commerce are; the quality of the sponsored ad text, ad position, search engine optimization (SEO), PageRank, yellow pages, and bidding etc.

REFERENCES

[1] Callen, T. and Chang, D. (1999). "Modeling and forecasting inflation in India", IMF working paper, September, WP/99/119.

[2] Chaudhry, Abhijit and Jean-Pierre, Kuilboear (2002). "Economics and e-commerce Infrastructure. Mc-GrawHill.

[3] Computer System & Applications, Dr. Faiyaz Gadiwala & Mukesh Tekwani, Sheth publishers Pvt. Ltd.

[4] Frieden, Jonathan D. and Rochee, Sean Patrick (2006), "E-commerce: Legal issues of the online retailer in Virginia. " Richmond Journal of law and technology, 13 (2).

[5] Khan, Mr. Yasir Zafar (Jan–Jul 2013). 'Challenges and Issues with e-commerce and the role of government in the development of ecommerce in India', *Journal of Information Sciences and Management.*

[6] Marc, J.R. (2002). Book review: E-learning strategies for delivering knowledge in the digital age. Internet and Higher Education, 5, 185–188.

[7] Meghna, Michelle (2008). "E-commerce trends for 2008 and 2009".

[8] Miller, Roger (2002). "The legal and e-commerce environment today", Thomson learning, pp. 741 pages.

[9] Nelasco, S., Nilasco, A. and Paul, A. (2007, November). ELearning for Higher Studies of India, *Fourth International Conference on eLearning for Knowledge-Based Society,* pp. 16.1–16.7.

[10] Nichols, M. (2003). A Theory for E-Learning, Educational Technology and Society, Vol. 6, No. 2.

[11] O'Connell, B. A poor grade for e-learning. Classroom students' did better. Workforce. 2002; 81: 1–15.

[12] Rajpal, S., Singh, S., Bhardwaj, A. and Mittal, A. (2008, March). E-Learning Revolution: Status of Educational Programs in India, *Proceedings*

of the International Multi-Conference of Engineers and Computer Scientists, ISBN: 978-988-98671-8-8, Vol. I.

[13] Rastogi, Rajeev; Country's report on e-commerce initiatives.

[14] Ruma Bhadauriya, E-learning—A boon for Indian Higher Education System International Journal of Engineering Technology, Management and Applied Sciences www.ijetmas.com February 2016, Vol. 4, Issue 2, ISSN 2349-4476.

[15] Sinha (April 2009). Economics in India—The Real Challenges.

[16] Smedley, J.K. (2010). Modelling the impact of knowledge management using technology. OR Insight (2010), 23, 233–250.

[17] Tatiana, Shopova, E-Learning in Higher Educational Environment, https://conference.pixel-online.net/edu_future/common.

[18] Turban, E., Lee, J., King, D. and Chung, H.M. (1999). "Electronic Commerce: A managerial perspective", Prentice Hall.

[19] Ubois, Jeff (1995). "Wheels of commerce—An interview with commerce", pp. 62–69.

[20] Wagner, N., Hassanein, K. and Head, M. (2008). Who is responsible for E-learning in Higher Education? A Stakeholders' Analysis. Educational Technology & Society, 11(3), 26–36.

[21] Wentling, T.L., Waight, C., Gallagher, J., La Fleur, J., Wang, C. and Kanfer, A. (2000). E-learning—a review of literature. Knowledge and Learning Systems Group NCSA, 9.1–73.

Challenges and Opportunities of E-Commerce in India: Future Perspective

Manorama Yadav[1] and Pankaj Singh[2]

ABSTRACT: Electronic commerce or e-commerce is a term for any type of business, or commercial transaction that involves the transfer of information across the Internet. It covers a range of different types of businesses, from consumer based retail sites, through auction or music sites, to business exchanges trading goods and services between corporations.

E-commerce is India's fastest growing and most exciting channel for commercial transactions. Indian e-Commerce is growing at an annual rate of 51% the highest in the world. The retail sector is also showing a promising trend of 11% Compound Annual Growth Rate (CAGR) and is expected to reach USD 1 trillion by 2020. E-Commerce industry is growing at an astounding rate in India and is expected to account for 1.61% of the global GDP by 2018. According to a report by Forrester, India is set to become the fastest growing market in the Asia-Pacific region with an expected growth rate of over 57% between 2012 and 2016. A.M.

There are various issues related to implementation of e-commerce. An April 2010 survey say AC Nielson found that news stories about identifies theft and fraud has confused many consumers about how to shop safely online. There are some barriers responsible for slow growth of e-commerce in India. Hamilton (2002) indicate some barrier in using e-commerce including security problems, lack of skills, cost etc. People do not yet sufficiently trust paperless, faceless transactions. For the growth of E-business in India it needs a focus and should to make country in the lines of E-business.

The future of e-commerce is difficult to predict. There are various factors responsible for the growth of e-commerce. There are some of serious challenges to be faced by the e-commerce industry. E-commerce is continuously progressing and is becoming more and more important to businesses as technology continues to advance and is something that should be taken advantage of and implemented. The paper examines

[1]Assistant Professor-Home Science.

[2]Assistant Professor, Economics, Govt. Girls P.G. College, Banda, UP.

certain important issues related to challenges and opportunity of e-commerce in India.

***Keywords:** E-Commerce, W.T.O., Bharat Interface for Money (BHIM), Artificial Intelligence (AI).*

1. INTRODUCTION

E-commerce has unleashed yet another revolution; which is changing the way businesses buy and sell products and services. E-commerce stands for electronic commerce and pertains trading in goods and services through the electronic medium. Electronic commerce or e-commerce is a term for any type of business, or commercial transaction that involves the transfer of information across the Internet. It covers a range of different types of businesses, from consumer based retail sites, through auction or music sites, to business exchanges trading goods and services between corporations. It is currently one of the most important aspects of the Internet to emerge. Electronic Commerce or e-commerce involves trade and transactions, the information of which is transferred through the internet. Today, e-commerce has grown into a huge industry. This paper is outcome of a review of various research studies carried out on E-commerce. The present study has been undertaken to analyze the present trends of e-commerce in India & examine the challenges & opportunities of e-commerce in India.

1.1 Definition

The buying and selling of products and services by businesses and consumers through an electronic medium, without using any paper documents. E-commerce is widely considered the buying and selling of products over the internet, but any transaction that is completed solely through electronic measures can be considered e-commerce. "E-Commerce is a concept covering any form of business transactions or information exchange executed using information and communication technology between companies and public administration."

2. REVIEW OF LITERATURE

Elizabeth Goldsmith and Sue L.T. McGregor (2000) analyzed the impact of e-commerce on consumers, public policy, business and education. A discussion of public policy initiatives, research questions and ideas for future research are given.

Andrew D. Mitchell (2001) examined the key issues that electronic commerce poses for Global trade, using as a starting point the General Agreement on Trade in Services (GATS), the World Trade organization (WTO) agreement most relevant to e-commerce.

Nir B. Kshetri (2001)—This paper attempts to identified and synthesized the available evidence on predictors of magnitude, global distribution and forms of e-commerce. The analysis indicated that the twin forces of globalization and major revolutions in ICT are fuelling the rapid growth of global e-commerce.

Jackie Gilbert Bette Ann Stead (2001) reviewed the incredible growth of electronic commerce (e-commerce) and presented ethical issues that have emerged. Security concerns, spamming, Web sites that do not carry an "advertising" label, cybersquatters, online marketing to children, conflicts of interest, manufacturers competing with intermediaries online, and "dinosaurs" were discussed.

Mauricio S. Featherman, Joseph S. Valacich & John D. Wells (2006) examined whether consumer perceptions of artificiality increase perceptions of e-service risk, which has been shown to hamper consumer acceptance in a variety of online settings.

Young Jun Choi1 and Chung Suk Suh (2005) examined the impact of the death of geographical distance brought about by e-marketplaces on market equilibrium and social welfare.

Prithviraj Dasgupta and Kasturi Sengupta (2002) examined the future and prospects of e-commerce in Indian Insurance Industry.

Arvind panagariya (2000) examined Economic issues raised by e-commerce for the WTO and developing countries. E-commerce offers unprecedented opportunities to both developing and developed countries.

3. BUSINESS MODELS FOR E-COMMERCE

The most common models of e-commerce are as follows.

1. **Business-to-Business E-commerce (B2B)**: B2B refers to online buying and selling of goods and services between two companies as seen in e-commerce between manufacturer and wholesaler.

2. **Business-to-Customer E-commerce (B2C):** B2C relates to exchanging of goods and services electronically in which customers buy goods from company.
3. **Customer-to-Business E-commerce (C2B):** C2B describes company pays for goods offered by the customers by means of online transaction. For example, authors providing a link back to Amazon.com in which the authors will get return on sale of the books.
4. **Customer-to-Customer E-commerce (C2C):** C2C E-commerce involves customers selling to customers using electronic media such as online auction. Its main benefit is that there is no need of company and as a result the cost is less as compared to above other models.

Today e-commerce is a byword in Indian society and it has become an integral part of our daily life. There are websites providing any number of goods and services. Then there are those, which provide a specific product along with its allied services multi-products e-commerce portals provide goods and services in a variety of categories, to name of few: Apparel and accessories for men and women health and beauty products, books and magazines, computers and peripherals, vehicles, software and consumer electronics, household appliances, jewelry.

E-commerce is India's fastest growing and most exciting channel for commercial transactions. Indian E-Commerce is growing at an annual rate of 51% the highest in the world. The retail sector is also showing a promising trend of 11% Compound Annual Growth Rate (CAGR) and is expected to reach USD 1 trillion by 2020. India's E-Commerce market is expected to nearly double to USD 1 trillion by 2020 from USD 600 billion in 2015, driven by income growth, urbanization and attitudinal shifts. While the overall retail market is expected to grow at 12 per cent per annum, modern trade would expand twice as fast at 20 percent per annum and traditional trade at 10 per cent. India's Business to Business (B2B) E-Commerce market is expected to reach USD 700 billion by 2020.

Online retail is expected to be at par with the physical stores in the next five years. India is expected to become the world's fastest growing e-commerce market, driven by robust investment in the sector and rapid increase in the number of internet users. Various agencies have high expectations about growth of Indian E-commerce markets.

4. RESEARCH METHODOLOGY

The process used to collect information and data for the purpose of making business decisions. The methodology may include publication research, interview, surveys and other research techniques & could include both present & historical information. The researcher has used only secondary data that has been collected from various articles, journals, books, websites etc. This has been used to study the conceptual framework, definition, present trends and some of the challenges and opportunities of e-commerce in India.

As per the findings of Internet and Mobile Association India the total value of E Commerce activities within India has Crossed ₹ 570 Crore during 2004–05. Internet and Mobile Association India a non-profit organization founded in January 2004 by leading Indian Internet portals, projects that e-commerce revenues in the country will reach ₹ 2,300 Crore in the 2007 financial year, growing at 95 percent over the year 2006. This pertains to the Business-to-Consumer (B2C) segment. Please refer below table:

Table 1: E-Commerce Market Size of India

Year	*2002–03*	*2003–04*	*2004–05*	*2005–06*	*2007–08*
Business to Consumer transaction in ₹ (Crore)	130	255	570	1,180	2,300
Percent Growth	–	96	124	107	95

Source: www.imai.in

According to the below table the total value of Business to Consumer transaction in India has Crossed ₹ 635.25 USD Billions in 2013. During four years total retail ecommerce value of business to consumer in India has crossed ₹ 1082.24 USD Billions in 2017.

Table 2: Total Retail E-Commerce Sales in India

Year	*2013*	*2014*	*2015*	*2016*	*2017*	*2018*
Total Retail E-commerce Sales in India	635.25	717.83	818.33	941.08	1082.24	1244.58
Percent Growth	3.59	5.3	7.69	10.69	14.14	17.52

Source: eMarketer, Dec. 2014 Figures in USD Billions.

5. CHALLENGES OF E-COMMERCE IN INDIA

5.1 Major Challenges Faced by E-Commerce Industry in India

1. Poor knowledge and awareness, 2. Online transaction, 3. Online security, 4. Tax structure, 5. Touch and feel factor, 6. Fear factor, 7. Cash on delivery, 8. Logistics and shipment services.

Internet based e-commerce has besides, great advantages, posed many threats because of its being what is popularly called faceless and borderless.

(a) Technological challenges
(b) Harmonization of laws and regulations
(c) Financial issues related to e-commerce.

Technological Challenges: (i) Internet facilities to common man, (ii) Availability of computers and software Access to telecommunication, (iii) Costly translation software's, (iv) Electronic data exchange, (v) Inadequate power supply, (vi) Computer illiteracy.

Harmonization of Laws and Regulations at National and International Level: (i) Security mechanism, (ii) Authentication, (iii) Electronic Contrary, (iv) Transaction processing mechanism Settlement of payment with e-money, (v) Intellectual and national tax transit issues, (vi) Licensing requirements, (vii) Universal trademark.

Financial Issues: (i) W.T.O. proposal to make e-commerce transaction tax-free. Government may lose control over money supply. (ii) No clarity in rights and responsibilities of various parties. (iii) Inadequate protection of public accounts.

6. OPPORTUNITIES FOR E-COMMERCE

Young Jun Choi1, Chung Suk Suh (2005) reported that the development of the internet in the 20th century led to the birth of an electronic marketplace or it is called e-marketplace, which is now a kernel of electronic commerce (e-commerce). An e-marketplace provides a virtual space where sellers and buyers trade with each other as in the traditional marketplace. Various kinds of economic transactions and buying and selling of goods and services, as well as exchanges of information, take place in e-marketplaces. E-marketplaces have become an alternative place for trading. Finally, an e-marketplace can serve as an information agent that provides buyers and sellers with information on products and other participants in the market. These features have been reshaping the economy by affecting the behavior of buyers.

6.2 Future Perspective

- **Social Media: Majority of online buying decisions are made on Social Media.** Social network like Facebook, LinkedIn, Twitter, Google+, Pinterest etc. have become a medium for easy log-in and purchase. Moreover, the clients can stay updated via the posts published on this media. Further, the advertising & promotions on these social sites has increased the chances of success of generating transactions to many folds.
- **Drone Delivery:** Companies have been working their way around to innovate the delivery process to shorten human effort as well as time. The answer to these problems is Delivery by Drones. DGCA is now fast tracking the process of issuing guidelines for the use of drones for civil purposes in India. If everything goes as per the plan, **then India might become the first country in the world to allow the use of drones for civil purposes.**
- **App only Approach:** Statistics suggest the future of internet lies in mobiles. Experts say more than 580 million people in India will use the Internet by 2018, and 70–80% of them will access the Web on mobile phones. This will cause all major players to switch to app only model. About two-thirds of its online traffic of Flipkart comes from users in small cities and towns. Flipkart's app-only approach assumes larger significance in these places where most people don't own desktop computers and have limited access to broadband.
- **Google's Buy Now Button:** Google is reportedly working on its own "Buy Now" style button that would allow e-shoppers search for products on Google and purchase them with a single click, right through Google's own search results page. The button will be displayed near sponsored search results beneath a "Shop on Google" heading at the top of the page. When users click on the Google's "Buy Now" button, they will be re-directed to another Google page that will allow them to choose specific item details, such as color and size, and then select a shipping route. Google would then pass on order information, including the customer's name and shipping address, to the retailer.

- **Artificial Intelligence:** As the ecommerce space gets saturated, investors looking for innovative use of technology are zeroing in on companies developing artificial intelligence (AI) solutions. Jet Airways is experimenting with one such solution devised by Vizury. It sifts through the individual's public content on the internet, as well as the customer's previous searches and creates an instant profile. Based on this information, the airline knows whether to package hotel deals, or simply stick with airfare discounts. The system also allows them to predict how likely is it for the customer to upgrade, and how flexible would the customer be to change travel location or date.

7. ESSENTIAL FACTORS FOR GROWTH OF E-COMMERCE IN INDIA

There are few online giants for shopping and travelling like flipkart.com, Snapdeal.com, Makemytrip.com who have overcome the challenges and represents the perfect growth trends of e-commerce in India. "E-commerce space is a booming space as internet audiences are likely to double in next two-three years and this industry will require talent from various sectors like technology, product, analytics, sourcing, general management talent, merchandising and marketing."

- **Customer Convenience:** Providing cash on delivery option service to the customers. A replacement guarantee should be there which offers 30 days replacement guarantee to their customers. The convenience of collecting orders post work while returning should be there. Low cost shipment should be there.
- **Adoption of Multi-Channel Investments:** Multi-Channel e-commerce business is an environment in which company can sell through two or more online channels. Cross channel investments are highly aggressive in augmenting both online and offline buying strategies.
- **Unique or Transparent:** Establishing a reputation and brand for quality products always drives demand. Booming rate of online credit card fraud, online shoppers only want to shop with secure, reputable online retailers.
- **Location based Services:** Getting the right content and targeting customers with crisp and relevant information is of upmost importance to users on the move. A dedicated 24/7 customer care centre should be there.
- **Multiple Payment Option:** Standard credit cards, debit cards and bank payment options should be there. Low credit card access and

low trust in online transactions has led to cash on delivery being the preferred payment choice also offered by e-commerce.

8. FINDINGS

The study indicates that e-commerce sector has huge growth potential in India.

E-Commerce in India-Opportunities and Challenges.

- Internet is the back-bone of e-commerce. But internet penetration in India is low compared to other countries.
- The growth of mobile internet is encouraging.
- There are some obstacles responsible for slow growth of e-commerce in India.

9. CONCLUSION

Electronic commerce or e-commerce is a term for any type of business, or commercial transaction that involves the transfer of information across the Internet. It covers a range of different types of businesses, from consumer based retail sites, through auction or music sites, to business exchanges trading goods and services between corporations.

E-commerce is India's fastest growing and most exciting channel for commercial transactions. Indian e-commerce is growing at an annual rate of 51% the highest in the world. The retail sector is also showing a promising trend of 11% Compound Annual Growth Rate (CAGR) and is expected to reach USD 1 trillion by 2020. E-Commerce industry is growing at an outstanding rate in India and is expected to account for 1.61% of the global GDP by 2018. According to a report by Forrester, India is set to become the fastest growing market in the Asia-Pacific region with an expected growth rate of over 57% between 2012 and 2016.

The future of e-commerce is difficult to predict. There are various factors responsible for the growth of e-commerce. There are some of serious challenges to be faced by the e-commerce industry. In general, today's businesses must always strive to create the next best thing that consumers will want because consumers continue to desire their products, services etc. to continuously be better, faster, and cheaper. In this world of new technology, businesses need to accommodate to the new types of consumer needs and trends because it will prove to be vital to their business' success and survival. E-commerce is continuously progressing and is becoming more and more important to businesses as technology continues to advance and is something that should be taken advantage of and implemented.

REFERENCES

[1] Andrew, D. Mitchell (2001). Towards compability: The future of e-commerce within the global trading system; *Journal of International Economic Law,* 2001, pp. 683–723.

[2] Callen, T. and Chang, D. (1999). "Modeling and forecasting inflation in India", IMF working paper, September, WP/99/119.

[3] Chaudhry, Abhijit and Kuilboear, Jean-Pierre (2002). "Economics and e-commerce Infrastructure. Mc-GrawHill.

[4] Computer System and Applications, Dr. Faiyaz Gadiwala & Mukesh Tekwani, Sheth publishers Pvt. Ltd.

[5] Dasgupta, Prithviraj and Sengupta, Kasturi (2002). E-Commerce in the Indian Insurance Industry; Electronic Commerce Research; Vol. 2, 2002; pp. 43–60.

[6] Elizabeth, Goldsmith and Sue, L.T. McGregor (2000). E-commerce: consumer protection issues and implications for research and education; J Consumer Studies & Home Economics; Vol. 24, No. 2, June 2000, pp. 124–127. Jackie Gilbert Bette Ann Stead (2001); *Ethical Issues in Electronic Commerce; Journal of Business Ethics;* Vol. 34, 2001; pp. 75–85.

[7] Frieden, Jonathan D. and Rochee, Sean Patrick (2006). "E-commerce: Legal issues of the online retailer in Virginia." *Richmond Journal of law and technology,* 13(2).

[8] Gowri Nair, A. and Aiswarya, K.M. (2015). Emerging Trends of E-Commerce & Challenges to the Consumer Protection Act, 1986.

[9] Jackie, Gilbert Bette Ann Stead (2001). Ethical Issues in Electronic Commerce; *Journal of Business Ethics;* Vol. 34, 2001; pp. 75–85.

[10] Khan, Yasir Zafar (Jan.–Jul. 2013) 'Challenges and Issues with e-commerce and the role of government in the development of ecommerce in India', *Journal of Information Sciences and Management.*

[11] Mandal, Shashi Nath (2016). "E-Consumers' Protection in India", *Global Journal of Management and Business Research: E-Marketing,* Vol. 16, Issue 5, Version 1.0, Year 2016, *Type: Double Blind Peer Reviewed International Research Journal Publisher: Global Journals Inc. (USA),* Online ISSN: 2249-4588 & Print ISSN: 0975-5853.

[12] Mauricio, S. Featherman; Joseph, S. Valacich and John, D. Wells (2006); Is that authentic or artificial? Understanding consumer perceptions of risk

in e-service encounters; *Information System Journal;* Vol. 16, 2006; pp. 107–134.

[13] Meghna, Michelle (2008). "E-commerce trends for 2008 and 2009".

[14] Miller, Roger (2002). "The legal and e-commerce environment today", Thomson learning, pp. 741 pages.

[15] Nir, B. Kshetri (2001). Determinants of the Locus of Global E-commerce; Electronic Markets; Vol. 11, No. 4, 2001; pp. 250–257. Jackie Gilbert Bette Ann Stead (2001); *Ethical Issues in Electronic Commerce; Journal of Business Ethics*; Vol. 34, 2001, pp. 75–85.

[16] Rastogi, Rajeev. "Country's report on e-commerce initiatives".

[17] Sinha (April 2009). Economics in India—The Real Challenges.

[18] Turban, E., Lee, J., King, D. and Chung, H.M. (1999). "Electronic Commerce: A managerial perspective", Prentice Hall.

[19] Ubois, Jeff (1995). "Wheels of commerce—An interview with commerce", pp. 62–69.

[20] Young, Jun Choil and Chung, Suk Suh (2005). *The death of physical distance: An economic analysis of the emergence of electronic marketplaces,* pp. 597–614.

Online Resources

http://www.investorwords.com/1637/e_commerce.html

Emerging Retail E-Commerce Export and India

B.B. Tiwari[1] and Anchal Singh[2]

1. INTRODUCTION

India the emerging global icon is one of the fastest growing economies of the world. In 2017, World Bank Group has given ranking to 189 economies for Ease of Doing Business where India is ranked at 130th position (Doingbusiness.org, World Bank Group, 2017). The existing Government is giving emphasis on various projects like Digital India, Make in India, Startup India etc. to improve this ranking. Retail export through E-commerce is becoming significant popular in last five years which can play a significant role in economy growth.

1.1 E-Commerce

Electronic commerce (ecommerce) is a type of business model, or segment of a larger business model, that enables a firm or individual to conduct business over an electronic network, typically the internet. Electronic commerce operates in all three of the major market segments: business to business, business to consumer and consumer to consumer. It can be thought of as a more advanced form of mail-order purchasing through a catalog. Almost any product or service can be offered via ecommerce, from books and music to financial services and plane tickets.

Electronic commerce emerged in the early 1990s, and its use has increased at a rapid rate. Today, the majority of companies have an online presence. In fact, having the ability to conduct business through the Internet has become a necessity. Everything from food and clothes to entertainment and furniture can be purchased online.

---

[1]Professor Shri Ramswaroop Memorial College of Engineering and Management Lucknow.

[2]Research Scholar, AKTU Lucknow.

Two familiar examples of electronic commerce companies are eBay and Amazon. Both of these companies allow consumers to purchase a variety of goods and services online from businesses and other consumers, while eBay also hosts online auctions. Consumers on these sites typically have numerous payment options, as well as choices for how their products are delivered.

1.2 Types of E-Commerce

B2C: The most common is **business to consumer**, in which a business sells products or services directly to consumers over the Internet. An example of a business to consumer e-commerce transaction would be an individual purchasing a pair of sneakers through Nike's website.

B2B: Another type of electronic commerce is **business to business**, where companies sell products or services to other companies over the Internet. An example would be the company GoDaddy, which sells domain names, websites, and hosting services to other businesses.

C2C: Finally, there is **consumer to consumer** e-commerce, which is where consumers sell products to other consumers. An example would be one consumer selling something that he or she no longer needs or wants to another consumer via a site like Olx or Quickr.

1.3 Retail E-Commerce Export

International trade and commerce has existed for centuries and played a very important part in the World History. However International Retailing has been in existence and has gained ground in the past two to three decades. The economic boom in several countries, coupled with globalization have given way to organisations looking at setting up retailing across borders. The advent of internet and multimedia has further changed the dimensions as far as International Retailing is concerned.

Retail E-commerce export or Global Retail can be defined as "All the activities involved in selling products and services to final international consumers for their personal consumption through e-commerce platforms" (Dana – Nicoleta Lascu, International Marketing: Managing worldwide operations in a changing International Environment).

2. LITERATURE REVIEW

In 2015, the global population amounted to around 7.3 billion people, of which 1.4 billion people purchased goods and/or services online at least once. In total, they spent $2,272.7 bn online, which results in an average spending per e-shopper of $1,582. Global B2C e-commerce sales have increased steadily since 2010. In addition, the growth rate has been quite consistent over the last few years as shown in the Figure below (Global B2C E-commerce Report 2016 by E-commerce Foundation).

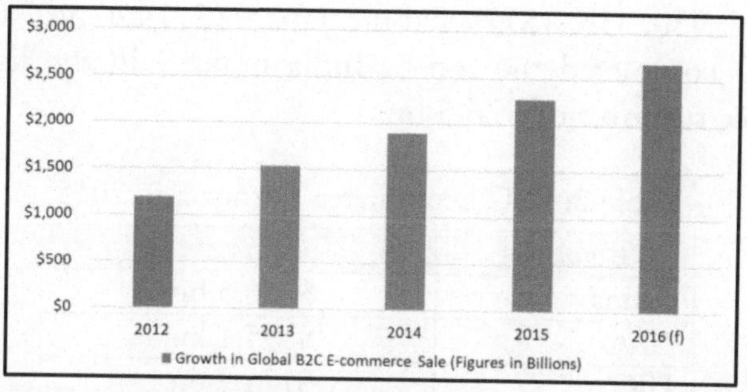

Fig. 1: Growth in Global B2C E-Commerce Sale (Figure in billions)

2.1 Internet Penetration Per Country

With regard to the countries covered in the report, the UK had the highest Internet penetration; 93% of its population had access to the

Table 1: Internet Penetration Per Country

Countries	*Internet Penetration*	*Online Population*
Top 10 countries	86%	612.3 mn
United Kingdom	93%	49.8 mn
Japan	91%	100.3 mn
Germany	89%	62.9 mn
USA	88%	229.6 mn
Canada	88%	26.6 mn
France	87%	47.0 mn
South Korea	85%	37.1 mn
Australia	85%	16.6 mn
Spain	80%	31.4 mn
Chile	76%	10.9 mn

Internet penetration per country.

Internet in 2015. It was followed by Japan (91%) and Germany (89%). However, with only 27% of its 1.3 billion inhabitants being connected to the web, India significantly lowered the region's average. In addition, at 51%, China's Internet penetration was also quite low.

2.2 B2C E-Commerce Turnover

In the category of B2C e-commerce sales, China and the United States are clearly at the top. In 2015, the Chinese in total spent $766.5 bn online, while the American B2C e-commerce turnover amounted to $595.1 bn. The UK ($174.2 bn), Japan ($114.4 bn) and France ($71.9 bn) completed the top 5. India ranks 9 in the list with the e-commerce turnover of $26.5 bn.

Table 2: B2C Ecommerce Turnover in 2015

Countries	*Total Turnover*
China	$766.5 bn
USA	$595.1 bn
UK	$174.2 bn
Japan	$114.4 bn
France	$71.9 bn
Germany	$66.2 bn
SouthKorea	$64.8 bn
Canada	$35.7 bn
India	$25.5 bn
Russia	$22.8 bn

Source: National Associations and Ecommerce Foundation, 2016.

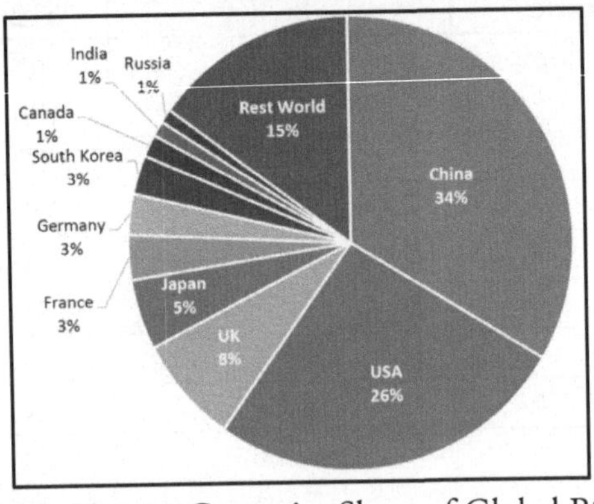

Fig. 2: Top 10 Countries Share of Global B2C E-Commerce Market

2.3 Retail E-commerce Opportunity for India

The Indian economy has consistently shown signs of proliferation, with the average Gross Domestic Product (GDP) growth rate at 7.5 per cent in 2015-16. The retail sector is currently demonstrating signs of rapid expansion at 11 per cent compound annual growth rate and is expected to grow from an estimated prevalent size of USD 600 billion to USD one trillion in the year 2020. Though, e-commerce spends in India is around one per cent of the total retail spending, e-commerce has become a key driver to create new markets in erstwhile unreachable geographies. Micro Small and Medium Enterprises (MSMEs) account for more than 98 per cent of the total industrial units in India. However, only limited numbers of MSMEs have the potential and readiness for Cross-Border Trade (CBT). Further, only 26000 Retailers are active in Cross Border Trade through E-commerce. There are few CBT categories like textile, apparel, leather, handicraft, gems and jewellery concentrated in clusters. It is, therefore, essential to map e-commerce (CBT) readiness to be able to attain focused and project based targets for CBT among MSMEs.

A new trend of boom in digitization amongst Indian MSMEs & Retailers is on the rise. Indian Retailers, particularly those with second and third generation entrepreneurs in the business are relatively quick to adopt technology, thus witnessing enhanced business efficiency. Such firms connect with customers digitally, trading globally through the e-commerce platform. This has further resulted in tremendous opportunities for them that earlier had limited marketing options and can now directly connect with the buyers across global markets. The encouragement to Retailers towards diversifying from offline to online mode also comes from intimations under the new foreign trade policy 2015–20 towards e-commerce exports.

2.4 Analysis and Assessment of CBT B2C E-Commerce for Indian Retailers

The increasing numbers of Global E-commerce turnover brings an unequivocal opportunity for Indian Retailers, both for existing as well as potential start up export units, to capture a portion of the rapidly expanding B2C e-commerce via marketplace giants such as eBay, Amazon and Alibaba. Although, B2C e-commerce sales in India stood at USD 25.5 billion, putting it at the ninth position followed by Russia as the tenth-ranked country, yet the Indian online retail surprisingly constitutes less than one per cent of India's total retail market. This is also reflected through poor Cross-Border Trade (CBT) via e-commerce (B2C) amongst Indian Retailers, which are still in the immature stage.

The overall export potential arising out of Indian products amounts to USD 302 billion, contributed by 93 product categories and is exported to 159 countries. There are numerous clusters in India that hold promising potential for MSME products that can be exported to various countries in North America (USA), Europe (UK, Germany, Italy and France), Australia and South East Asian countries (Thailand, Singapore, Philippines and Malaysia). Although products like petroleum, machinery, iron and steel, etc. cannot be addressed through B2C e-commerce exports, nevertheless the addressable retail export through B2C ecommerce is only worth USD 52 billion, contributed by only 20 product items like gems and jewellery, finished leather goods, handloom products, handicrafts, auto accessories etc.

2.5 Factors Affecting the Performance in Retail Export

- Lack of awareness about the growing opportunities in international market
- Resist to Change—to adopt e-commerce as a retail practice
- Inability to export
- Lack of awareness of export procedure
- Regulatory challenges
- Physical Infrastructure unavailability
- Financial Concerns
- Transportation medium—high shipping cost
- Lack of trust.

3. CONCLUSION

Hence forth, it is visible that India is not yet grasping full evident advantages of the at-hand e-commerce opportunities. Considering the rapid rise in the number of internet users, culminating in increased buying and selling of goods and services from Business to Consumers (B2C), the online international trade is flourishing. This is something that Retailers can benefit from directly. Therefore, there is a dire need to understand the status, challenges and opportunities of e-commerce exports from India, which depends on the e-commerce readiness of the Indian Retailers and the limiting factors within the retail Export sector via e-commerce from India.

REFERENCES

[1] Bhragab, Kalita (2016). Impact of E-commerce on Indian Economy. www.internationaljournalssrg.org, 280–283.

[2] Dana–Nicoleta Lascu, International Marketing: Managing worldwide operations in a changing International Environment.

[3] Deloitte (2014). Online Retail in India: Clicking Towards Growth.

[4] Doing Business (2017). A world Bank Flagship Report. Retrieved from: http://www.doingbusiness.org/~/media/WBG/DoingBusiness/Documents/Annual-Reports/English/DB17-Report.pdf

[5] E-commerce in India: A game Changer of the economy by The *Confederation of Indian Industry (CII) 2016.*

[6] Ernst & Young (2012). Rebirth of E-commerce in India.

[7] Export.gov "India E-Commerce: https://www.export.gov/article?id=India-e-commerce

[8] Foreign Trade Policy 2015–2020.

[9] Global B2C Ecommerce Report 2016 by E-commerce Foundation, by E-commerce foundation, retrieved from https://www.ecommercewiki.org/wikis/www.ecommercewiki.org/images/5/56/Global_B2C_Ecommerce_Report_2016.pdf

[10] International Trade Centre (2016). Bringing SMEs onto the E-commerce Highway.

[11] Kearney, A.T., Global Retail E-commerce Index 2016.

The Effectiveness of Online Advertising: Impact on Purchase Decision

Priyanka Khare[1] and Syed Haider Ali[2]

ABSTRACT: Over the past decade, Internet media have emerged as successful platform for advertising in the market. Increased web usage among consumers have strengthens the position of online advertising among consumers. Online advertising uses the internet media to target customers for delivering promotional marketing message to customers for product/services. The study examines the effectiveness of online advertising and its impact on purchase decision. The main aim of this article is to reveal the influence of online advertising on purchase decision of consumers. The results of the study will be helpful for the marketers in assessing the attitude of consumers towards internet advertising and formulating their future marketing strategy accordingly. The study is carried on 100 internet users with structured questionnaire to achieve the aim of the study.

Keywords: *Online Advertising, Purchase Decision.*

1. INTRODUCTION

Internet has emerged as versatile upcoming media for advertisement through it's online content. The online customer are growing tremendously in the current decade, the reason behind it is advancement of technology, flexibility, interactivity of online companies in the market. The revolution of online market has led to the emergence of online advertising for the target customer. Online business has transformed the mode of business. In the current scenario a number of companies had adopted online advertising for their product/services. Online advertising had emerged as a most effective direct marketing channel for the customer. On the customer perspective online

[1]Research Scholar at Dr. A.P.J. Abdul Kalam Technical University, Lucknow, India. E-mail: Priyanka.khareincvns@gmail.com

[2]Professor in Department of Business Administration at K.M.C.U.A.F., University, Lucknow, India. E-mail: Syedhaideraliabidi@gmail.com

advertisement provide an ease in accessing information regarding product/services. Online advertisement contribute to pull marketing strategy for the companies offerings. Customer gets flexibility in accessing unlimited range of products in addition to reduced time and effort on shopping. Customer themselves plays an important role in online search of information influenced by advertisement. It is customer response regarding advertisement the way how they interpret, analyse and form purchase decision regarding the product/services.

2. ONLINE ADVERTISING

Over the time span of recent years the online advertising is being popularised among internet users. Various research has been carried out to discuss and explain the research problem related with effectiveness of online purchasing and role in making the purchase decision. Online advertisement are checked while browsing and they effects customer in buying the product/services. According to Aqsa & Kartini (2015) online advertisement also influences the attitude of customer. Online ads provides information regarding the product, which form customer attitude and effect their interest in buying online. More positive the customer attitude, the stronger the interest of the customer in buying the product. Kalia and Mishra (1016) revealed from the study that customer purchasing the product not necessarily prefer online advertising. Visual graphics and animation containing ads are more preferred as compared to other online ads. Discounts showing ads are mostly preferred by the customers. In the clutter of online advertising rectangular banner ads and skyscraper ad in vertical formats gain attention of internet users. According to Lim *et al.* (2011) Malaysian consumers response to internet advertising with positive attitude. They utilise online advertisement in making purchase. The study reveals that only online advertising can be proved as a effective marketing tool, so the marketers can focus on online ads to enhance their profit and sale. Online ads should be made more attractive and consumer oriented to draw their attention. Interest, arousing curiosity and attention-seeking ads enhances memorising and recall ability of customers.

Zourikalatehsamad *et al.* (2015) also conducted a study to evaluate the effect of online ads on purchasing behaviour of consumers. The study reveals that consumers are positively influenced by online advertisement and therefore their purchasing behaviour is influenced by online advertisement. Online advertisement has its own advantage for customer which draw their attention towards it, such as cost saving, convenience, customised product or services.

2.1 Online Advertising and Social Sites

Internet users for social sites are also exposed to online ads and for different perception regarding online advertising. Studies has been conducted on users of social sites regarding their response for online advertising while operating in twitter, Facebook, YouTube etc. Verma (2016) focussed the study on online advertisement via YouTube. According to the study the number of YouTube view is high, which is mostly operated through mobile phones. Maximum number of response come across advertisement which is viewed through YouTube videos. Customer are influenced through online ads and even they buy the products which they don't need actually. Srivastava (2012) analysed that Customers mostly access internet for email checking and seeking information, they do window shopping but very less of them make purchase online. Online ads are not always entertained by internet users it irritates users of all age group. Online advertisement is considered as informative but still the credibility is not so high. The study by Pikas & Sorrentino (2014) revealed that online ads on social network sometime becomes annoying. Users are not always receptive for ads on social sites. They are not likely to be exposed to ads and marketing information. Users prefer video commercial as compared to others on YouTube. Online ads if properly designed can target a huge customers who spent their maximum time on social sites. Users mostly overlook the advertisement on social sites and skip the commercials.

2.2 Impact of Online Advertising on Customer and their Purchasing Decision

Further Gilaninia *et al.* (2013) studied advertising through internet and behaviour of consumer in purchase of product. Internet advertising is cost-effective way to target customer. Internet advertising provides sufficient amount of information for the product range, which contribute to purchase decision making of customer.

Saravanan and Sajitha (2016) analysed the perception of customer regarding online advertisement. According to the study customer are aware of online advertisement, mostly customer consider online ads as a disturbance and also as a economic marketing effort. They also consider online ads as a effective medium for purchasing of products and time saver. Online advertising influence customers in purchase of product as they are also considered as reliable medium for purchasing.

Md. S. *et al.* (2016) focussed the study on banner advertisement and purchase intention of consumers. A contingency framework was proposed which suggested the introduction of moderating variable which measures various consequences of the dimensions on consumer purchase intention influenced by online banner ads. The major contributing factor affecting purchase intention were discussed. According to McCoy *et al.* (2004) inlining of ads effects retention of website information Pop ups were found less effective as compared to inline ads. Online ads interfere online contents. Users are disturbed due to interference of ads during their task.

Rzemieniak & Iannuli (2015) assessed effectiveness of settlement models for online campaign. The study was carried out for small and medium sized companies on a polish market. Majority of companies were running their advertising campaign online. CPC model (cost per click) was found as more effective and popular model for campaign settlement followed by CPS and CPM. Search engine advertising is most effective according to majority of respondents, since it is mostly preferred for searching information. News portal and social media advertising are also becoming effective. Dencheva (2009) analysed the effectiveness of online advertisement by discussing model for effectiveness of online advertisement. Banner ads manages the relationship with the customers individually. A well designed ads appeals users which performing their original task, clicking on online ads is their secondary task. Banner ads becomes more effective due to media factors such as media dispersion, CPM, length of campaign etc. Anusha (2016) studied the effectiveness and usefulness of online advertising. Customer mostly prefer advertised products and online advertisement are preferred as compared to any other advertisement. Video advertisement is more popular among consumers. Customer spend very less time on online purchase and they are also scare of online fraud and malpractices.

This research work is in continuation with the former research work it discerns the behaviour of consumers regarding online purchasing. Since internet has its immense presence in current scenario due to which online marketing and online advertising has gained importance among consumers. The research paper emphasises the relationship between internet user checking ads on web and their participation in online advertising. The behaviour of consumer regarding online ads whether the accept it positively or consider it as interference in browsing. The study also analyses the purchasing of product/services due to online ads.

3. CONCEPTUAL FRAMEWORK OF THE STUDY

Online advertisement: Online advertisement can be defined as "The activity of attracting customer towards product/services through electronic media. It is a economic and profitable method for promotion of product/services. There are specialized companies in the market known as 'Advertising firm' that manages online marketing campaign. Advertisement through electronic media has geared towards defining modern form of business through unique and useful application.

3.1 Types of Online Advertisement

There are major four types of online advertising which are very popular in business world and among customers:

- **Display and Banner Ads:** Banner ads comprises of some text (eye catching image or headlines). A click on banner ads ends on advertising websites due to hyperlink. It provides relevant information to the customers and propel them to buy the product. Display ads are visual ads that appears on websites related with the content/services.
- **Classified Ads:** Typically short messages which can be popularly seen in newspaper, periodicals etc. These are cheaper than large display advertisements.
- **Search Advertising:** The method of placing the online ads on the web pages is search advertising. When the internet user type a particular keyword in the search engines for the product/services the ads appears on the web page.

- **Media/Video Ads:** Ads which can be seen parallel while watching content. These are online video ads consist of text, display and video of product/services.

4. RESEARCH HYPOTHESIS

1. H_0: There is no significant relationship between checking ads while browsing and interference in browsing due to online ads.

   H_1: There is a significant relationship between checking ads while browsing and interference in browsing due to online ads.
2. H_2: There is no significant relationship between checking ads while browsing and participating in online advertisement.

   H_2: There is a significant relationship between checking ads while browsing and participating in online advertisement.
3. H_3: There is no significant relationship between checking ads while browsing and purchasing product online after watching the advertisement online.

   H_3: There is a significant relationship between checking ads while browsing and purchasing product online after watching the advertisement online.

5. OBJECTIVE OF THE STUDY

- To study the impact of online advertising on Internet users.
- To analyse the impact of online advertising on purchase of product.
- To study the consumer behaviour regarding online advertising.

6. RESEARCH METHODOLOGY

The Research on this topic involve collection of both Primary and secondary data. The primary data was collected through survey method. The secondary data was collected through various sources such as books, journals and Internet. A well-structured questionnaire was used as research tool for collection of data from 100 respondents. The respondents were from 18–35 age group and they were net savvy. The primary data was collected through convenience sampling from the Lucknow city. The collected data was presented through graphical presentation.

Nonparametric test is used for analysing the data. Bivariate Correlation is applied to the test which measures the strength of association between variables. Two type of bivariate correlation is applied for testing the data in this research work:

- Kendall's tau-b (τ_b) correlation coefficient (Kendall's tau-b).
- Spearman's rank correlation coefficient (Spearman's rho).

Variables Used in the Study: There are four variable considered to study and analyse the effectiveness of online advertisement on consumers and impact on purchasing decision:

- Checking ads while browsing
- Interference in browsing due to online ads
- Participating in online advertisement
- Purchasing product online after watching the advertisement online.

7. RESULT AND DISCUSSION

The accomplishment of data collection on this topic involves data collection through well-structured questionnaire.

Table 1: Demographical Characteristics of Respondents

	Variable	*Total*	*Percentage*
Gender	Male	69	69%
	Female	31	31%
Education	High School	15	15%
	Intermediate	24	24%
	Graduation	45	45%
	Post- Graduation	16	16%
Place of residence	Rural	22	22%
	Urban	78	78%

H_1: There is a significant relationship between checking ads while browsing and interference in browsing due to online ads.

Table 2: Showing the result of correlation bivariate analysis for relationship between checking ads while browsing and Interference in Browsing Due to Online ads

			Check ads while browsing	*Interference due to online advertising during browsing*
Kendall's tau-b	Check ads while browsing	Correlation Coefficient Sig. (2-tailed) N	1.000 . 100	.651** .000 100
	Interference due to online advertising during browsing	Correlation Coefficient Sig. (2-tailed) N	.651** .000 100	1.000 . 100
Spearman's Rho	Check ads while browsing	Correlation Coefficient Sig. (2-tailed) N	1.000 . 100	.651** .000 100
	Interference due to online advertising during browsing	Correlation Coefficient Sig. (2-tailed) N	.651** .000 100	1.000 . 100

**. Correlation is significant at the 0.01 level (2-tailed).

The results are present in above matrix, as it can be seen. Nevertheless tabular presentation shows the Kendalls's tau-b correlation and Spearman's rho correlation, its significance value and the sample size on which the calculation was based on. In the above matrix we can see that Kendalls's tau-b correlation and Spearman's rho correlation is 0.651 that is statistically significant. The significance, 2-tailed level is. 000 which shows there is significance between checking ads while browsing and interference in browsing due to online ads and the relationship is positive 65.2% which means that as one variable goes up or down so will the other one.

$H_{2:}$ There is significant relationship between checking ads while browsing and participating in online advertisement.

Table 3: Showing the result of correlation bivariate analysis for relationship between checking ads while browsing and participating in online advertisement

			Check ads while browsing	*Participation in online ads*
Kendall's tau-b	Check ads while browsing	Correlation Coefficient	1.000	.024
		Sig. (2-tailed)	.	.808
		N	100	100
	Participation in online ads	Correlation Coefficient	.024	1.000
		Sig. (2-tailed)	.808	.
		N	100	100
Spearman's rho	Check ads while browsing	Correlation Coefficient	1.000	.024
		Sig. (2-tailed)	.	.810
		N	100	100
	Participation in online ads	Correlation Coefficient	.024	1.000
		Sig. (2-tailed)	.810	.
		N	100	100

The results are present above in matrix, as it can be seen. Nevertheless tabular presentation shows the Kendalls's tau-b correlation and Spearman's rho correlation, its significance value and the sample size on which the calculation was based on. In the above matrix we can see that there is no correlation between the variables and the result is insignificant, which means that the variable have no effect on each other. There is no relationship between checking ads while browsing and participating in online advertisement.

H_3: There is a significant relationship between checking ads while browsing and purchasing product online after watching the advertisement online.

Table 4: Showing the result of correlation bivariate analysis for relationship between checking ads while browsing and purchasing product online after watching the advertisement online

			Check ads while browsing	*Purchase of product after watching online ads*
Kendall's tau-b	Check ads while browsing	Correlation Coefficient	1.000	.106
		Sig. (2-tailed)	.	.293
		N	100	100
	Purchase of product after watching online ads	Correlation Coefficient	.106	1.000
		Sig. (2-tailed)	.293	.
		N	100	100
Spearman's rho	Check ads while browsing	Correlation Coefficient	1.000	.106
		Sig. (2-tailed)	.	.295
		N	100	100
	purchase of product after watching online ads	Correlation Coefficient	.106	1.000
		Sig. (2-tailed)	.295	.
		N	100	100

The results are present above in matrix, as it can be seen. Nevertheless tabular presentation shows the Kendall's tau-b correlation and Spearman's rho correlation, its significance value and the sample size on which the calculation was based on. In the above matrix we can see that there is no correlation between the variables and the result is in-significant, which means that the variable have no effect on each other. There is no relationship between checking ads while browsing and purchasing product online after watching the advertisement online.

8. CONCLUSION

From the data and analysis of data it can be concluded that checking ads while browsing the websites and interference due to online advertising are related to each other. Checking ads interferes browsing. Internet users checks online ads they are attracted towards banner ads pop-ups and video advertising is the most popularised form of online advertising. The internet user checking the online ads sometime participate in online advertising but there is no correlation between checking ads and participating in advertising. It is not necessary that people purchase the product after watching the online advertising. There are a lots of online buyer which even not seen the online ads but they buy the product. Now customer are well aware of online marketing and advertising through internet. Customers encounter these online ads while browsing social sites, informative sites, news sites etc. and they have a positive attitude towards it but still online channel needs time to grasp consumers online.

REFERENCES

[1] Anusha, G. (2016). Effectiveness of Online Advertising. *International Journal of Research – GRANTHAALAYAH.* Vol. 4(3), 14–21.

[2] Aqsa, Muhammad and Kartini, Dwi (2015). Impact of Online Advertising on Consumer Attitudes and Interests buy Online (Survey on Students of Internet Users in Makassar). *International Journal of Scientific & Technology Research.* Vol. 4(4), 230–236.

[3] Busen Salem, Mohamed S., Mustaffa Che, Su and Bahtiar, Mohamad (2016). Impacts of online banner advertisement on consumers" purchase intention: A theoretical framework. *Asia Pacific Journal of Education, Arts and Sciences,* Vol. 3(1), 75–82.

[4] Dencheva, Silvena (2009). Effectiveness of Internet advertisement. *3rd Central European Conference in Regional Science – CERS.*988–994.

[5] Gilaninia, Shahram; Taleghani, Mohammad and Karimi, Houman (2013). Internet Advertising and Consumer Behavior in the Purchase of Products. *Journal of Research and Development,* Vol. 1(1), 45–52.

[6] Kalia, Gitanjali and Mishra, Ashutosh (2016). Effects of online Advertising on Consumers. *IOSR Journal of humanities and social science,* Vol. 21(9), 35–41.

[7] Lim, Yet-Mee; Yap, Ching-Seng and Lau, Teck-Chai (2011). The Effectiveness of Online Advertising in Purchase Decision: Liking, Recall and Click. *Australian Journal of Basic and Applied Sciences,* Vol. 5(9), 1517–1524.

[8] McCoy, Scott; Everard, Andrea; Galletta, Dennis and Polak, Peter (2004). A Study of the Effects of Online Advertising: A Focus on Pop-Up and In-Line Ads. *Proceedings of the Third Annual Workshop on HCI Research in MIS, Washington, D.C.*, December 10–11, 50–54.

[9] Pikas, Bohdan and Sorrentino, Gabi (2014). The Effectiveness of Online Advertising: Consumer's Perceptions of Ads on Facebook, Twitter and YouTube. *Journal of Applied Business and Economics,* Vol. 16(4), 70–81.

[10] Rzemieniak, M. and Iannuli, F. (2015). The Effectiveness of Online Advertising of Companies in Poland. *Polish Journal of Management Studies,* Vol. 12(2), 130–138.

[11] Saravanan, M. and Sajitha, S. (2016). Consumer Perception Towards Online Advertisement. *International Research Journal of Engineering and Technology,* Vol. 3(11), 197–202.

[12] Srivastava, Priyanka (2012). A Study on Impact of Online Advertising on Consumer Behavior (With Special Reference to E-mails). *International Journal of Engineering and Management Sciences,* Vol. 3(4), 461–465.

[13] Verma, Supriya (2016). Study on the Effect and Behavior of People Toward YouTube Advertisements. *International journal of management and economics invention,* Vol. 2 (2), 541–546.

[14] Zourikalatehsamad, Naser; Payambarpour Seyed, Abdorreza; Alwashali, Ibrahim and Abdolkarimi, Zahra (2015). The Impact of Online Advertising on Consumer Purchase Behavior Based on Malaysian Organizations. *International Scholarly and Scientific Research & Innovation,* Vol. 9(10), 3417–3422.

Big Data Analytics for E-Commerce

Prateeti Johari*

1. INTRODUCTION

You are thinking of buying a few fitness gear and accessories products, so you open your browser and search for it. After browsing for quite a while, you get back to you daily chores. You probably would have noticed similar products, popping up on every new tab that you open, including your social networking sites. This eventually would lead to you buying that particular product. This might be understood as target marketing but, it has a more complex concept backing it up. It is all brought together as a result of data science. This process uses data science to bring about such great revenues for online marketplaces, is, in layman's terms known as data analytics. Big Data is all about the non-traditional ways of dealing with the modern digital data.

Big data analytics is the way toward looking at huge and varied data i.e., BIG DATA to reveal shrouded designs, obscure connections, market trends, customer inclinations and other valuable data that can enable organizations to make more-educated business decisions. These data sets are vast and complex and without a doubt overwhelming, that traditional data processing is not capable to process them. Big Data is being utilized in practically every sector, except it is most widely being utilized in e-commerce sector, which primarily deals in B2B, B2C and C2C arenas.

Any big retail firm would value this data extremely as it helps them in predicting the user interest, their likes and dislikes and provide their customers relative search results when they shop on their site, so that they attract the customer by giving them the required and relevant searches of the products or items. These preferences are all generated through Big Data analytics.

And it goes a long way for the organization by aiding them for future—big decisions and contingencies, whenever they do arise. As far

*Lucknow University. E-mail: prateeti.johari@gmail.com

as short term gains are concerned, the profits have notably increased. It has been ascertained that e-commerce firms that inject big data analytics (BDA) into their value chain, experience 5–6% higher productivity than their competitors (McAfee and Brynjolfsson, 2012).

While the use of emerging internet-based technologies provides e-commerce firms with benefits (e.g., real-time customer service, personalized offers or improved interaction) (Riggins, 1999), BDA can further solidify these impacts by enabling informed decisions based on critical insights (Jao, 2013). Specifically, in the e-commerce context, "big data enables merchants to track each user's behavior and connect the dots to determine the most effective ways to convert one-time customers into repeat buyers" (Jao, 2013, p. 1).

2. ESSENTIALS OF BDA

In 2001, Gartner's Doug Laney first presented what became known as the "three Vs of big data" to describe some of the characteristics that make big data different from other data processing.

2.1 Volume

With high volume of data-structured or unstructured, comes a way bigger responsibility of sorting it and further storing it securely. Now due to large size of various organizations and their work requirements, it exceeds the capabilities of a single computer and availability of limited storage. This high volume of data/information becomes a challenge of pooling, allocating, and coordinating resources from different sources. And as such cluster management and algorithms capable of breaking tasks into smaller pieces and speedily working through it, in the most efficient manner become increasingly important.

2.2 Velocity

The difference between big data systems and other data systems is the speed of information going through the system at any given point of time. Data is constantly being added, filed, processed and analyzed so as to keep up with the influx of new information and to bring up the relevant data when required to understand it and take decisions accordingly by updating the current information.

This changing focus on almost instant feedback has forced big data practitioners to move from a batch processing and feedback approach to a real-time streaming and operating approach. And this requires systems which are robust and can handle heavy data.

2.3 Variety

Data is collected from various sources and as such this data can be useful or useless depending upon the nature of organization. This data is collected from internal systems like applications and server logs, from social media as well as other external sources. BDA seeks to handle and manage potentially useful data regardless of its source and it consolidates all the useful information available into a single storage area. Any transformation and changes in the data take place when the need arises during the time of processing.

2.4 Other Characteristics

Besides the aforementioned characteristics, some more have been pointed out and they are:

- **Veracity:** The variety of sources and the complex processing can lead to skcpticism and challenges in understanding and evaluation of the quality of the data and therefore, the quality of the resulting analyzed information.
- **Variability:** Variation in the data leads to differences in quality. Additional resources may be required to identify, process, or filter low quality data to make it more useful and accurate.
- **Value:** The ultimate aim of big data is to deliver value or valuable information. Often, the systems and processes are so complex, resulting in difficulty in using the data and extracting value out of it.

3. BIG DATA—THE HYPE (GLOBAL GROWTH OF BIG DATA)

Big data is an emerging topic which has uncertain origins. Diebold (2012) argues that the term "big data… would have most probably originated during lunch-table conversations at Silicon Graphics Inc. (SGI) in the mid-1990s." Despite its references in mid-nineties, this term and concept became popular in the start of this decade, i.e.

2011 (Figure 1). The current build-up and hype about this can be accredited to the promotional activities done and initiatives taken by IBM and other leading technology companies who invested in creating an analytics market.

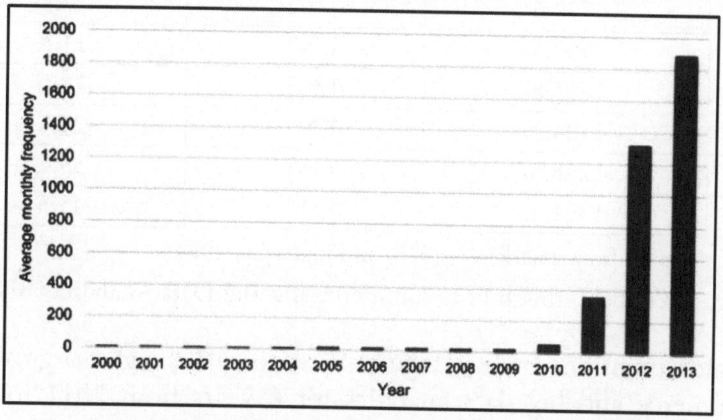

Fig. 1: Frequency Distribution of Documents Containing the Term "Big Data" in ProQuest Research Library

Big Data is a topic whose definitions have evolved swiftly. An online survey was conducted of 154 C-suite global executives conducted by Harris interactive on behalf of SAP in April 2012 ***"Small and midsize companies look to make big gains with big data,"*** 2012. Figure 2, above shows how different executives had different understanding of big data, wherein some definitions focused on what it is, while others tried to answer what it does.

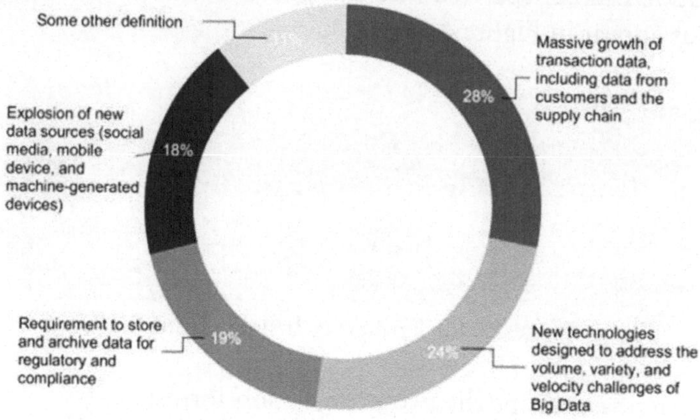

Fig. 2: Definitions of Big Data Based on an Online Survey of 154 Global Executives in April 2012

Year	*Growth in the number of e-commerce customers worldwide (in millions)*	*Growth in e-commerce sales per customer worldwide (in US$)*	*Growth in big data analytics (BDA) market worldwide (in billions)*
2011	792.6	1162	7.3
2012	903.6	1243	11.8
2013	1015.8	1318	18.6
2014	1124.3	1399	28.5
2015	1228.5	1459	38.4
2016	1321.4	1513	45.3

Source: Adapted from emarketer (2013) and Piatetsky, 2014).

Fig. 3: Global Growth in E-commerce and Big Data Analytics (BDA)

The aforementioned table (Figure 3) represents the global growth in e-commerce and big data analytics for 6 years from 2011 to 2016 showing an increase in e-commerce customers and sales per customers and likewise a growth in sales in BDA market worldwide.

4. BIG DATA ANALYTICS PROCESS

Enormous data is useless in a vacuum. Its potential value is expanded just for exact decision making. To empower data/evidence-based decision making, organizations require highly proficient procedures to turn high volumes of quick moving and diverse data into meaningful information. The general procedure of gaining insights from enormous information can be separated into five phases (Labrinidis and Jagadish, 2012), as appear in Figure 4.

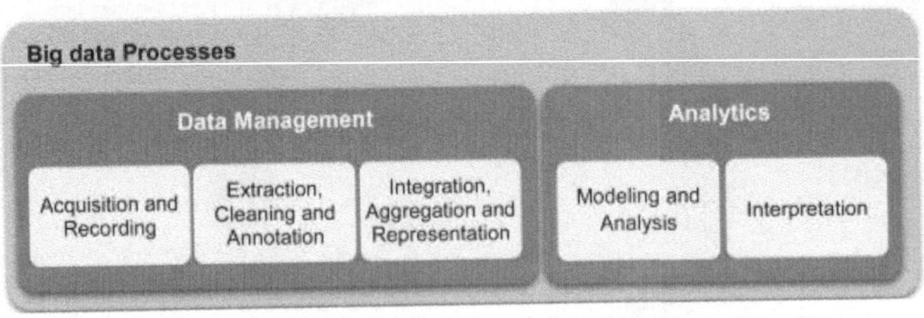

Fig. 4: Processes for Extracting Insights from Big Data

These five phases shape the two primary sub-forms:

- Data Management
- Data Analysis

Data management includes procedures and supporting advances to procure and store information and to plan and recover it for examination. Data analytics, refers to methods used to dissect and gain insight from huge information. Subsequently, enormous information examination can be seen as a sub-process in the general procedure of 'knowledge extraction' from huge information.

5. FUNCTIONS SUPPORTED BY ANALYTICS IN E-COMMERCE INDUSTRY

E-commerce companies use Big Data in two ways. One is to analyze past behavior of customers to find patterns, and the other is real-time analysis, that is, reacting when the customer is shopping online," said Asheet Makhija, country leader-information management, International Business Machines Corp. (IBM) India/South Asia. This list covers broad roles in E-commerce industry.

5.1 Supply Chain Management

This incorporates overseeing information for items appropriate from distribution center to the client. Internet business enterprises utilize analytics widely to oversee Inventory. Additionally a critical bit of work is done into advancing transportation and estimating delivery price.

5.2 Merchant/Customer Fraud Detection

Despite the fact that the E-Commerce organization may have nothing to do with this misrepresentation, they are the people who pay for it. Notwithstanding, fakes are not generally from the trader side. Despite the fact that it is uncommon, clients likewise make false claims in cheats. At first every one of these fakes were taken care of physically, yet with time E-Commerce is moving towards creating prescient calculation to recognize fakes and keep away from them if conceivable.

5.3 Merchant Analytics/Online Marketing Analysis

Traders shape the center of E-Commerce industry. In the event that the vendor develops, E-trade supplier additionally develops. So E-Commerce players do broad examination for Merchants to get into new markets or set the correct cost for their products. For example, Amazon can prescribe a Cricket Bat merchant to keep Hockey sticks as a result of a developing interest in his area. Such choices would have been significantly more costly for the merchant, had they not joined forces with E-Commerce players.

5.4 Recommender Systems

Recommender frameworks in E-Commerce industry are not altogether different from those of YouTube. These engines fill in as blueprint for clients to explore through the store of this virtual environment. Recommender engines have been one of the strongest contributors to technological analytics.

5.5 Pricing

E-commerce companies need to have the ability to constantly change pricing on millions of products on a daily basis based on their consumption, competition, demand for products, substitute goods etc.

5.6 Personalization

According to Harvard Business Review, Research shows that personalization can deliver five to eight times the ROI on marketing expenditure and lift sales 10% or more. This Personalization can be delivered through data analysis.

5.7 Make Big Predictions

Huge data analysis makes it workable for you to acquire a top to bottom look at a wide range of channels in your organization, from stock/inventory to sales. You can, for example, utilize enormous information analysis to take a look at the season of year in which certain products of your company sell better. You would then be able to take this data and ensure that you have enough stock accessible to capitalize on this surge in demand. By utilizing huge information to make predictions, you can guarantee that your business is constantly prepared for occasional surges, and make the most out of the items you offer.

6. HADOOP—THE TECHNOLOGY FOR BDA

It consists of a distributed file system called HDFS, with a cluster management and resource scheduler on top called YARN (Yet another

Resource Negotiator). Batch processing capabilities are provided by the MapReduce computation engine. Other computational and analysis systems can be run alongside MapReduce in modern Hadoop deployments.

Hadoop is the exceedingly progressed and broadly utilized technology and makes it feasible to run applications on systems with a huge number of hardware nodes, and to deal with a large number of terabytes of data. Its circulated record framework encourages fast information exchange among nodes and enables the system to keep working, should there be an occurrence of a node malfunction. This approach brings down the danger of disastrous system failure and unforeseen big data loss, regardless of the possibility that a large number of nodes end up inoperative. Hadoop has rapidly evolved as a base for big data processing tasks, for example, scientific analysis, business and deals arranging, and processing colossal volumes of data. Following quite a while of improvement inside the open source group, Hadoop 1.0 became publically accessible in November 2012 as a major aspect of the Apache project sponsored by the Apache Software Foundation.

Innovations like **Apache Sqoop** can take existing information from social databases and add it to a major information framework. Additionally, **Apache Flume** and **Apache Chukwa** are ventures intended to aggregate and import application and server logs. Queuing systems like **Apache Kafka** can likewise be utilized as an interface between different information generators and a major information framework.

7. SUCCESSFUL CASES OF VARIOUS E-COMMERCE ORGANIZATIONS

7.1 Snapdeal

It has been one of the early movers in Big Data analytics for personalization and recommendation so as to make product searches easier, also said that real-time analytics has become a key focus area for companies. It makes use of a multi-tier system, which they call the Hadoop-based farm. Snapdeal, which has over 20 million subscribers and generates terabytes of data through the interactions that happen with customers in addition to a catalogue of over 5 million, churns

15 million data points (related data set like a consumer shopping on specific days for a particular thing) within two hours, using Hadoop. About 35% of its orders come from recommendation and personalized systems, and the conversion rate of such orders is 20-30% higher than normal orders, the company claims.

7.2 Amazon

Amazon's recommendation engine generates 'you might also want' prompts to identify possible needs of customers based on the analysis of transactions history and book views.

7.3 Macys

Macys, an e-retailer in the US, has developed an analytics infrastructure that can optimize pricing of 73 million items in just over one hour (Davenport *et al.*, 2012). Macy's also analyzes data at the stock keeping unit (SKU) level to ensure that products of different assortments are readily available.

7.4 Netflix Inc.

It created various customer segments (e.g., adventures, crime movies, family features, movies on books etc.) by analyzing over one billion reviews in categories such as liked, loved, hated, etc. Using a visualization and demand analytics tool, Netflix introduced "House of Cards", "Iron Fist" program in the United States (USA) which is a huge success as a new product.

8. CONCLUSION

BDA has emerged as the new field which improves decision making capability of the organizations by understanding the behavior of customer, which ultimately helps in knowing about their interests and this information acquired can then be used by the e-commerce vendors and websites which show customers the products they like. BDA has revolutionized the way modern day e-commerce websites/web-portals operate. The vendors value the information, analyze it and then take decisions accordingly.

This is a process which deals with data, sources, skills, and systems in order to create a competitive advantage for the organization and its product. As explained above leading firms Snapdeal, Amazon, Netflix are already taking huge advantage from it and improving their hold in the market and experiencing high growth. Other organizations should also follow suit use the BDA accordingly, so as to play in the big leagues.

BIBLIOGRAPHY

[1] Ellingwood, J. (2016, 09 28). *An Introduction to Big Data Concepts and Terminology*. Retrieved 08 2017.

[2] Haider, A.G. (n.d.). Beyond the hype: Big data concepts, methods, and analytics. *International Journal of Information Management.*

[3] Pavithra B., D.N. (2016). The Study of Big Data Analytics in E-Commerce. *International Journal of Advanced Research in Computer and Communication Engineering,* 6.

[4] Samuel Fosso Wamba, S.A. (2016). Big data analytics in e-commerce: A systematic, 54.

[5] Srivastava, M. (2014, July 13). *Using Big Data to net online buyers.* Retrieved august 2017, from livemint.com.

Competitive Advantage Assessment of E-Business in India[#]

Swati Jain*

ABSTRACT: E-business in India having exceptional growth in past ten years; drift towards online marketing laying down foundation to achieve more in future. It is distributing economic growth and employment opportunities from big cities to small town at large. Though, small and medium businesses facing tough competition with growing market, investments, liberal state policies. This article investigates the linkages among e-business benefits and competitive advantage; elucidate theoretical model for economic analysis of e-business in India: The Porter's competitive advantage model for economic assessment of the factors that influence e-business. This model not only distills the factors as the dynamic forces of e-business but also provides insight to smooth the progress of the assessment of e-business and identification of the competitive advantages of this emerging business model. The model is effectively proficient to be the frame for enhanced policymaking process by the public and private sectors; to envisage modifications in the swiftly growing e-business. Thus, model may be integrated into broader research framework construction for the analysis of e-business development and its role in gaining competitive advantage. This competitive advantage is the key to industry and stakeholders of any business model, i.e. consumers (national, regional and local) and governments.

Keywords: *Competitive Advantage Model, Drivers of Inclusive Development, E-Business.*

1. INTRODUCTION

ICT has become the driving force for business in the Globalisation era. It has also enhanced the dissemination of information to the uninformed but prospective entrepreneurs. E-Commerce transactions facilitated by digital networks have not only forced all types of business to become competitive but has equally made them efficient and

[#]Paper submitted for "International Conference on e-Business" 2017, organized by SRMGPC and SRMU, Lucknow.

*Assistant Professor, Department of Economics, University of Allahabad.
E-mail: jswati2008@gmail.com

integrated. In case of India E-Commerce transaction (as a subset of e-business) is expected to be growing at a rate of 28 percent and reaching USD 67 billion by 2020 (IBEF September 2017 update). According to Government Ministry, the ecommerce segment has been estimated around USD 33 billion in 2017 (Economic Times July 28, 2017). Internet and Smart Phone penetration, young demographic profile, better economic performance and supportive government policies are assumed to be the factors behind this growth. More importantly, this growth has laid down the foundation for e-business. There have been several research studies analyzing the positive impact of use of ICT for business process in developing countries like India.

The term E-Business was initiated by IBM in 1997 to describe businesses run on internet or use internet technologies to improve its productivity & profitability. E-Business has been defined as procurement, financial as well commercial transactions based on information technology. In other words e-business is the easiest way to reach all involved in the supply chain. It has also been explained as application of information technology tools and processes for various internal and external dimensions of a business. E-Business w@tch,[1] defines e-business as an "automate business processes (both intra-and inter-firm) over computer mediated networks". In the E-business automation and optimization practices are adopted for each type of business process. Thus efficiency and effectiveness of various business processes such as procurement of raw material and equipment, information about markets and vendors improved management of resources; time efficiency in supply chain and logistics, improved internal and external communication, management of distribution networks, reduced costs and the many others benefits can be achieved (OECD: 2002; Dwivedi *et al.,* 2005). The Porter's theory of global competitiveness has emerged as a new conceptual model for effective analysis of E-Business (Porter 1998; Porter, M & Kramer 2006).

2. RELEVANCE OF PORTER'S MODEL OF COMPETITIVE ADVANTAGE FOR E-BUSINESS

According to Porter the emerging global business environment provides to the firm as well as entrepreneurs, necessary market information, factors of production, technology and scope to compete.

[1]European Commission Market Observatory launched in 2002.

Further, the limitation of the natural factor driven competitiveness has been questioned and thus competitiveness based on skill and factors acquired is propagated. Despite the country's situation, individual firm's capacity and competitive advantage is more crucial. Porter's Diamond Model incorporates factors related to global supply and demand, industry structure, level of competition in the input and output markets and strategies of rivals in a general equilibrium framework. Thus in the given set of internal and external factors affecting the business, the interaction between the four interrelated and mutually reinforcing forces have been presented in the Diamond Model as mentioned below in Figure 1.

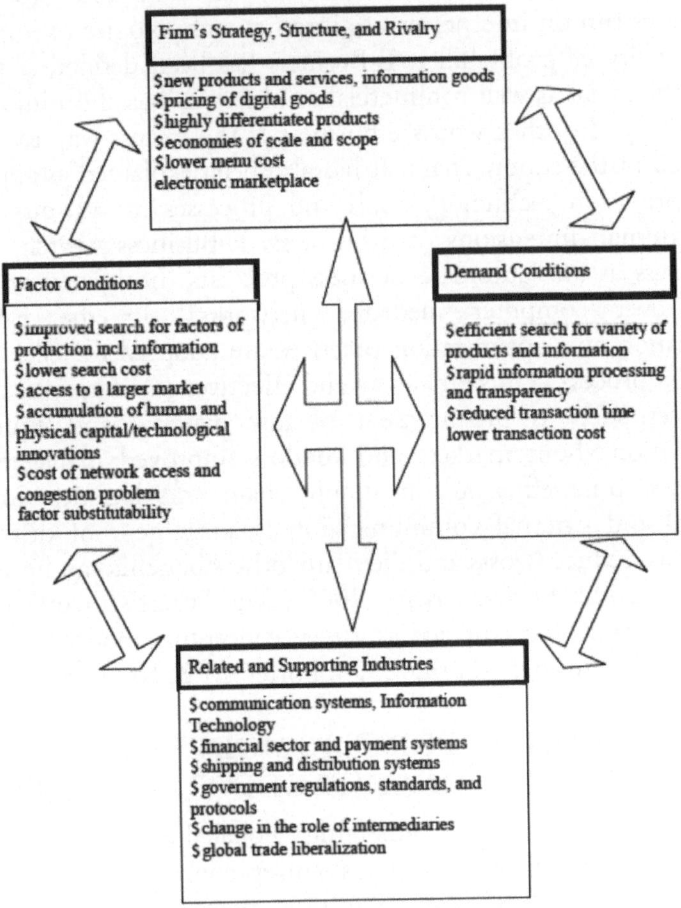

Fig. 1

Source: Adopted from Yousefi, A (2009).

Porter initially discussed five forces, which form firm's competitive advantage in the industry: threat of new entrants, threat of substitutes, bargaining power of suppliers, bargaining power of buyers and competition between competitors. Later it was argued that competitive advantage is based on the various functions and process which a firm undergoes in its day to day business. The relevance of this model has been elaborated under five segments as follows:

2.1 Improved Availability, Accumulation and Access of Factors of Production

Factor conditions should be understood as the availability as well as access of resources such as human capital, physical capital, technology and information. Labour force through accumulation of skills as well as managerial knowledge is transformed into human capital. It is the single most important factor that is instrumental for e-readiness and the success of e-commerce. Human capital in any country is the result of targeted public investment and R&D expenditures by profit-seeking firms and governments specifically in countries like India. (Kenneth 2002; Dwivedi *et al.*, 2005; Dossani *et al.*, 2005; Niavand & Zia: 2017) This is due to the fact that acquiring ICTs and maintaining productive use is a costly affair for private firms and entrepreneurs. Costs of ICTs often emerges as a substantial barrier to entry for firms and entrepreneurs but it may help in lowering the cost in medium to long term in a labour force abundant country. E-Business takes place when the producers, consumers, intermediaries, and all business processes undergo fundamental changes though market interaction. Information dissemination though internet and digital platform improves economic efficiency of search for required factors for any business. Such efficiency results not only due to the speed and ease with which information is obtained, but also due to volume and quality available to all market participants. Given the appropriate infrastructures and logistics, firms can participate and compete in such an environment, which brings about both unprecedented opportunities as the digital space is without boundary and restriction. Further, the digital platform creates value in many ways. It reduces the search costs and empowers producers and consumers by making the global market accessible to them virtually at one click. Proponents of the Resource Based theory argued that when factors are valuable, heterogeneous, non-transferable, owned exclusively by the organization, and hard-to-copy by competitors, may provide positive outcomes, such as reduced costs or increased revenue. Further, the innovation-imitation complementarity due to their positive externalities, create larger value.

2.2 Cost and Time Efficient Search for Demand Conditions

Entrepreneurs derive incentive for investment and innovation if there is a large scope for demand of a product or service offered in the market. Demand largely depends on population size, level of per capita purchasing power and income accrual, relative prices of products in competition. Potential demand evolves continuously over time and in different dimensions. The recent developments and promotion of digital technology and networks has lowered the cost of search for buyers and sellers and also the opportunity cost of price and market discovery. Use and benefits of ICT are not only limited to search and supply of final products and services but equally to intermediate products and services. Transaction cost in terms of storage, delivery, follow-up services have all been reduced and the process has become transparent. Such an environment reduces the risk of market failure by lowering information asymmetry about product characteristics such as price, quality, and the like.

2.3 Related and Supporting Industries, Intermediaries and Firm Structure

ICT based businesses requires proper marketing structure, banking and transportation facilities, and other infrastructures such as communication systems, distribution channels, intermediaries between buyer and seller. Further along with the availability, affordability of these services, existence in the digital space, information security lowers the business risk and enhances the willingness to participate among the probable entrepreneurs and firms. E-Business relies heavily on distribution systems for the physical delivery as well as electronic delivery. Digital technology allows products to be distributed quickly at a very low cost (Shapiro & Varian, 1999). Perhaps, government policy in terms of government regulations, standards and protocols, becomes the most important factor affecting communication networks, transportation and distribution systems. The nature of information goods necessitates government involvement for protecting intellectual property rights, information privacy, and fair competition (Shapiro & Varian, 1999). In the E-Business scenario role of intermediaries has undergone a paradigm shift. Particularly in case of rural entrepreneurs and business ventures, online intermediaries can play a very important role in not only reducing the distance between buyer and seller but reducing the network costs as well. In the new role of intermediaries, they are also the provider of bundle of services in the market such as travel, tourism, real estate and many others. It is important to note that E-Business integrates and focuses more on B2B and B2G along with B2C, thus strengthening the business process. It helps in making the interaction of a particular firm to government and its backend and frontline suppliers more efficient and cost effective. E-Tenders, E-Sewa, E-Governance, E-Banking are such platforms which have been contributing significantly in the current business process.

2.4 Business Strategy, Organizational Structure, Rivalry and Threats

Rivalry and threats are an integral part of business and helps in strengthening firm's competitive advantage by making augmentation of investment and updation of production processes compulsory. According to Porter (1990), rivalry, especially a domestic one, is a major contributor to the global competitiveness of a firm. E-business and associated technologies continue to have a major impact on the way organizations conduct business. However, in the current environment which is conducive for imitative behaviour, organizations find it increasingly difficult to create competitive advantage by simply implementing pervasive e-business solutions. Sharing of innovation related know-how helps in avoiding technology based rivalry among entrepreneurs. Although innovation inimitability may be important for first movers to protect generated advantage, it has the potential to spur an innovation substitution cycle that cannot protect advantage sustainability (Troshani & Rao 2007).

In addition pricing of digital goods or information goods and product differentiation are the two factors which affects the business strategy in this environment. Pricing as an important part of business strategy not only becomes easy but becomes real time. Participants in such an environment must inevitably adapt a new set of organizational and procedural rules. For firms to enjoy a global competitive advantage, internalization of domestic and foreign practices and well as facilitiating role by the government is also essential. The governments should engage in harmonizing practices at the international level and disseminate useful information. Certain factors which affect each and every modern business, such as, Intellectual Property Rights, domain name registration, internet security, service protocol, Web host, Application service provider, ERP, SAP also has to be integrated and utilized for the usual business process. E-business applications are considered to be an enabling mechanism that enhances organizational competencies, thereby allowing organizations to deliver traditional and new services more effectively and efficiently. Studies have shown that e-business solutions are gradually becoming prone to commoditization. In this context, e-business solutions no longer provide organizations with strategic differentiation. Many argue that investments in e-business are a competitive necessity rather than a source of competitive advantage.

3. CONCLUDING REMARKS

Porter (1985) argues that competitive advantage can be generated through a cost leadership, a differentiation strategy or a niche market strategy that in turn can lead to better market performance and profitability. Specifically, four theories provide a theoretical foundation for competitive advantage namely, the resource-based view; the transaction cost theory; agency theory and resource dependence theory that are used for explaining competitive advantage,

It can thus be concluded that ICT has transformed the nature of business. Porter's theory emerges as an appropriate model for E-Business. It can also be instrumental in examining the factors which are hindering growth of e-commerce in developing countries. In case of India, special attention has to be given to the ICT-skilled labor force, structural deficiencies as well as institutional bottlenecks. With the rapid growth of the ICT sector in India, there is an urgent need for appropriate there is an urgent need for appropriate data and information about use of ICT. More importantly measuring and identifying the digital divide and its linkage with employment and income levels have to be researched and analysed in detail. There are opportunities as well as challenges for e-business in India arising from certain recent developments. One being the fact, that almost 12000 rural post office branches are now digital and moving towards payment banking facility. The adoption of digital villages and e-governance as a policy measure will contribute to the enhancement of the competitive advent-age of the probable entrepreneurs. According to studies by CII, IBEF, FICCI and ASSOCHAM digital India plan can boost GDP upto $ 1 trillon by 2025. As per the World Bank report, a 10 percent increase in mobile and broadband penetration can increase per capita GDP by 0.8 to 1.5 percent. India being the second largest telecom market and third largest internet market has still a huge untapped market in rural India. E-Business is supposed to create large social impact in forms of e-education, healthcare, financial inclusion and economic empowerment. More importantly, digital platforms can help farmers to develop their competitive advantage in this global business environment.

REFERENCES

[1] Dossani, R., Jhacri, R. and Misra, D.C. (2005). Enabling ICT for Rural India, published by Asia Pacific Research Centre and National Informatics Centre.

[2] Dwivedi, R. and Momaya, S. a. (2005). E-Business in India: Early evidence from Indian Manufacturing Industry. In S. Kamel (Ed.), *Electronic Business in Developing Countries: Opportunities and Challenges* (pp. 393–411). Idea Group Publishing.

[3] Kenneth, K. (2002). Grassroot ICT projects in India: Some Prelimnary Hypothesis. *ASCI Journal of Management*, 31 (1&2).

[4] Niavand, H. and Zia, F.H. (2017). A New Method of Rural E-Business, Information and Communication Technology Development in India. *International Journal of Networks and Communication, 7(2)*, 33–39.

[5] OECD (2002). ICT, E-Business and SMEs.

[6] Porter, M. and Kramer, M. (2006). Strategy and Society: The Link between Competitive Advantage and Corporate Social Responsibility, Harvard Business Review, December.

[7] Porter, M.E. (1998). Competitive Advantage: Creating and Sustaining Superior Performance, Free Press, London.

[8] Porter, M.E. (2001). Strategy and the Internet, Harvard Business Review, 79(3), 63–78.

[9] Troshani, I. and Rao, S. (2007). Enabling E-Business Competitive Advantage: Perspectives from the Australian Financial Services. *International Journal of Business and Management, 2*(1), 80–103.

[10] Yousefi, A. (2009). An Economic Framework for the Assessment of E-Commerce in Developing Countries, Chp 12 in *Emerging Markets and E-Commerce in Developing Economies,* IGI Global.

Women Empowerment and E-Commerce: Challenges and Prospects in India

Leena Singh[1], Surojeet Das[2] and Veena Singh[3]

ABSTRACT: In today's world all facets of human lifestyle have become dependent on virtual solutions. In such circumstances information and communication technology has been a radical force in transforming social considerations like gender equality. Despite of the fact that there have been numerous studies on the role of Information Communication Technology in woman empowerment, there is a shortage of knowledge remaining for the same in terms of e-commerce. In the current times women have emerged to be major economic factor for the development of the country. E-commerce has brought a great revolution in the context of women empowerment and has greatly facilitated women to gain financial independence. The e-commerce sector in India has the potential to empower women as it provides them the opportunity to work from home and is poised to eradicate social inequalities from the society. Today e-commerce provides an efficient platform for the qualified and technically sound women to develop entrepreneurial values. As e-commerce has emerged to be a powerful tool for gender empowerment it is important to study the opportunities and constraints to woman empowerment through e-commerce. The paper is motivated by the potential contribution of e-commerce in the empowerment of women in India. Set in local context, the paper discusses the main obstacles faced by woman in the developing and developed parts of the world with major focus on India. Finally, taking learning points from the already successful models and policies, it suggests practical strategies to address the challenges and suggests ways to implement simplistic model for e-commerce driven woman empowerment in India. We are hopeful that the paper will be effective both for purposes of understanding the effect of e-commerce on empowering women through the extensive review of literature and also provide insight for effective program development.

[1,3]Institute of Management, Commerce and Economics, Shri Ramswaroop Memorial University, Barabanki–225003, Uttar Pradesh, India.
E-mail: [1]leenasingh010@gmail.com; [3]drveenasingh27@gmail.com
[2]Institute of Bioscience and Bioengineering, Shri Ramswaroop Memorial University, Barabanki–225003, Uttar Pradesh, India. E-mail: surojeetdas010@gmail.com

Keywords: *Information Communication Technology (ICT), Women Empowerment, E-Commerce, Entrepreneurship, Growth Factors.*

1. INTRODUCTION

Technology is a crucial factor in furthering the socio-economic development of a country. In this era of information, access to new and advanced developments in the area of information and communication (ICT) has offered us with numerous opportunities to make our lives better, societies to develop and economies to prosper (UNCTAD, 2011). ICTs are also regarded as one of the key solutions for the empowerment disadvantaged groups, like minorities and women. In recent times, e-commerce has proven to be a modern blessing of ICT for developed and developing economics. E-commerce is the application of digital information processing technology and electronic communication in business transactions which creates, transforms and redefines relationships between organizations and individuals. Ever since the dot-com boom and bust in the 90s the application of e-commerce has promptly gained acceptance globally. This is due to the fact that e-commerce has the potential to go beyond the international boundaries enabling the creation of virtual market-place in the process. Hence, e-commerce has evolved itself from being a mere tool for selling stuff online; it's now a highly efficient and productive online resource to do better business.

E-commerce has also provided immense value from the gender standpoint. The 2002 annual report of UNCTAD report regarded e-commerce as a "potential goldmine" for women of developing nations. Reports have shown that half the customers in the e-commerce market are women. It can be attributed to the fact that women prefer online trading to tradition trading, where there are chances that they may be intimidated by male brokers. It has also been observed that e-commerce has facilitated stay-at-home or single parents who can have ease of managing time with their children by shopping online (Tanaka, 1998). A large number of women entrepreneur prefer opting for e-tail sites to sell across various sectors like home furnishing, health care, handicrafts, fashion apparels, jewelry etc. The emergence of such a trend could be attributed to the fact that the e-commerce platforms require minimum investments, global reach, ease of working and financial independence (Padmannavar, 2011). Owing to all this developments the literature on the enormous opportunities which e-commerce can provide for woman empowerment is wide ranging and vibrant. In this paper we review the literature on the use of e-commerce for empowering woman in India. We anticipate that the study would be useful for effectively developing future programs and policies in this direction.

2. THE E-COMMERCE WAVE

Advent of the e-commerce era can be dated back to 1960s when for the first time exchange of data was possible through electronic medium. It was until 1990s, that the e-commerce sector actually began to take shape. The first secure online purchase was carried out in '90s. The e-commerce saw its first major success when in 1997 announced a single day sale record of $1 million online. In the early 2000s, introduction of broadband lead to more people having access to internet resulting in more exposure to online shopping. According to an article at E-Commerce Times (2003), online sales increased by 26% in 2003 and Amazon alone reported a 28% hike in sales increase year on year. Year 2013 marked the rise in mobile commerce and social media exposure which resulted in shifting of the way ecommerce operates. Social medial and smart phones has changed how consumers shop and select retailers online. These platforms have made brands more accessible to the consumers and changed the way they communicate with the business. Currently, the global online sales are growing exponentially and are estimated to reach 8.8% of total retail expenditure by 2018 as compared to 7.4% in 2016 (Patil *et al.*, 2009; Mellita *et al.*, 2012; Padmannavar, 2011).

3. E-COMMERCE AND INDIA

India has one of the largest and rapidly growing populations of internet users in the world. The growth in the internet user base in India has trended exponential. In 2017, India has an internet user base of 333.77 million which is expected to grow to 511.89 million by 2022 (Figure 1A). India has the second largest population of internet users only behind China. This growth can be credited to the rapid expansion of telecom companies in rural India, increased number of affordable data-enabled handsets, and increasing need and awareness of internet. The majority of India's internet users constitute of mobile phone internet users. In 2006 India had 320.57 million (about 24.3 percent of the country's population) internet mobile phone users which is estimated to reach 492.68 million by 2022. According to a report by Nasscom and Akamai Technologies the increased internet penetration in India has fueled the growth of the online market, which accounts for two-thirds of the total e-commerce market. The report stated that by 2020, India will garner an estimated 702 million smartphones and mobile phones would be the preferred device for shopping leading up to 70 percent of the total online shopping. It has also been reported that digital buyer penetration in India was 43.8 percent in 2016 (Figure 1B).A total of 43.8 percent of internet users in India are accustomed to online purchasing in 2016 and this figure is expected to grow to 64.4 percent by 2019 (Figure 1C). At the beginning of 2016 retail e-commerce sale amounted to about 16 billion US dollars and this figure is projected to increase exponentially and surpass 45 billion US dollars in 2021 (Figure 1D).

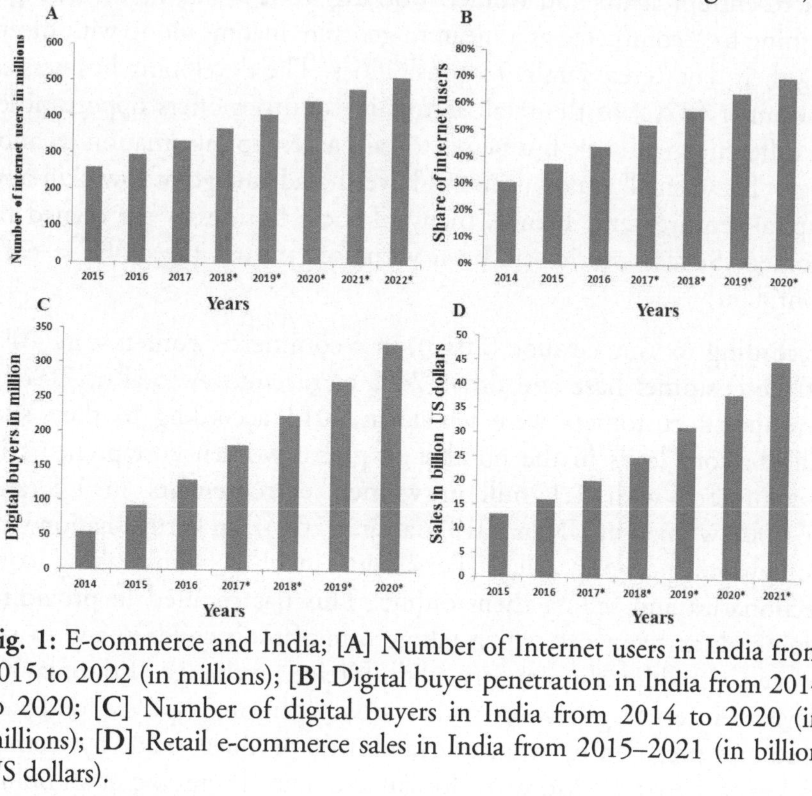

Fig. 1: E-commerce and India; **[A]** Number of Internet users in India from 2015 to 2022 (in millions); **[B]** Digital buyer penetration in India from 2014 to 2020; **[C]** Number of digital buyers in India from 2014 to 2020 (in millions); **[D]** Retail e-commerce sales in India from 2015–2021 (in billion US dollars).

Source: Statista.com

This proves the fact that the opportunity window for online retailers in India is huge. The main catalyst behind this is rapid urbanization, increased literacy levels, a high percentage of young population, increased adoption of computers and the growing rate of internet accessibility.

4. E-COMMERCE AND WOMEN: GLOBAL SCENARIO

The e-commerce sector has introduced women around the globe to a world of endless opportunities. But to seize these opportunities these women have to overcome the obstacles of infrastructure, finance and education. Though women have tapped into the growing demand of outsourced services, they find themselves at the lower end of the salary and skill spectrum. This leads to the increased risk of them being replaced by new technologies if they and their concerned government do not prepare themselves up for the task. Self-employed women, both micro-entrepreneurs and women working from home are increasingly turning to e-commerce as a mean to generate income along with meeting their day to day family responsibilities. The developing business to consumer (B2C) or the retail sectors in countries offers opportunities to different small scale businesses to gain access to information technology. These small scale businesses have the advantage of low skill and capital requirement. Hence, many of these businesses are owned by women. Success stories are been witnesses around the globe in each continent.

According to Gilt Groupe (2013), in e-commerce women were 70% of the customer base and drove 74% of revenue. A total of 77% of Groupon's customers were female in 2013 according to their site. Alibaba.com leads in the number of global women entrepreneurs in e-commerce with 1.1 million women entrepreneurs in US and 261,000 women in UK in 2013 (Sabrina, 2014). In Peru, a nationwide housewives network called Tortasperu involves with baking confectionaries and selling them online. This has resulted in providing women lucrative work which taking care of their children and in the process provides the country with foreign exchange. Ethiopia has devised internet gift shop which sells traditional spices, food and costumes prepared by women. Handmade products made by women in Egypt, Lebanon, Morocco, Jordan and Tunisia are sold at an online shop like Elsouk. Opportunities like this are particularly significant for women in Asia, where 35% of the small and medium sized enterprises are owned by women. In such countries IT enabled or remote services and business process outsourcing of conventional back office operations have shown exponential growth. It has been observed that such e-commerce is limited to certain market segments which are dictated by a country's trading strength and infrastructure. Freelance women journalists in Malaysia and India provide their services online. It has been reported, that at Alibaba which is one of the world's largest e-commerce platform there are 40% of the management and 60% of the employees (UNCTAD, 2002).

5. E-COMMERCE AND WOMEN: INDIAN SCENARIO

As per a report published by Morgan Stanly, India will had around 50 million online shoppers in 2015, this number is going to reach 320 million by 2020. Women constitute around 20% of the 1 million sellers online platforms that form $12 billion online retail industry of the country. IndiaShop an e-market place has eliminated the middleman in selling of saris. According to a recent report by IAMAI-IMRB and Nielson Informate suggests that in 2016 there was a 30% growth in woman shoppers in urban India and a massive 157% growth in woman shoppers in rural India. The reports also predicted that 42% of all the online shoppers in India would be women by 2020. According to a report in The Hindu (2016), it was reported that 15–17 percent of entrepreneurs in e-commerce are women. According to a report by Indianonlinesellers.com (2014), in 2013 women contributed to 26% which was around half a billion dollars to the countries e-commerce revenue. Nair (2015) reported that women have started adopting e-commerce in their business ventures at an early age of 25 years. Though a majority of the Indian women entrepreneurs are from tier I cities, a significant rise has been reported in women entrepreneurs from tier II and tier III cities (Digitalerra, 2016).

E-bay has been promoting women entrepreneurs in India and has registered more than 5000 women sellers (Nair, 2015). Amazon India has collaborated with Nagaland Government and National Skill Development Corporation (NSDC) to help enable women entrepreneurs of the state to sell their product online. Under this collaboration, Amazon India will conduct skill development and training workshops to help women prepare for online selling. At Alibaba.com Indian women entrepreneurs manage a diverse set of industries ranging from gems and jewelry, hair and beauty and machinery to food processing.

6. OPPORTUNITIES FOR INDIAN WOMEN IN E-COMMERCE

In recent times, India has witnessed a paradigm shift in e-commerce scenario due to the increasing number of upcoming women entrepreneurs of the country. These e-commerce ventures are changing the face of the country as we know and efficiently helping the country's economy to grown and many sectors to bloom. The main reasons which attribute to the increased preference of women for choosing online market are:

1. *Global Exposure:* E-commerce has expanded the horizons of women entrepreneurs where there are able to sell their product to any part of the world. This has enabled them to establish newer market for their products.
2. *Ease of Operation:* E-commerce business provides the facility to work from home and provides proper security and privacy to every transaction made through the implementation of passwords.
3. *Cost-effective:* E-commerce business eliminates the middle man and the entrepreneurs are directly able to contact the consumers and sell their products. Overheads such as travelling, mail and the need for extensive manpower is also eliminated.
4. *Time Saving:* The e-commerce sector takes advantage of unimaginable technical speed, accuracy and memory provided by use of modern day technology. This helps in finalizing transactions at a faster rate and helps customers receive immediate replies for their queries. This in turn has led to tremendous time saving in commercial transactions and delivery of products.
5. *Ease in Flow of Information:* As the internet is a hub of information, any women entrepreneur can access internet through the e-business route and float information about the products, its specifics with greater ease and speed.

7. CHALLENGES FACED BY INDIAN WOMEN IN E-COMMERCE

With the increasing popularity of the e-commerce sector, India is witnessing quite a few number of women entrepreneurs who have made a mark in the industry. Despite of this overwhelming growth, the e-commerce sector faces several problems. The challenges arise primarily due to lack of proper education and training along with lack of financial and social support. These roadblocks lead to slower rate of technology adoption by women entrepreneurs as compared to their male counterparts (Jethwa, 2016). Especially women entrepreneurs have to face several challenges in their ventures like:

1. ***Problem in finding a proper niche:*** It is widely believed that e-commerce chiefly involves finding people of suitable niche who are willing to transact over the internet for the targeted product.
2. ***Customer acquisition:*** One of the biggest challenges which the e-commerce sector faces is the problem in retaining customers. E-commerce businesses require investing large sums of money in marketing and advertisement to attract attention from customers. Hence, there is a constant need of funds and investments. This has been the biggest challenge to most e-commerce startups as cited by market experts.
3. ***Good supply chain and reliable logistics:*** Failure in proving reliable logistics to the customer leads to detrimental damage to company's reputation. E-commerce sector relies on customer trust and any damage to the reliability of an e-commerce company can prove to fatal for its existence.
4. ***Raising sufficient amount of funds:*** For women entrepreneurs it's a big challenge to raise constant funds for the smooth running of the company. Unless there is a constant flow of funds it becomes tough to run a successful e-commerce venture.
4. ***Good and effective customer service:*** Maintaining a good reputation to the existence of an e-commerce company. There may be instances where the delivered goods may not be up to the expectations of the customer which can lead to dissatisfaction and must be giving utmost priority. Hence, a combined team effort is needed to meet the expectations of every customer.

8. WHY E-COMMERCE IS A BETTER ROUTE FOR WOMEN ENTREPRENEURS?

Going the e-Commerce way provides a number of benefits that are not high up with regular professions. It allows women to multitask and earn a living along with running their household and honoring their family obligation. Few points which were predominant during interview conducted by Indian Online Seller with upcoming women entrepreneurs:

1. Easy to manage a business by using only a laptop which can be carried anywhere.
2. Online work can be managed while taking care of household chores.
3. Opens up many channels of Business to Business selling and International business as well.
4. Online selling facilitates greater geographic reach which is far better than targeting for one customer at a time in one region.
5. A growing sector with ample opportunities.
6. Being a woman helps business as they tend to have an eye for detail which helps them understand little things a customer may be looking for giving them an edge.

9. GOING FORWARD

There are several factors which collectively shaped up the present trend of the e-commerce market and will continue doing so in the years to come. Some of the trends which are going to a positive influence for the growth of women in the field of e-commerce are (Figure 2):

1. ***Better Support Networks:*** Business women's associations are been created which will provide development opportunities for female e-commerce entrepreneurs to scale up their business ventures. Government initiatives such as National Skill Development Corp (NSDC) has also paved the way in providing female entrepreneurs with adequate digital platforms to broaden their horizons.
2. ***More Role Models:*** In recent times there have been a large number of women stepping into their power. Hence, the increased number of role models has had a positive impact in terms of creating a greater acceptance of e-commerce culture amongst women.
3. ***Businesses are Becoming Less Hierarchical:*** Businesses today are becoming less siloed and more structured along flatter hierarchies. Hence, this produces more favorable work atmosphere for women. These results in, women having a better position to make a more personalized work plan and take command of their venture's integration.

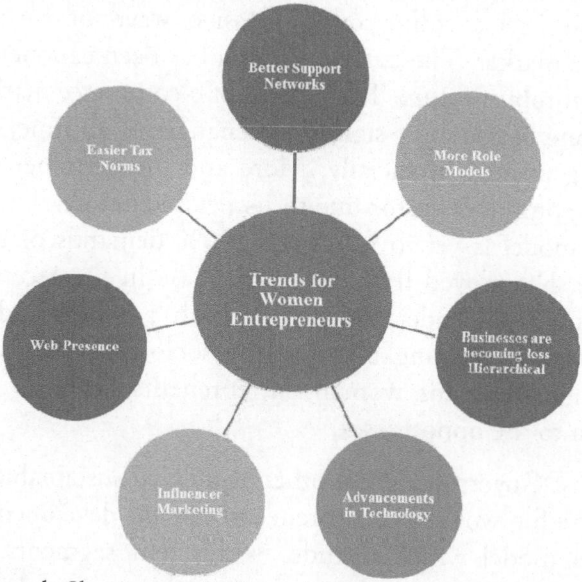

Fig. 2: Trends Shaping-up E-Commerce Sector for Women in Future

4. ***Advancements in Technology:*** The introduction of advanced technologies has greatly decreased the cost of starting a venture. It has now become possible to create businesses that are entirely online. Social media plays an important role in opening new dimensions for marketing and customer engagement, offering more impact with less financial outlay.
5. ***Influencer Marketing:*** There has been an exponential growth in influencer marketing from 2016 to 2017. This has resulted in influencer marketing being regarding as an efficient marketing strategy.
6. ***Web Presence:*** The increased penetration of internet has provided women to have better control over their brand development, marketing and customer engagement. Internet tools provide attainable and affordable solutions for small businesses in every industry. 2017 has witnessed a mammoth increase in Web based business amongst women entrepreneurs.
7. ***Easier Tax Norm:*** The introduction of goods and service tax (GST) in the 2017 budget has introduced a centralized tax system which is on tenterhooks. It has been predicted that women entrepreneurs can be a part of consideration in corporate taxes and loans in the near future.

India at present is riding on a massive wave of success in the e-commerce market. The current growth has been exponential with a prediction of robust future. The growth of e-commerce market has also witnessed one of the most significant changes of all time, and that is empowering women financially. More and more women are testing waters in e-commerce sector due to its flexible nature. The current e-commerce model is yet to fulfill the 100% demands of the market. The market has moved from phase to phase in the recent years. As already quoted—"Gender Equality is both a moral and economic must". However, keeping in mind the socio-economic structure in India, sustainability for women entrepreneurs becomes difficult in comparison to the opposite sex.

With help of Government and other agencies a sustainable model for e-commerce for women entrepreneurs can be developed. We have proposed a model which includes 4 different segments to be emphasized to create a long term entrepreneurship (Figure 3).

1. Product and Customer Base
2. Government Role and Participation
3. Payment and infrastructure
4. Continuous Improvement.

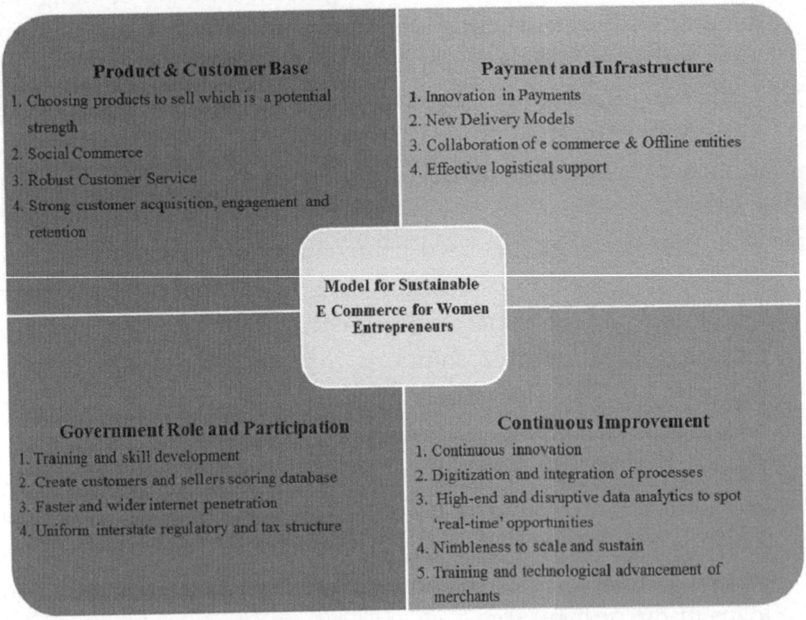

Fig. 3: Model for Sustainable E-Commerce for Women Entrepreneurs

10. CONCLUSION

The main goal of this paper was to establish the prospects the thriving e-commerce industry holds for empowering women financially and thereby understand the tailback faced by women in getting the maximum as entrepreneurs from the e-commerce business. e-Commerce unfurls many opportunities for all genders. But, success comes to only those who make the efforts to achieve it. The tussles of ecommerce are common for all genders and success or failure is directly proportional to a person's creativity and drive. What makes online selling distinctive for women is its flexibility. What follows is hugely dependent on their grit, expertise and skills they possess. Gender equality is both a moral and economic must. Closing the gender gap must be a central part of any strategy to create more sustainable and inclusive economies and societies. It is about fairness and equity, the realization of individual aspirations, economic empowerment around the world and growth. Ecommerce is helping women to level out the gender continuum and is thereby empowering Indian women socially and financially. Women make up nearly 45% of the Indian population. Effective steps are needed to provide entrepreneurial awareness, orientation and development roadmap to women. The role of women entrepreneur in economic development is now being acknowledges and robust steps are being taken by the Government and other voluntary agencies to promote women entrepreneurship. Most importantly, the e-Commerce boom has provided women with a flexible option to step into a field of entrepreneurship which predominantly was controlled my men. The need of the hour is to promote and help women recognize their entrepreneurial traits and skills to meet the changes in trends, challenges global markets and also be competent enough to sustain and strive for excellence in the entrepreneurial arena.

REFERENCES

[1] Digitalerra (2016).Women Marches E-commerce In India. Retrieved from https://www.digitalerra.com/women-marches-e-commerce-in-india

http://bwdisrupt.businessworld.in/article/Trends-That-Will-Shape-eCommerce-Sector-in-2017/27-02-2017-113532/#gist

https://www.digitalerra.com/7-key-trends-in-2017-for-women-entrepreneurs

https://www.statista.com/statistics/251631/number-of-digital-buyers-in-india

https://www.statista.com/statistics/251631/number-of-digital-buyers-in-india

https://www.statista.com/statistics/261664/digital-buyer-penetration-in-india

https://www.statista.com/statistics/289770/india-retail-e-commerce-sales

[2] Jethwa, M. and Mishra, C. (2016). A study on status of women entrepreneur in e-commerce environment in India. *Review of Research Journal*, 5(8), 1–7.

[3] Mellita, D. and Cholil, W. (2012). E-Commerce and Women Empowerment. Palembang.

[4] Padmannavar, S.S. (2011). A Review on E-Commerce Empowering Women's. *International Journal of Computer Science and Telecommunication*, 2(8), 74–78.

[5] Patil, A., Dhere, A.M. and Pawar, C.B. (2009). ICT and Empowerment of Rural and Deprived Women of Asia. Asia Pacific Journal of Rural Development, 1–27.

[6] Sabrina, A. (2014). Role on E-Commerce in Women Empowerment. Retrieved from https://www.academia.edu/6586964/Role_of_e_commerce_in_women_empowerment

[7] Tanaka, J. (1998). From Soups to Lunch: Shop for Groceries without Leaving the Den. Newsweek. 16 March. United Nations Conference on Trade and Development (UNCTAD) (2002). Opportunities rising for women in e-commerce. New York and Geneva: United Nations.

[8] United Nations Conference on Trade and Development (UNCTAD) (2011). E-commerce and development. New York and Geneva: United Nations.

Socially Responsible Leadership as a Driver for Sustainable Growth in the World of Electronic Commerce

Ratna Singh[1] and Anushree Singh[2]

ABSTRACT: Digitalization also leads to globalization which in due course reduces entry barriers. In such a scenario it is necessary that leaders should not be obsessed by returns in terms of money but also in terms of social value. In addition to this employees, are also interested in not only doing work for the organization but also doing meaningful work for the society. CSR can be taken as a carrier for this meaningful work and social value. It can be taken as a way of flowing from economic model leading to maximizing shareholder value to another ethical, social and humanistic model for greater number of stakeholders including the society. Keeping the relevance in view, this paper is an exploration of literature for responsible leadership including Indian case studies and secondary data. It will provide an outcome for better understanding of requisite ethics, CSR and responsible leader.

***Keywords:** Social Responsibility, Socially Responsible Leader, CSR, E-Commerce and CSR.*

1. INTRODUCTION

Globalization as seen by Beck (2000); Giddens (1990) can be said as a formalization of cross-border and cross-region relationship between people, players of distant locations and of increasing trans-border interdependence of fiscal and social activities. This amplified cross-border, cross-country exchange is made conceivable owing to technological inventions of telecommunications, internet etc.

One of the carriers of such exchange is electronic commerce leading to a global marketplace with low entry barriers and walls but elevated competition. In this situation various challenges crop which are of transnational nature and cannot be handled unilaterally by a single

---

[1]Research Scholar, Shri Ramswaroop Memorial University, Lucknow, India.
[2]Assistant Professor, Shri Ramswaroop Memorial University, Lucknow, India.

government. Some of these issues may include global warming, cyber-crime and terrorism, diseases etc.

Now in this set of environmental variables, Corporate Social Responsibility (CSR) is a way to lever societal pressures and make the organization a moral agent, mobilize regulation and convert the business from totally revenue driven to increased value to all stake-holders including society (De Winter, 2001; Marchand, 1998). In this context Shamir (2004) stated that MNCs should stress on volunteerism rather than taking it as an obligation. Ougaard (2006: 243) stated that when businesses engage themselves in voluntary efforts of CSR they allocate scarce resources for societal purposes.

Corporate world should focus on long term returns rather than stressing on quarterly earnings. In fact when an organization desires to get and retain top employees then they need to create a culture where the employees feel that their work output is meaningful and bestows a sense of purpose. Work that benefits society satiates employees more as compared to not engaged in such work. In addition to this according to Barker, 2014; Thottam, 2005, having meaning in your life increases life satisfaction twice as much as wealth. A Professor from Wharton states that productivity of employees increases when they are able to connect their work some meaningful task which also increases sustainable performance.

2. LITERATURE REVIEW

2.1 Sustainable Performance and Growth

Sustainability is building an optimum balance between economic, social and ecological objectives of the firm. In elaboration it needs sustaining financial growth, generating enhanced shareholder's value, goodwill, brand prestige, reputation, customer relationship and maintains good quality of goods and services with pursuance of ethical business structures, processes and procedures and looking after the needs of under privileged. Figure below extends the areas on which a company should focus so as to develop sustainable strategy.

Today corporates need to make compliance with national and international regulations covering environment, human rights, personnel standards and corporate governance. But sustenance not only requires compliance but also making contribution to the society.

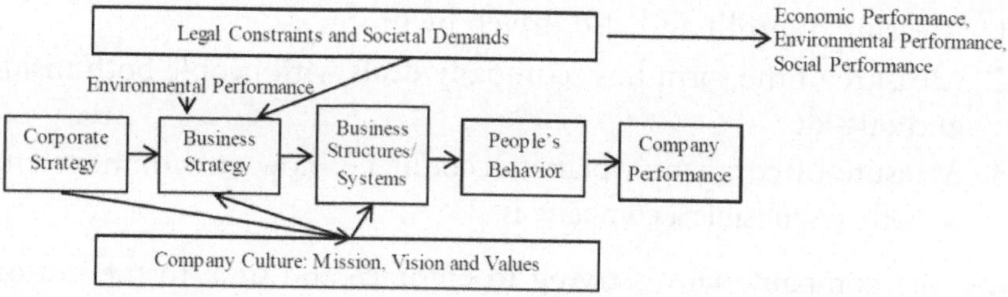

Fig. 1: Assessing the Sustainable Performance of a Company

Source: Francisco Sze'kely, Marianna Knirsch (2005). Responsible Leadership and Corporate Social Responsibility: Metrics for Sustainable Performance. *European Management Journal,* Vol. 23(6), pp. 628–647. Elsevier Ltd. Great Britain. doi: 10.1016/j.emj.2005.10.009

2.2 Corporate Social Responsibility

"CSR is the continuing commitment by business to behave ethically and contribute to economic development while improving the quality of life of the workforce and their families as well as of the local community and society at large"—As extended by World Business Council for Sustainable Development (WBCSD) (1999).

Shrivastava and Venkateswaran (2000) extended that CSR is broadly culture specific, the issue is of prioritization. The CSR goals of a firm should focus on benefiting people and communities who are not included into their legal obligatory contract.

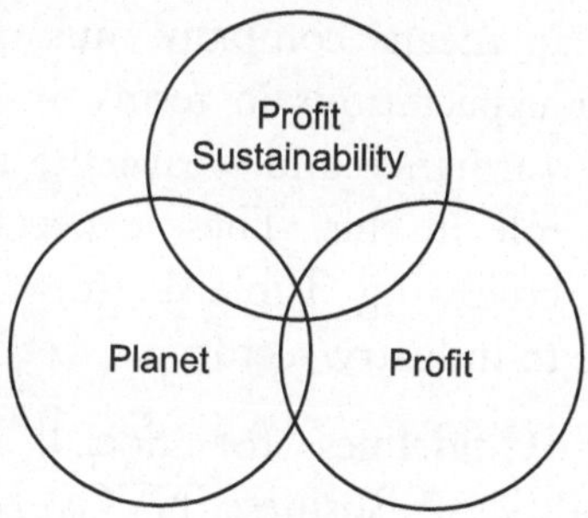

Fig. 2: Pillars of John Elkington's Triple Bottom Line Model to Sustainable Businesses

2.3 Sustainability and Corporate Social Responsibility

The relationship between sustainability and CSR can be best understood by triple bottom line model John Elkington. This model suggests that company is preparing for three different results.

1. Measure of profit and also driven by profit.
2. Measure of the form how company deals with people both inside and outside.
3. Measure of company's planet account i.e. how environment and socially responsible a company is.

Now the company who is trying to embrace and stick to the notion of sustainability then it is responsible for not only its shareholders but stakeholders. These stakeholders push the circles of the model for themselves thereby increasing the overlap.

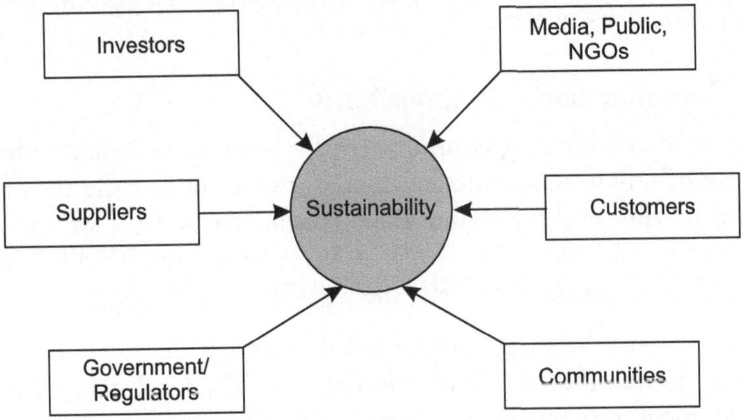

Fig. 3

This increasing overlap means company must map its stakeholders and understand their expectations in terms of environment, society and also financial performance and weave the business accordingly. CSR plays a pivotal role in this. These expectations are also called sustainability issues. Following Table 1 shows the list which can change in accordance to industry/sector.

National Voluntary Guidelines for Social, Environmental and Economic Responsibilities of Business (NVGs) issued by the Ministry for Corporate Affairs, Government of India, in 2011 contains nine principles that define the meaning of responsible business. The eighth principle states that, "Business should support inclusive growth and equitable development". Hence the relationship between CSR and sustainability can be elaborated as follows:

- CSR is a vital component of sustainability. Responsible business deals with one of the most important stakeholder i.e. communities.

- CSR explains that 'what is done with profits' while sustainability states firstly how the profits are made.

Table 1: Stakeholders and their Societal and Environmental Issues

Stakeholder	*Social Issues*	*Environmental Issues*
Suppliers	Wages and benefits Conditions of work Safety	Emissions, effluents and waste Carbon footprint Water consumption
Investors	Managing community expectations Social issues in the supply chain Product safety	Environmental performance Security of supply of natural resources
Employees	Occupational health and safety Freedom of association Capacity building	Environmental conditions at the workplace Emissions, effluents and waste
Customers	Product safety Product performance	Resource consumption during usage Packaging material disposal
Communities	Infrastructure development Better livelihood opportunities Improved quality of life	Emissions, effluents and waste Natural resources availability—water, forests

2.4 Socially Responsible Leadership

According to Tom Karp, a company who can be defined as Socially Responsible can be identified by the following:

- Responsible to its stakeholders'
- Accountable for the broader effects of its business activities by aiming to deliver shareholder, societal and environmental values together,
- Accountable and transparent in all aspects of its business operations.

And, Socially Responsible Leadership is a type of leadership of a commercial business enterprise with the objective of developing a Socially Responsible Company as aforesaid.

According to Maak and Pless (2006), responsible leadership is the art and ability involved in building, cultivating and sustaining trustful relationships to different stakeholders, both inside and outside the organization, and in co-coordinating responsible action to achieve a meaningful, commonly shared business vision.

Socially Responsible Leadership can be defined as, "the use of power and influence to mobilize forces to address a myriad of social issues".

2.5 Relationship between Socially Responsible Leadership and Company Performance

Basic definition of leadership says that about making people to do something. So an effective and ethical leader can move the organization to immense growth and maturity. Although the moral standards for leaders should not be set too high or too low; rather it should be similar to all others.

An interesting relationship between SRL and CSR was given by Shuo Wang, Wei Huang, Yuhui Gao, Sean Ansett, Shiyong Xu. They demonstrated a positive relationship between organizational performance and CSR. The characteristics of SRL integrity, morality, and stakeholder relationship are closely to CSR.

Oxford Library of Psychology in the Oxford Handbook of Leadership and Organizations edited by David V. Day deliberate that responsible leadership is at a very nascent stage and following model was propounded.

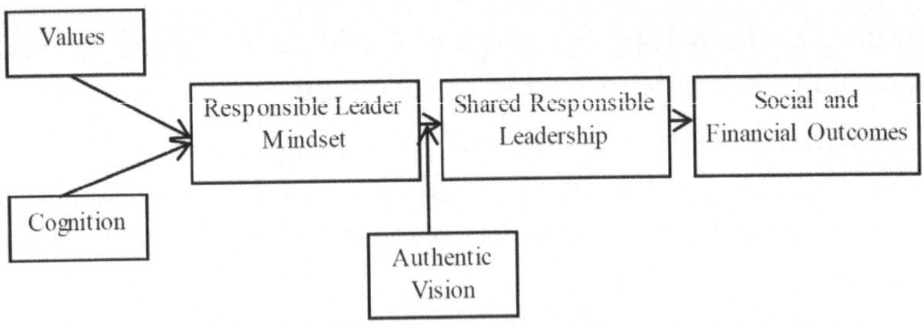

Fig. 4: A Model of Responsible Leadership and its Effect

Shared facets of responsible leadership like shared vision, strategic consensus and servant leadership will give a positive outcome for firm in terms of both financial and non-financial performance.

There are numerous advantages associated in context of performance for implementation of CSR:

- Enhanced corporate trust, relationship and reputation among different stakeholders.
- Increased demand for ethical products.
- Accessibility to financial markets.
- Achieve possible fiscal, economic and other incentives which the government could introduce so as to reward ethical companies.

2.6 Relationship between Socially Responsible Leadership and Sustainability

Pingali (2016) built a framework at five levels that demonstrate how a leader who is responsible can lead the organization to sustainable growth.

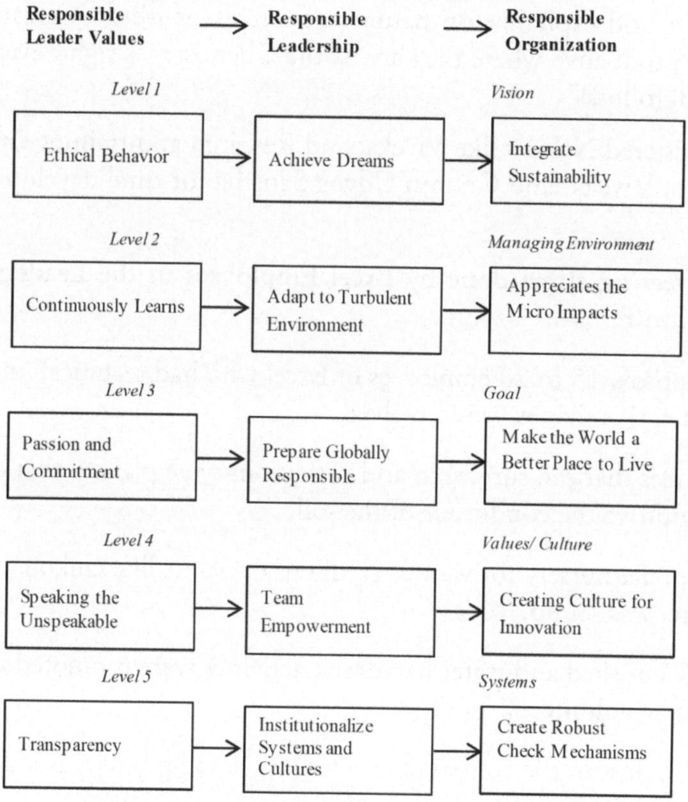

Fig. 5: Framework for Responsible Leadership

2.7 Indian Cases of Socially Responsible Leaders having Sustained Growth

A. *Shree K.C. Shroff (Kaka)—Excel Industries—Ecommerce interface: http://www.excelind.co.in*

He is the Chairman to Excel Industries. He originally belonged to the barren lands of Kutch where he converted all the challenges into opportunities not only for the society but also for the company. He believed in the interdependence of the planet, people and profit.

In his words,

"This means owning up the responsibility for the health of the planet. This means learning to be responsible and relevant. This means joining hands with like-minded people, locally and globally. If we do, we can conserve and capitalize on nature's resources. If we do we can make people productive where they are. If the Chemistry is right, everything else will follow!"

He registered NGO's like Vivekanand Research and training Institute, Shrujan, Vivekanand Gramin Udyog Sanstha for rural development.

Volunteering effort done by Excel Employees in the Leadership of Shri Shroff:

1. Approx. 15 to 20 employees of Excel who had technical knowhow of agri activities were involved.
2. Trees that can survive in arid conditions were planted that can also improve the conditions of the soil.
3. Special nursery for various seedlings of plants like chikoo, coconut etc. was set up.
4. Water shed and water harvesting activities were promoted through these volunteers.
5. Progress in the construction of dams, small ponds was made.
6. Recharging of individual wells was developed.

Table 2: Framework Developed by Shri Shroff

Work	*Activities*	*Responsibility*
Development of near about Villages	• Setting up of Preschools • Micro enterprise units for women • Health and educational camps • Awards and recognition to school going children	Employee Volunteers HRD Department Executives
Development of Kutch	• Horticulture development. • Training of farmers • Water management activities • Activities to improve quality of rural life.	VRTI VGUS
Disaster Management	• Relief and rehabilitation	Employee volunteers and NGO staff
Donations to other NGOs	• Influence of policies of State and Center	Top management of Excel and NGO staff

B. *Mr. Pehr Gyllenhammmar—Aviva Plc.—Ecommerce interface https://www.aviva.com*

Aviva describes its policy of CSR as incorporated in the corporate DNA. Following are the important initiatives extended by Aviva:

- Insuring the comparatively weaker sections of the society like the self-employed women, artisans etc.
- Employees are encouraged to participate in volunteering exercises like visiting slums, educating them, teaching basic hygiene etc.
- The employees are also encouraged to participate in various local NGO activities. Like in Asansol, Burnpur, the employees associated themselves to a trust for mentally challenged girls.

In addition to this there are also innumerable efforts extended by Aviva in this direction under the leadership of various department heads. They motivate and engage employees by these CSR activities that only engages them into meaningful work but also places Aviva into a place of most good places to work for.

C. *Ratan Tata—Tata Industries—Ecommerce interface http://www.tata.com/company/profile/Tata—Industries*

Ratan Tata is the leader who focused on "triple bottom line model John Elkington" for sustainable business model.

The volunteering program of Tata is listed among the top 10 volunteering program in the world under the title TATAENGAGE. It aspires to touch million volunteering hours each year. As the founder believes that CSR of Tata is rooted in the fact that corporates have a onus to empower and permit all living beings a fair piece of planet's resources. This is implemented through the way that Tata employees donate their time, skill and experience to serve the under privileged.

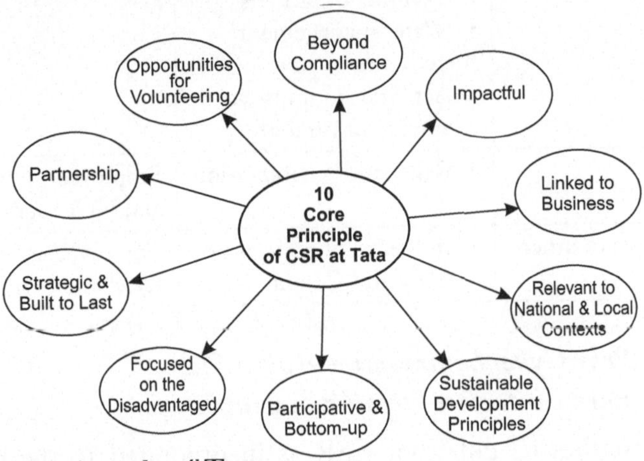

Sustainability Agenda of Tata

Tata group apexed the Sustainability Leaders Survey 2016 conducted by GlobeScan and SustainAbility in partnership with Sustainable Brands. It is a demarcation of Tata Group's effort to embed sustainability in its business strategy i.e. they are committed to incorporate environmental, social and ethical concerns into its core business and hence enhancing shareholder's value.

D. *N.K. Chaudhary—Founder Jaipur Rugs— Ecommerce interface: http://www.jaipurrugsco.com*

They impact the society by following ways:

(a) *Alternative Education Program:* Under this program illiterate artisans are given basic functional primary education, basic calculations, hygiene, and family planning etc. This provides them with self-confidence leading them to self-reliance. The centers for this education are located in the village itself so that people can attend the daily classes. In fact the teachers are also locals who were trained before.

(b) ***Financial Inclusion:*** One of the main reasons for which rural Indian population lags development is the lack of banking and financial services. Keeping in view the fact and the vision of Mr. N.K. Chaudhary Jaipur Rugs helps artisans and weavers to open bank accounts and access other services. In fact the firm has aided to open about 2000 bank accounts in last five years. With penetration of mobile phones they are also helping the artisans to do such transactions through services like M-Pesa.

(c) ***Health & Eye Camps:*** Jaipur Rugs Foundation also organizes various health camps with cheap diagnostic services also at intervals throughout the year.

(d) ***Artisan Engagement Program:*** A Responsible Leader is highly concerned with well-being of the weavers. He wants that the weavers have their dignity and self-respect. They considered themselves as laborers and were disconnected from the main stream. Weavers who have hard core knowledge of the technique were designated as designers. Up till 2014, 800 women were trained transforming their own lives but also of their family.

(e) ***Leadership Training:*** Jaipur Rugs provides management and leadership skill trainings to women of age group 18–35 in collaboration with British Council and Diageo Foundation so that they can utilize their tacit leadership capability. This led to eradication of male by female ones with experience and direct looms were given to weavers. This young women social development initiative transforms the conventional gender biasness prevalent in rural communities.

3. DISCUSSION

An interesting study on parcel and logistics study by Lee and Seo indicate that volunteer practice of CSR augments organizational identification but also aids in getting a cutting edge in the industry. Now there are innumerable corporations practicing CSR but through contributing a bit to the society can make the company move to higher levels of competition. Now as it is said that where the front wheel goes rear follows so the implementation can be through a person or in more refined way a leader who can lead the organization to practice of CSR. That leader will induce the fact that CSR is not a cost that is incurred; rather it is company's way of projecting its concern about the society and giving back to it from where it is reaping benefits.

This paper attempts to extend the importance of such leader that is a Socially Responsible Leader in the booming times of ecommerce and have sustainable performance.

4. CONCLUSION

A Socially Responsible Leadership (SRL) is the art and ability involved in building, cultivating and sustaining trustful relationships to different stakeholders, both inside and outside the organization, and in co-coordinating responsible action to achieve a meaningful, commonly shared business vision—according to Maak and Pless (2006). So this is a leader who handles all stakeholders of the business including the society. In this paper an attempt is being made to understand the role and importance of leader in practice of CSR by the company. The strategy followed for this is firstly the meaning of SRL and then various papers were reviewed for understanding its importance. In addition to this various live case studies are also being studied to understand the role of responsible leader in Indian CSR situation.

So it can be said that first and foremost CSR is of profound importance if a corporations wants to have a competitive edge in business and standout in the myriad of similar business and ecommerce websites. CSR should not be considered as a cost but it should be considered as a way of giving back to the society. It not only adds value to stakeholder (society) but also increases employee engagement and satisfaction leading to increased motivation and throughput giving an image of responsible corporation to the world thereby increasing its visibility. It has been proved by various studies that a responsible corporation has loyal customers than others.

Future studies can explore the exact role played by SRL in employee volunteering and corporation participation. The main issue with the current is that it explores secondary data which can be biased.

REFERENCES

[1] Baxi, C.V. and Prasad, A. (Eds.) (2005). Corporate social responsibility: concepts and cases: The Indian experience. Excel Books India.

[2] Gupta, V. and Montgomery, V.W. (2015). *Leadership across the globe.* Routledge, 468-470

[3] Karp, Tom (2003). Socially Responsible Leadership. *Foresight,* 5(2), 15–23. Retrieved from http://www.emerald insight.com/1463-6689.htm

[4] Lee, S.Y. and Seo, Y.W. (2017). Corporate Social Responsibility Motive Attribution by Service Employees in the Parcel Logistics Industry as a Moderator between CSR Perception and Organizational Effectiveness. *Sustainability, 9*(3), 355.

[5] Levy, L. David and Kaplan, Rami, Corporate Social Responsibility and Theories of Global Governance: Strategic Contestation in Global Issue Arenas. In Crane, Andrew; Matten, Dirk; Abagail, McWilliams; Jeremy, Moon; and Siegel, S. Donald, *The Oxford Handbook of Corporate Social Responsibility.* England: Oxford University Press.

[6] Miriam, Gerstein and Friedman H. Hershey (2017). A New Corporate Ethics and Leadership Paradigm for the Age of Creativity. *Journal of Accounting, Ethics and Public Policy,* 18(2)

[7] Pingali, V. (2016). Responsible leadership: learning from Indian case studies. *Asian Journal of Business Ethics, 5*(1–2), 139–147.

[8] Scherer, George Andreas and Palazzo, Guido (2008). Globalization and Corporate Social Responsibility. In Crane, Andrew; Matten, Dirk; Abagail, McWilliams; Jeremy, Moon; and Siegel, S. Donald, *The Oxford Handbook of Corporate Social Responsibility.* England: Oxford University Press.

[9] Shamir, R. (2004). Between Self-Regulation and the Alien Tort Claims Act: On the Contested Concept of Corporate Social Responsibility. *Law & Society Review,* 38, 635–664. https://doi.org/10.1111/j.0023-9216.2004.00062.x

[10] Tata Industries (2012). *Responsible Leadership, Conscious Capitalism.* Retrieved from http://www.dnaindia.com/money/report-ratan-tata-responsible-leadership-conscious-capitalism-1782230 accessed on 1 August 2017.

[11] Tata Industries (2012). *Tata tops corporate sustainability survey.* Retrieved from http://www.tata.com/sustainability/articlesinside/sustainable-development-tata-group and http://www.globescan.com/news-and-analysis/press-releases/press-releases-2016/103-press-releases-2016/389-co mmunicating-purpose-through-brand-among-top-drivers-of-corporate-leadership-new-poll-of-experts.html. Accessed on 9 Aug 2017.

[12] Tencati, A., Perrini, F. and Pogutz, S. (2004). New tools to foster corporate socially responsible behavior. Journal of Business Ethics, 53(1), 173–190.

[13] Venkateswaran Shankar, Chief Tata Sustainability Group (2014). Retrieved from http://www.tata.com/article/inside/Sustainability—demystified. Accessed on 1 Aug 2017.

Digitalization in the Bancassurance Model of Distribution—Opportunities and Challenges

Mugdha Relan*

ABSTRACT: Indian Life Insurance sector is growing at a faster pace. It has given a platform for economic growth, financial inclusion which has increased the employment opportunities in Indian economy. With many players in business, the Insurance Regulatory and Development Authority (IRDAI) came with innovative and customer focused guidelines for both products and services. The basic idea is to compensate the financial losses of a family when the main bread earner is no more due to certain eventualities in life. Bancassurance is one of the most common models of the distribution of life Insurance products among Agent Selling Model and Direct Distribution.

The research will focus on how time has been changed and the Industry is following the latest wave of Digitalization, Big Data Analytics and Artificial Intelligence. A recent change in the economy like Cashless India/Digital India is giving a boost to every economic and financially viable product including Life Insurance. There are digital startups which are launched specially for Insurance products which could receive seed funding from the investors which are acclaimed internationally famously known as InsurTech. The research will focus on problems that after innovation and technological advancements why still the Insurance penetration is so low in India which is 3.69% as against the global penetration of 6.13% (Swiss Re Sigma Report 2018). The study will also investigate that why still 55% of the population prefer buying Insurance through a traditional channel like Agents selling model instead of web aggregators and other digital set ups. The research will also include a comparison of a developed and successful model of Bancassurance in an international market. The primary data will be mainly collected through various sources like structures questionnaires, direct interviews and interaction with the staff and policyholders of bank and life insurance companies. The sample size will be more than 500 policyholders.

*Institute of Management Commerce and Economics, IMCE, Shri Ram Swaroop Memorial University, Lucknow. E-mail: mugdha.relan@gmail.com

The Research statistical tools for analyzing the data applicable will be variance tests, chi square test and factor Analysis.

***Keywords:** Life Insurance, Bancassurance, Digitalization, Insurtech, Insurance Penetration & Density, Protection Gap.*

1. EVOLUTION OF THE INDIAN INSURANCE SECTOR

In 1956 to 1972 all life insurance companies were nationalized to form LIC in 1956 to increase penetration and protect policy holders from mismanagement. In 1993 to 1999 Malhotra Committee recommended opening up the insurance sector to private players IRDA, LIC and GIC Acts were passed in 1999, making IRDA the statutory regulatory body for insurance and ending the monopoly of LIC and GIC. In 2000–2014 post liberalization, the insurance industry recorded significant growth; the number of private players increased to 46 in 2017. In December 2014, Government approved the ordinance increasing FDI limit in Insurance sector from 26 per cent to 49 per cent. This resulted in attracting investment of US$ 7–8 billion. In 2015, Government introduced Pradhan Mantri Suraksha Bima Yojnaand Pradhan Mantri Jeevan Jyoti Bima Yojana. Government introduced Atal Pension Yojana and Health insurance in 2015. Then in 2017 onwards National Health Protection Scheme launched under Ayushman Bharat, as per Union Budget 2018–19. Insurance companies raised more than US$ 6 billion from public issues in 2017. Life insurance in India has a huge growth potential. By 2020, it is expected to account for 35 per cent of India's total savings. Gross premium collected by life insurance companies in India increased from ₹ 2.56 trillion in FY12 to ₹ 5.78 trillion in FY19. Premium from new business of life insurance companies in India have increased at a 14.44 per cent CAGR to reach ₹ 1.94 trillion. In FY19, premium from new life insurance business increased 10.73 per cent annually (*Source:* IBEF Report October 2019).

2. UNDERSTANDING BANCASSURANCE

Emilia Clipici & Catalina Bolovan (2012) defines the term bancassurance, for the first time, in France and indicate that it's simple distribution way of insurance products by bank branches, which is one of the most dominant and successful modeling European and other countries.

Hughes (1994) defines the bancassurance model as the coming together of enhanced selling skills of the insurance concepts and strong customer building relationships through being loyal to own bank.

Leach (1993) explains that bancassurance is a set up mainly in the involvement of banks, and building the base for marketing and sourcing various insurance products.

Yuan (2011) stated bancassurance is the process where a bank source insurance products manufactured by insurance subsidiaries and companies.

Jeffery (2007) highlighted that the actual formalized event of a bank entering the insurance industry happened when Barclays Bank created Barclays Life in 1965.

Artikis ***et al.*** (2008) mentions that documented version the used term "bancassurance" was completed in France, in the 1980s where it was perceived with the development of the consumer and as well as the liberalization of the financial markets. Established and successful model in Europe the concept is relatively new for Asian countries having emerged only in 2002.

Wu ***et al.*** (2008) highlight, bancassurance is a synergy of two financial services: banking and insurance that is defined as the insurance distribution model where insurance products are sold through banks.

Dr. C. Paramasivan and C. Kalpana Naidu (2014) investigated the reasons for Entering Bancassurance set up is an excellent way so as banks feel they fulfill the three major requirements for a successful Insurance business that is a set management, investment skills and capital adequacy.

3. RISE OF DIGITALIZATION

In the course of digitalization, a company's digitized resources (such as online mode, tools operational with digital sensors, cloud-based systems) are altered into new areas of revenue and operational excellence. It's been observed that almost all the enterprises have undergone some elementary dynamic changes which have resulted in transforming their functions, operations and processes. Today, most of the companies are using digital technology. Hence, companies are stressing on Digitalization *not as alternative but an opportunity for their steady long term augmentation and survival.*

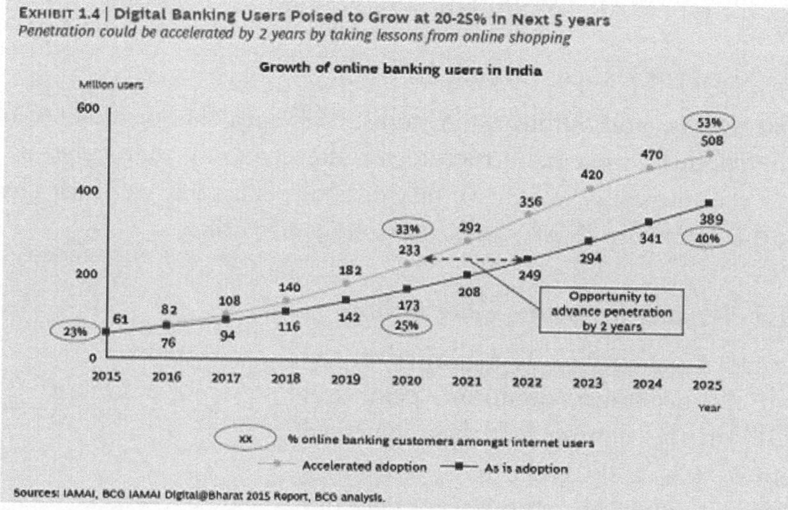

Fig. 1

Source: www.bimabazaar.com

The rise in digital banking is also because of increased mobile banking transactions. According to the RBI, the number of users in 2013–14 is 12.96 million. The RBI's technical committee on mobile banking accentuated that, in terms of per-transaction or per-branch costs, mobile banking transaction is economical compared to the traditional banking channels and hence mobile banking channel should be encouraged for long-term economic gains. A game changer the digital revolution in India has disrupted the business environment in all today's scenario is no exception. Escalating Internet penetration (with the number of users in India expected to rise from 429 million in 2017 to 829 million by 2021 at the rate of 17.9%) will continue to persuade the insurance business as well as other industries.

4. COMPARISON OF INDIAN INSURANCE INDUSTRY WITH THE GLOBAL LANDSCAPE

The Indian insurance sector is underperforming as compared to that of developed and emerging economies. Insurance Penetration and

Density, are the key performance indicators of the insurance industry, are especially very low in India. Further, there is a noteworthy gap between insurance coverage and value, which highlights the high-risk state of country. Since these essential parameters are improving at a stagnant growth rate, there is a long way to go.

4.1 Need for Bancassurance in India

Lalat K. Pani and Sukhmaya Swain (2013) speak about the need of a well-appointed financial structure for the economy that helps us to grow economically. When we talk of about statistics, we must check out the ***Insurance density*** and ***Insurance penetration.***

4.1.1 *What is Insurance Penetration?*

Insurance penetration is measured as the ratio of insurance premium paid and GDP of the country. It has increased from 2.71% in 2001 to 3.69% in 2017 in India. Although this is significant development considering the volume of business, it lags the penetration levels in the rest of the world at (6.13%) and emerging Asian economies at (5.62%).

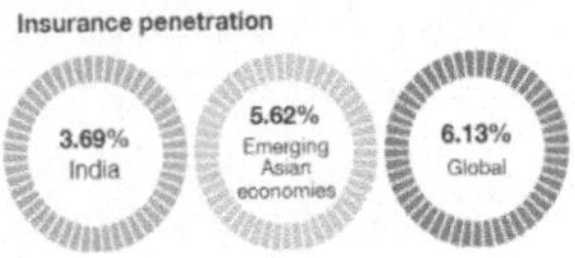

Fig. 2

Source: Swiss Re Institute (July 2018).

4.1.2 *What is Insurance Density?*

Insurance Density is calculated as the ratio of premium (in US $) to the total population (per capita premium).

Fig. 3

Source: Swiss Re Institute (July 2018)

5. STATEMENT OF PROBLEM

The literature review depicts that there is a huge gap between the bancassurance channel and the purpose of technology in the banking channel is a great concern. The digital wave can help the banks to sell more policies to the customers and is a better way to connect the customer for various banking and Insurance solutions. A deep comparative study must be done between the perception of consumers towards the bancassurance and the traditional selling module. Despite rising computerization in banking there is a lack of IT enabler for the Life Insurance distribution through banks. The previous research has not listed out the ways that how can technology be the most significant factor to amplify the revenue and lead generation for the partnership. Previous research focuses well on why the bank should tie up with the life insurance company or why life insurance should expand its business through a tie up with the bank. It also concludes that consumer have wider benefits to procure the policies through the banks like easy accessibility of multi products through genuine channel of distribution. However, it has not focused how three variables or Independent entities banks Insurance companies and the consumer benefit if all the three are amalgamated through the digital disruption.

Arpita Khare (2012) concludes is a scope of future research that how the three variables will react once they are on digital platform and final goal should be of bridging the protection gap. The previous research depicts that how the technology can help the banks to tap more clients for the life Insurance products.

6. OBJECTIVES OF THE STUDY

- The Research will focus on, why still major population prefer buying Insurance through a traditional way like agents instead of web aggregators and other digital set ups despite of companies investing heavily on technology.
- The Research will be focused on how three variables The Bank, The Insurance Company and The Customer are on the same platform through Digital Interventions through a scalable model.
- The Research will involve comparing of a successful international model of bancassurance and how can we execute in Indian Context.
- To build up and standardize a measured model to evaluate investment pattern in life insurance through Bancassurance.

7. CONCLUSION

In our country, the society's observation on life insurance should be changed. For example, insurance is sold just as savings, investments or tax savings but not as protection. Pure Protection or Term Insurance Policies are gaining momentum through the innovative advertisements by the private life insurers. Moreover, these term insurance policies are being sold online by majority of the private life insurers. Bancassurance is already a well-established channel of distribution, but still its achievement is far from other Asian countries. For instance, Bancassurance contributed just 8% of total new life insurance premium during 2016 in India, however in Malaysia it was 49%, China 64% and in Singapore it was 27%. Life insurers in India should strengthen their Bancassurance models in urban areas to increase the ticket value of life insurance premiums, which in turn will help the country to achieve greater life insurance penetration and density.

REFERENCES

Journals

[1] Artikis, P.G., Mutenga, S. and Staikouras, S.K., "A practical approach to blend insurance in the banking network", *Published in The Journal of Risk Finance,* Vol. 9, No. 2, pp. 106–124,2008.

[2] Cappiello, A. (2018). *Digital Disruption and Insurtech Start ups: Risks and Challenges.*

[3] Chang, Pang Ru; Peng, Jin Lung and Fan, Chiang Ku (2011). A comparison of Bancassurance and Traditional Insurer Sales Channel, *Published in the Geneva Papers,* 36 (76–93).

[4] Hughes, J. McGoldrick, P.J. and Greenland, S.J. (Eds), "The financial environment", *Published In* Retailing of Financial Services, McGraw-Hill, London, 1994.

[5] Jaffer, S. Islamic Insurance: Trends, Opportunities and the Future of Takaful, *Published in Euro money,* London, 2007.

[6] Khare, Arpita (2012). *Customer Behaviour toward online insurance services in India* 2012, *Published in* Macmillan Publishers Ltd., 1741–2439, Vol. 19, 10–133.

[7] Leach, A., "European Bancassurance: Problems and Prospects", Published *in Financial Times Business Information,* London, 1993.

[8] Nithya, D. and Chitra, B. (2019). On Recent Trends and Growth in Bancassurance Business in India: *Published in Paripex-Indian Journal of Research,* Volume 8, Issue 4, April 2019.

[9] Pahuja, Anurag and Verma, Rajesh (2006). Reinventing Insurance Distribution through Bancassurance.

[10] Pani, Lalat K. and Swain, Sukhmaya," Bancassurance and Indian Banks". *Published in* International *Journal of Research and Development—A Management Review (IJRDMR),* Volume 2, Issue 1, 2013.

[11] Paramasivan, C. and Naidu, C. Kalpana, "A Study on Role of Bancassurance in Indian Life insurance Business", *Published in SELP Journal of Social Science,* Vol. V, Issue 20, April–June 2014.

[12] Satsangi, Rupali (2014). An Analysis of effectiveness of Bancassurance as a distribution channel, *Published in* Delhi *Business Review,* Vol. 15, No. 1 (January–June 2014).

[13] Shetty, Abkitha and Basri, Savitha (2018). Assessing the Technical Efficiency of the Traditional and Corporate Agent in the Indian Life Insurance Industry: Slack based data Envelope Analysis Approach, *Published in Global Business Review-Sage Publications,* 21(I) 1–17.

[14] Stoeckli, Emanuel; Dremel, Christian and Uebernickel, Falk (2018). Exploring characteristics and transformational capabilities of Insurtech innovations to understand insurance value creation in a digital world, *Published in Springer,* 28:287–305.

[15] Wu, C.R., Lin, C.T. and Lin, Y.F., "What forms of the bancassurance alliance model is customers' preference?" *Published in Journal of Modelling in Management,* Vol. 3, No. 3, pp. 207–219, 2008.

[16] Yuan, Y. "US financial services integration: evidence in banking and insurance", *Published in Academy of Banking Studies Journal,* Vol. 10, No. 1, pp. 53–109, 2011.

Online Resources

[1] https://www.swissre.com/dam/jcr:a160725c-d746-4140-961b-ea0d206e9574/sigma3_2018_en.pdf

[2] https://blog.policystreet.com/reasons-you-need-life-insurance

[3] https://www.insurancefunda.in/indian-life-insurance-industry-2018-19

[4] https://www.irdai.gov.in/ADMINCMS/cms/Uploadedfiles/english_hindi_ annual report 2018 webcopy.pdf

[5] https://www.asiainsurancereview.com/News/View-NewsLetter-Article/id/39211/Type/eDaily/India-DBS-is-first-bank-to-adopt-open-bancassurance-model

[6] https://www.pwc.in/assets/pdfs/consulting/financial-services/competing-in-a-new-age-of-insurance.pdf

[7] https://www.ibef.org/industry/insurance-sector-india.aspx

[8] https://www.swissre.com/dam/jcr:a160725c-d746-4140-961b-ea0d206e9574/sigma3_2018_en.pdf

[9] https://inc42.com/resources/how-can-ai-assist-streamline-insurance-laims-management-process/

[10] What is Bancassurance Model? https://www.leadsquared.com/bancassurance-model

[11] Bancassurance in India and Digitization, http://www.bimabazaar.com/bancassurance-india-digitalization

Advertising Strategies for Online Marketplace

Prachi Srivastava[1] **and P. Joseph Antony**[2]

ABSTRACT: This paper considers the allocation of "shelf space" in the context of online marketplaces, where item's positions are linked to advertising. While featuring advertised products makes search less efficient, lowering transaction commissions, it incentivizes sellers to compete for better placements via advertising. We consider this trade-off by considering both sides of the platform. On the demand side, we consider aspect of search (impressions), consideration (clicks), and choice (demand). On the supply side, we consider sellers' advertising competition under various fee structures and ranking algorithms. Considering buyer, seller, and platform dynamics, we find that strategies trade off for advertisement fees to be considerate. On the seller side, the high advertising commissions create an incentive for sellers to advertise items in the hope of selling them elsewhere with lower fees.

Keywords: *Online Advertising, E-Commerce, Two-Side Market.*

1. INTRODUCTION

Online marketplaces are economically consequential and growing. The market capitalization of Alibaba, the world's largest online marketplace, is around $190 billion, and that of Amazon, the largest online retailer in the US, is over $330 billion in the second quarter of 2018. Amazon sold more than 2 billion items worldwide in 2018 and approximately 50% of the units were sold by more than 2 million third-party sellers (or called marketplace sellers). It is now believed that an important part of Amazon's business future is being the world's biggest online retailer acting as a platform for goods. With recent developments in mobile website browsing, online marketplaces are expected to continue the rapid growth in coming years. With buyers on one side, and third party merchants on the other, online

[1]NET, MBA, Head, Department of Business Administration, Sacred Heart Degree College, Sitapur.

[2]C.A., M.Com, Assistant Professor, Sacred Heart Institute of Management and Technology, Sitapur.

marketplaces are a two-sided platform (Rochet and Tirole 2003, Armstrong 2006, Weyl 2010) of substantial economic importance. In this paper we address both sides of the platform by considering i) how online marketplace shelf space allocation decisions (i.e., the listings' ranks) affect the consumers' search (impression), consideration (click) and demand for merchant goods, and ii) how payments for better allocations affect advertiser behavior and profits for both the advertiser and the platform. Advertiser payments are a growing source of revenue for these marketplaces; owing to its wealth of consumer knowledge, Amazon is now the seventh largest seller of online advertisements worldwide, exceeding Twitter, Pandora and LinkedIn.

1.1 Literature Review

The Weitzman's sequential search models or funnel shaped consumer search model provides the base model to analyse probable advertising strategies in online marketplace. Online market place is a phenomenon evidencing differential consumer stimulus and quick reaction patterns. Frequent visits to the pages, memberships, discount policy, feedback mechanism, live chat, advanced searches make it a lively and viable place for marketers.

There has been considerable attention allocated to search and purchase, both in theoretical and empirical work of Economists. In online environments, empirical research has mostly focused on the demand side of the platform (Kim *et al.*, 2010, Koulayev 2013, Ursu 2015), price elasticity of demand and price dispersion amongst internet retailers (Chevalier and Goolsbee 2003, Ellison and Ellison 2009, Smith and Brynjolfsson 2001, Einav *et al.*, 2013a), or recommendation system (Bodapati 2008, Ansari *et al.*, 2000).

1.2 Online Market Place—A Differential Phenomenon

Moving away from traditional market model online market place is completely different. Physical market place due to geographical distances and proximities quite often encourages a consumer to buy a less satisfying product or encourage to buy which is readily available. Where as in an online market place a consumer is exposed to more items at a click. Another feature is of independent or assisted approach. In physical market quite often human involvement plays a vital role for ensuring re-visits, where as in online place these features are substituted by website designs, displays, texts and review etc. The following dimensions explains it more.

1.2.1 *Physical Search*

Navigating through physical markets consumer is exposed to a set of attributes. More over what matters is being it a multi-product or single-product search. For buying expensive single items it is observed that consumer before making a purchase decision will sample all stores and will spent more time in extensive search. Whereas for inexpensive multi-product purchase consumer often finds feasible to buy from a multi-product store even though costly and finds comfort more important than search cost.

Other considerations for making choices are the availability of model, design and delivery. A consumer is often confronted with these issues while being in the buying process.

1.2.2 *Online Search*

Online search facilitating product availability on the click and delivery at the door step is a very dynamic platform. In less time more products and pages are visited where also variations in designs and models are available. A consumer need to be focused while search and purchase decisions because online marketplace is filled with advertisements and recommendations.

Quite often search time is invested in divergent products which are catchy and are readily displayed.

1.2.3 *Components of Online Advertisements*

The online advertisement is built of three components **buyer, seller and platform, where all three** respond differently when in online marketplace. Lets analyse the dynamics

2. PLATFORM DYNAMICS

Consumer is motivated through ease of buying, analysing and viability of interface. We consider mainly three aspects of the platform structure: the design of its pages (i.e., how attributes are allocated across the product listing and product detail pages), the ranking algorithm used to display products to consumers, and the fees charged for advertising.

2.1 Website Design

When a consumer visits the site, they arrive on the main landing page. On this page, the platform displays 10 product listings in a sequential product feed format, of which a subset of items are visible depending on the size of the screen. Consumers can scroll down to view more items or can interrupt search by clicking upon a specific product to access its product detail page and to gather additional information. Upon continuation of search, the platform loads 10 more products at a time in response to scroll down requests, and the main page product feed continues until the consumer stops searching. Because 10 products are loaded per request, we do not observe where the product search exactly ends within the loaded products. Thus in the empirical analysis, consumers are assumed to have searched all items that are loaded from the requests.

2.2 Ranking Algorithm

Product recommendations appear based on the search history and purchase decisions made by the consumer. The websites based on data analysis make items most visible and apparent to the consumer according to their taste. It includes and plays a vital role in platform aspect and interface between seller and buyer.

2.3 Fee Charged

The online platform providers charge fee either for listing or for transaction only. Amazon charges as per following formula.

Paid for by the customer {
Item Price $$
+ Shipping Charges
+ Gift Wrap Charges
}
- Referral Fee
- Variable Closing Fee
- $0.99 Per Item Fee

Total Merchant Revenue

2.4 Purchase Decision

Upon visiting the website, the consumer is presented an ordered list of items, one product at a time, where the arrival order of the products is exogenously determined by the platform's ranking algorithm. Faced with this list, a consumer can either click on a link to the rest item's product detail page by incurring a consideration cost, or move to the next alternative on the list while incurring a search cost; that is we presume a sequential search process. This leads to the following sequence of steps.

2.4.1 *1st Stage: Consideration (Product Detail Page Click) Decision*

The consumer is presented with t^{th} positioned product (starting at t = 1), with some subset of the tth item's attributes available on the product listing page. Having this partial information about the product's attributes, the consumer decides whether or not to add the tth product into the consideration set by accessing (clicking) its product detail page. Once considered, the consumer gathers all information on the product detail page's, and the matching value with price, and fully resolves any product uncertainty with regard to its utility. Once the consideration decision is made, the consumer decides whether to search the $(t + 1)^{th}$ position product.

2.4.2 *2nd Stage: Search or Exit Decision*

Conditioned on the information obtained in searching so far, the consumer decides whether or not to continue search for the $(t + 1)^{th}$ product. If the consumer decides to continue search, partial information on $(t + 1)^{th}$ product is revealed. The consumer incurs a search cost, and the consumer moves to the 1st stage of $(t + 1)^{th}$ step. If the consumer decides not to continue, the entire search process terminates.

2.4.3 *3rd Stage: Choice (Purchase)*

Once the search process terminates, the consumer has a consideration set that consists of the items whose product detail pages have been visited (clicked) and the outside option. The consumer rationally chooses the highest utility alternative among the ones considered.

3. ADVERTISEMENT STRATEGIES

Based on the above stated dynamics we propose the strategies which are again subjective to the seller's choice. Of course, even the online market place is becoming dense and loaded with rapid growth and rivalry amongst firms and necessarily firms are supposed to choose the suitable trade off between strategies to compete with.

3.1 Specify Your Market Segment

Specifying the focus on a specific market segment of the online platform will help firm to ensure reaching target audience. Start-ups that are targeting all segments end up reaching no segments. Amazon started by specifying their platform in the market segment of books. When you specify a smaller market segment, this allows you to build and design our niche skilfully. Dedicate resources adequately to a more specific segment always ensuring you are able to execute on your performance objectives of speed, quality, costs, flexibility, dependability due to an initially uncontrollable size. As you scale your customer base, ensure to drive your ability to learn as an organisation. Sustainability scalability involves continuous improvement to maintain performance standards for a growing marketplace of increasing numbers of peers. A conscious scaling process ensures continuous satisfaction among platform peers as well as efficient use of organisational resources including time, effort, and financial reserves. To begin, specify your online platform's market, and focus all resources to succeed in this segment. The more specific your market segment becomes, the better you can ensure you are reaching your targeted group. If you want to create an online marketplace for sustainable fashion apparel? Try focusing on a specific section such as women's leisure wear out of bamboo. Starting as an expert in a smaller field will allow you to perform at high levels which will give your brand credibility and the chance to establish as the best in field. As you gain trust and enlarge your customer base, look into sustainable scaling.

3.2 Know the Personas of Your Marketplace

Initially **your marketplace** will cater to specific personas of buyers and sellers. Explore who these specific **personas** are and draw up the key characteristics that make up the essence of these figures. Personas are there to raise the question who is this marketplace for? Why do buyers and sellers choose our online platform?

In our buyer persona analysis services, we include key questions which you can apply to **get to know** the buyers and platform:

- Who is your buyer demographically?

- What objectives motivate your buyer?
- How can you help your buyers?
- What are the driving pain points of your buyers?
- What does an empathy map of both buyers and sellers look like according to research based findings?

3.3 Strengthen Existing User Relationships First

Strengthen existing user relationships, that you've spent time, money and resources acquiring. It's a lot more expensive to get new users than to keep and grow existing user relationships. 80% of new leads never translate into sales and companies that excel at lead nurturing generate 50% more sales ready leads at a 33% lower cost. Strengthening your existing user base is all about user relationship management. Incentivise your existing user base to engage regularly in your online marketplace. Email Marketing has proven to be particularly successful and cost-effective here. Actively and regularly inform users with relevant content such as personally targeted offers.

3.4 Fostering Trust to Drive Meaningful Engagement

Essential to your marketing strategy will be to transmit trust to buyers and sellers of the online platform in order to drive meaningful engagement. User engagement will see less barriers as users begin to have trust in your reputation. As you build your reputation, remember that to foster trust, all company actions and behaviours should represent extension of the company values. Ensure that actions are in line with your organisational values. On a more practical level, foster quality engagement through prioritising performance objectives of speed, quality, costs, flexibility, dependability. Get the most out of your efforts by making them visible. Use seals of approval and testimonials to make your efforts transparent and build your reputation. This in turn will foster a sense of trust among both buyers and sellers, inviting them to meaningful engagement.

3.5 Story Telling Over Selling

Don't sell, tell a story. Inbound marketing, is a natural way of sharing knowledge and build relationships without looking in need of **selling** yourself. Successful inbound marketing will engage with your platform buyers and sellers by making use of their persona profiles to educate, excite, and empower these. Create content and stories that focus on your specific market segment needs as opposed to focusing on your business needs as an online marketplace.

Craft your content in an engaging language that leads your audience through a story, whilst continuously making clear the value add that you are providing. Users know what they are looking for, so make titles representative of your content, steering clear of clickbait titles and headlines. With creating effective titles, it is essential to analyse periodically the most relevant metrics and make all changes and tests necessary for finding the most appropriate title.

As a content marketer, your main goal should be to make your content that is relevant and adds value. Create stories that are helpful, informative or entertaining and transmit your company values. Engage your target audience at an emotional level by letting go of the mindset to sell, and adopting the mindset of telling a story.

3.6 Viral Marketing

Viral marketing means promoting the growth, for example through targeted marketing in online communities and social media groups, so that new customers are generated. To carry out a **viral marketing campaign**, create valuable content for your users that is attractive to share on their own social networks. So called 'referral marketing' has also proven to have viral effects. This is where users are incentivised to refer your online marketplace through receiving a personal benefits when one of their contacts arrives on your site. Try adding elements to incentivise sharing such as discounts and promotions for your users to get them to refer you. This can save time, effort, and financial resources in your marketing department.

3.7 Network Effects of Popular Platforms

Popular platforms are attractive. Buyers want committed sellers, and sellers want committed buyers. More buyers attract more sellers, and more sellers attract more buyers. Online marketplaces and **platforms gain attractiveness as they grow**, this is called the **network effect.** The question is, where do we start?

Taking the case of the online fashion apparel marketplace, a bamboo cloth sock manufacturer, a bamboo handbag crafter and a bamboo jewellery maker all share a common problem. Each are specialists in their individual craft, but neither know how to reach their target audience. Marketing is what attracts the right consumers who want to pay for their products and services. Platforms and marketplaces are a way of using the individual offerings, to offer buyers a better overall shopping experience.

Start with inbound marketing strategies through useful and relevant content. Over time, this will attract prospects and credible buyers. This way meaningful transactions can commence as soon as you introduce your first seller onto the platform. On the contrary, if you invest efforts into attracting sellers first, you run the risk of having your efforts go to vain in the absence of credible buyers. The bottom line is, sellers come where the buyers are, so focus on customer development first.

3.8 Transmitting Your Values Using Social Media

Use **social media** to engage with your various online marketplace personas. Allow buyers and sellers to create an emotional bond with your platform by getting them to understand your values and **transmitting** your intentions. Social media is where you can define your company culture, share relevant content, and allow your behaviour to be an extension of your organisational values.

Show your appreciation to buyers and sellers by maintaining active engagement. Check your social media accounts daily and keep them up to date with user engagement. Post links to new content on your blog or site, and establish a presence as an active, friendly company.

Make use of existing social media groups. These are a filtered space for your specific market segment. Social media groups potentially hold the future peers of your online platform. Dedicate resources to transmiting your commitment and credibility and convert members into enthusiastic buyers and sellers of your online marketplace.

More than 450 million people are already visiting groups on Facebook to buy or sell every month. Established groups can be used to your advantage and growth. Provide useful, informative content and users will do the sharing for you.

3.9 Community Development

Transform users into a **loyal community** through creating expectations for high quality content regularly. Succeed as a company manager and keep users coming back for more by keeping them up to date on key events, new ideas and innovative industry insights. BuzzSumo is an analytics tool that analyses performance of content topics among a particular demographic. Getting your users to feel part of a community further develops an emotional dimension to the relationship and will foster customer loyalty.

3.10 Search Engine Optimisation

Search Engine Optimization (SEO) determines your ranking on Google. Have users find you in the moment they are looking for the relevant product by ranking in search engine result page positions.

Make it a joint effort by creating guidelines for seller offerings on your platform to ensure their content is SEO optimised. Give your sellers the opportunity to provide detailed product descriptions. Search engine optimised content will allow the data stored on your site to be more easily accessed by search engine algorithms, and score you a higher ranking.

Your search engine results page ranking will score higher the higher the quality of your content. Get your online community to improve your SEO score for you by engaging them to publish their own content such as product reviews, interacting with FAQs, leave comments on the platforms content, or blog about industry insights they are finding too.

Whilst your buyers and sellers can contribute their part, most commonly, it is the online marketplaces and platforms themselves who have the responsibility to position their site. Providing the users of your online marketplace with a high SEO positioning is your way of communicate that you are putting in the effort to gives them the recognition they deserve. Search engine optimisation is a profession on it's own, but a great place to start is by dividing your products into categories and subcategories—this makes it easier for search engines to review and list your individual pages.

4. CONCLUSION

This paper considers the role of advertisement in the context of online marketplaces.

To achieve this aim, we consider all three agents in the two-sided network; i) the platform who sets the advertising fees and designs the website in regards to information structure (whether to present attributes on the search page or the consideration page) and placement of items listed on the market, ii) the sellers who make advertising decisions conditioned on platform's policies and expected consumer behavior, iii) consumers who search, consider and make purchase decisions given the preferences, search/consideration costs and information. The above stated dynamics clearly engraves the possibilities ant threats of online advertisements. Weather the buyer, seller or the platform provider, all need to be considerate in decision making. In absence of clearly defined strategy and objectives none of the participants will be able to maximize gains.

REFERENCES

[1] Ansari, A. and Mela, C.F. (2003). E-customization. *Journal of Marketing Research*, 131–145.

[2] Arcidiacono, P. and Miller, R.A. (2011). Conditional choice probability estimation of dynamic discrete choice models with unobserved heterogeneity. *Econometrica* 79 (6): 1823–1867.

[3] Argentesi, E. and Filistrucchi, L. (2007). Estimating market power in a two-sided market: The case of newspapers. *Journal of Applied Econometrics* 22 (7): 1247–1266.

[4] Armstrong, M. (2006). Competition in two-sided markets. *The RAND Journal of Economics* 37 (3): 668–691.

[5] Chen, Y. and He, C. (2011). Paid placement: Advertising and search on the internet. *The Economic Journal* 121 (556): F309–F328.

[6] Dréze, X., Hoch, S.J. and Purk, M.E. (1995). Shelf management and space elasticity. *Journal of Retailing* 70 (4): 301–326.

Comparative Analysis between Netflix and Amazon Prime

Shraddha Verma[1], Aparna Rawat[2] and Ayushi Shrinate[3]

ABSTRACT: Entertainment has always been a necessary part of our lives from historic times till now. Television also has been a long-standing source of entertainment. But with the advent and introduction of internet, web television and streaming television has been taking over our everyday lives and replacing the once traditional domination of TV networks with its anytime, anywhere watching content options. Netflix and Amazon Prime are two of the major players in the online video streaming market. Since its inception in 1997, Netflix has had an ever-increasing number of subscribers. With its introduction in 2005 Amazon Prime has also been competing in the market and offering a number of exclusive content deals from comedy shows to movies to originals in order to differentiate its service. This paper presents a study on comparative analysis of these two major players of online video streaming market. In this paper we are trying to explore their strategies which they have used to capture the market and become dominant players. Through this study we will be able to find out the reasons of success of these players. For this we have explored data from both primary and secondary sources.

Keywords: *Comparative Analysis, Online Video Streaming Market, Marketing Strategies.*

1. INTRODUCTION

Streaming media is multimedia that is constantly received by and presented to an end-user while being delivered by a provider. The verb "to stream" refers to the process of delivering or obtaining media, the term refers to the delivery method of the medium, rather than the medium itself, and is an alternative to file downloading, a

[1]Assistant Professor (Department of BBA), Shri Ramswaroop Memorial College of Management, Lucknow. E-mail: shraddhav19@gmail.com

[2,3]BBA II year Student, Shri Ramswaroop Memorial College of Management, Lucknow.

E-mail: [2]rawataparna1008@gmail.com; [3]ayushi.shrinate@gmail.com process in which the end-user obtains the entire file for the content before watching or listening to it. With the increased average broad-band speed, video streaming has become a custom for many users. The introduction of Amazon Prime has become a game changer for Netflix by being its major contender. Both these platforms offer a 30 days free trial and then offer services based on their subscription plans. Video services from both Amazon & Netflix can be accessed by downloading their mobile applications and on devices such as Smart TV, laptops & desktops. This research study provides a distinction between the two key players of online video streaming applications and the services they offer.

2. NETFLIX

Netflix, Inc. is an American media-services provider and production company headquartered in Los Gatos, California, founded in 1997 by Reed Hastings and Marc Randolph in Scotts Valley, California. The company's primary business is its subscription-based streaming service which offers online streaming of a library of films and television programs, including those produced in-house. As of April 2019, Netflix had over 148 million paid subscriptions worldwide. Netflix's initial business model included DVD sales and rental by mail, the company focused on expanding its business in 2010 with the introduction of streaming media while retaining the DVD and Blu-ray rental business. The company expanded internationally in 2010. Since 2012, Netflix has taken more of an active role as producer and distributor for both film and television series, and to that end, it offers a variety of "Netflix Original" content through its online library. Netflix has various subscription plans in India it gives subscription as: Basic—₹ 500/month, Standard plan—₹ 650/month, Premium—₹ 800/month. Netflix has worked a lot on its market strategy it has named it as 'Taste Doppelgangers' they use it in place of traditional market strategy of differentiating the market on geo-graphical basis. 'Netflix and chill' has become the new cool as of content Stranger Things, Sex Education, Bird Box and Perfect Date are some of the recent popular series and movies on Netflix.

3. AMAZON PRIME

Amazon Prime is a paid subscription service offered by Amazon that gives users access to services that would otherwise be unavailable, or cost extra, to the typical Amazon customer. This includes free two-day delivery, two-hour delivery for a fee through Prime Now, streaming music and video, and other benefits. In April 2018, Amazon reported that Prime had more than 100 million subscribers worldwide. The service debuted on September 7, 2006 as Amazon Unbox in the United States. On September 4, 2008, the service was renamed Amazon Video on Demand. The Unbox name still refers to the local program, which as of August 2014 is no longer available for downloading purchased instant videos. On February 22, 2011, the service rebranded as Amazon Instant Video. It provides subscription plans in India as ₹ 129/month and ₹ 999/year. Amazon Prime is trying to capture more market by giving prices that are ideal for everyone. Also, Amazon has been known for its incredible value that they provide to their customer so, it helps the customer think well of its prime services. Some popular shows that stream on amazon prime are Orphan Black, Mr. Robot, Made in Heaven, Comicstan.

4. LITERATURE REVIEW

4.1 Amazon *vs.* Netflix: Who will Win Indian Battleground?

Video streaming is becoming part of our modern daily lives, which means no domination of TV networks. Amazon and Netflix are the two major players in the online video streaming market. Netflix has been world's leading online streaming network since 1997 while Amazon prime video was launched in 2006 in the US. Subscribers can watch anytime, anywhere, on nearly all devices connected with internet-connected. To keep pace with the competition, Amazon has introduced a number of exclusive content deals to differentiate its service. This paper presents a case study on the comparative analysis of the two main players and the strategies they use to capture the Indian market.

4.2 Netflix *vs.* Amazon Prime Video: A Battle of Streaming Giants

There's a reason Netflix has more subscribers than any other streaming video service—and by a very wide margin. It's a fantastic way to watch ad-free movies and TV shows, and the company's investments in both licensed and original content mean there's always something worth watching. If having access to the best selection of video content, delivered via a well-thought-out and consistent interface, matters to you, we think it's the best choice. However, even Netflix Standard can still put a dent in your budget, so if you've already got an Amazon Prime membership for its various other benefits, it makes a lot of sense to see if Prime Video can quench your entertainment thirst. After all, you're already paying for it.

4.3 Netflix *vs.* Amazon: Which Streaming Service Deserves Your Cash?

Has Amazon Video caught up with Netflix after years of trailing behind a bit? In most of the ways that count, yes it has.

Netflix no longer steamrolls the Amazon rival in terms of its library, though we'd argue it still has the edge on the consistency and stunning highs of its original content. Amazon has improved considerably in this regard over the past 12 months or so, and there's every sign that it's going to continue to do so. Amazon has also improved its platform and app support in recent times, but it's still not as cohesive or ubiquitous a service as Netflix, which has one of the most identifiable and user-friendly interfaces around. Netflix's edge has never been as slight as it is now, but it still gets our nod in a straight-up fight. Of course, at present there's no reason why you can't skip between the two. Each has TV series worth getting hooked on, so why not play the field?

4.4 Amazon Prime Video *vs.* Netflix: Which is Worth Your Money?

Amazon Prime Video, a popular online streaming service and one of the biggest rivals of Netflix, is now available to users in 200 countries including India. The availability of Prime Video enhances the options for Indian users looking for quality international content. Like Netflix, Prime Video is a subscription-based service but is a lot more affordable compared to the former. It has a single annual subscription plan of ₹ 499 which works on smartphone, tablets, Microsoft Xbox, Sony PlayStation, TV and PC. This means a user is actually paying ₹ 41.50 every month for multiple devices. In comparison, Netflix presents its users with more subscription options but charges a lot more. Even the Basic Subscription plan costs ₹ 500 per month allows a user to access content in Standard Definition (SD) resolution on only one device at a time. Both Amazon Prime Video and Netflix allow free access to their content for the first 30 days after subscription. The current price structure gives Prime Video an upper hand over Netflix, but it won't be an easy choice as both of them have unique content to offer.

4.5 Amazon Prime Video *vs.* Netflix: Which is the Better Streaming Platform for You?

Although Netflix is arguably the original media streaming service, it is by no means alone in the industry. There are many streaming services out there all vying for your monthly subscription dollars. One of those services is Amazon Prime Video, which begs the question: which service should you get? The Amazon Prime vs. Netflix decision isn't easy. After all, an Amazon Prime subscription doesn't just give you access to streaming movies and TV; there are many more perks on offer too. If you want to get the most out of your dollars, our suggestion would be to go with Amazon Prime. If you want to spend the least amount of money possible, we suggest going with Netflix. Ultimately though, we highly recommend going with the Basic Netflix plan and Amazon Prime. If you do, you'll get the incredible selection of content Netflix offers as well as the content and perks Amazon Prime offers. If you can afford to spend $228 per year—or around $19 per month if you budget it out for yourself—this is the ideal situation.

5. OBJECTIVE

1. To explore the usage of online video streaming apps.
2. To study the influence of online video streaming apps on the personal and professional lives of people.
3. To understand the pros and cons of online video streaming apps.

6. HYPOTHESIS

1. H0 - Parameters of online video streaming apps cannot be predicted.

   H1 - Parameters of online video streaming apps can be predicted.

2. H0 - Online video streaming apps will not affect the personal and professional lives of people.

   H1 - Online video streaming apps will affect the personal and professional lives of people.

3. H0 - Positive and negative aspects of online video streaming apps cannot be predicted.

   H1 - Positive and negative aspects of online video streaming apps can be predicted.

7. RESEARCH METHODOLOGY

This paper incorporates the quantitative approach to study the research objectives. Sampling has been done effectively and the tool that has been employed to work on the data collection is particularly questionnaires where the questions were both open ended as well as close ended. A survey was conducted to study the patterns of consumer behavior in relation to both these apps. The sample was mainly taken from Lucknow city. In total 200 questionnaires were filled and enthusiastic responses were received by the respondents.

8. ANALYSIS

The data collected through questionnaires provided varied degree of responses in various aspects. On being asked which online video streaming app they preferred the target audience responded by choosing both (Netflix and Amazon prime) as the leading choice with 43%, followed by Amazon Prime only with 30%, and then ending with Netflix only with 27%. This hereby proves that due to very similar content offering, running platforms provided and not drastically different price points the maximum amount of audience is inclined towards availing the subscriptions of both Netflix and Amazon prime video (Figure 1).

Collection of personal information through the questionnaire revealed that maximum of the audience belongs to a general category of student. These students include both schools and colleges. The student group was followed by the working class with less than half the numbers, working class covered all jobs. Then there was the category of housewife with a bare minimum 2 to 3 entry. The age group data showed that majority of the audience belonged to the age group of 15 to 25 (Figure 2).

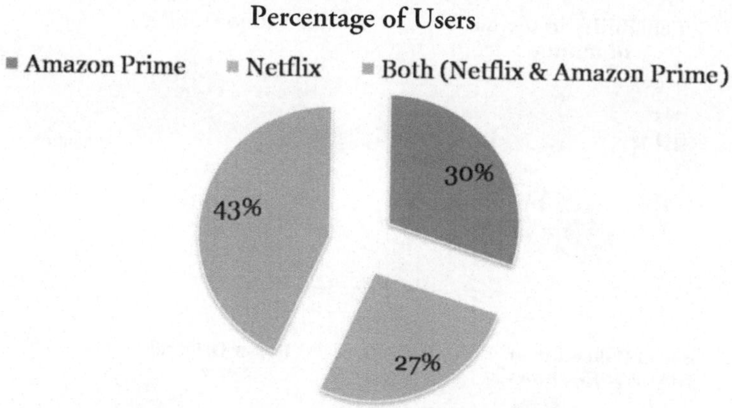

Fig. 1

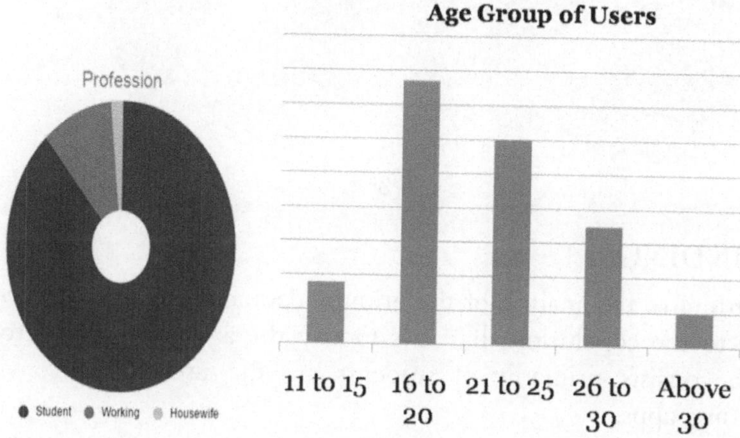

Fig. 2

In order to dive deep and actually figure out the choice of audience between the two applications another round of questions were given in which the audience had to choose one of the two options. These questions were strictly closed ended.

The responses to these questions revealed that the audience preferred Amazon prime video in terms of feasibility of money as it scored 60% votes followed by Amazon with 40%. But at the same time the respondents liked the video quality of Netflix better and it scored a 74% as opposed to Amazons' 26%. Further in terms of better collection of movies and TV shows and also original series the audience preferred Netflix both times (Figures 3 & 4).

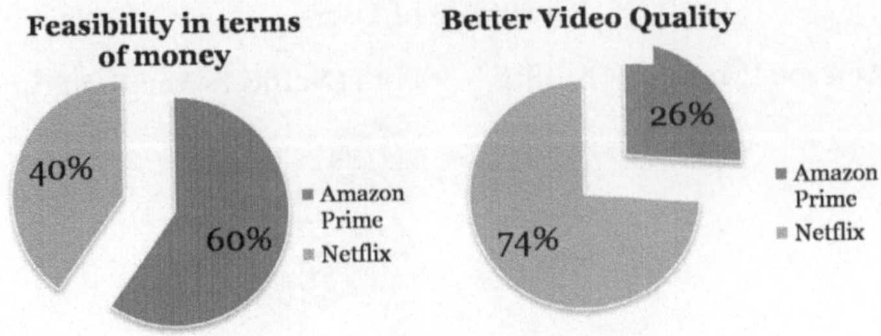

Fig. 3

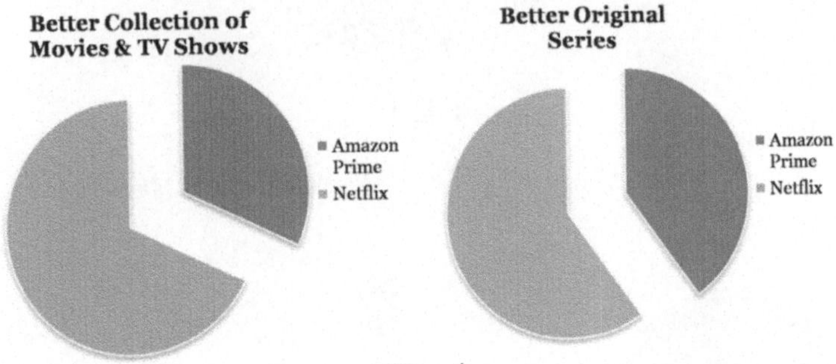

Fig. 4

9. FINDINGS

According to the analysis of the primary data and literature review we come to the conclusion that it is mostly the age group of 15 to 25 which consists primarily of students are the users of these video streaming apps.

It has several benefits i.e. it provides entertainment and helps you escape the humdrum routine work, but also has various negative effects like lack of socializing, lack of concentration in youth and various health problems.

The scope of the online video streaming apps is bright as with time more people are moving towards the online entertainment and the growth and the profit is dependent on the no of subscribers which is rising.

10. CONCLUSION

The primary objective of the research was to throw light on the usage of online video streaming apps and how it affects the personal and professional life of people and also to analyze its pros and cons. With reference to the study it was found that the majority of the users of these apps belonged to a certain profession i.e. students and a certain age group i.e. 15 to 25. Through the aid of the data that was collected and analyzed quite a few conclusions have been drawn down which can be detailed and elaborated as follows—The parameters of measuring the performance of online video streaming apps can be very well predicted and the performance measured accordingly. Secondly the effects on both personal and professional lives can be seen by the amount of time an individual spends on these apps. There is eventually loss of social contact and increased health problems relating to eyes and obesity due to inactivity of the individual. People also experience loss of concentration, loss of focus in work and daily tasks. Thirdly and finally we observe that there are both positive and negative impacts of such applications.

Through the analysis of data gathered in doing this research it can be positively concluded that as the competition increases between Netflix and Amazon prime so does the number of paid subscribers for each app. It is rather difficult to state with surety which application the audience prefers but we can state that the audience eagerly awaits further developments in technology by both apps and the offers that they can provide to lure in more subscribers. As per the research there are certain aspect where Netflix emerges as the winner like in terms of library collection and video quality whereas Amazon Prime emerges as a winner in terms of prices they offer.

REFERENCES

[1] Sabharwal, Karan (2018). "Amazon Vs Netflix: Who will win Indian battleground?". *International Journal of Multidisciplinary Research and Development*, 5(2):140–142.

[2] https://thecollegeinvestor.com/20686/amazon-prime-vs-netflix-compare

[3] https://www.digitaltrends.com/home-theater/netflix-vs-amazon-prime

[4] https://www.trustedreviews.com/opinion/netflix-vs-amazon-prime-instant-video-2918310

[5] https://www.androidauthority.com/amazon-prime-vs-netflix-1005748

[6] https://www.livemint.com/Leisure/2kL7ZsG8AcO5mFmcmFGbRO/Amazon-Prime-Video-vs-Netflix-Which-is-worth-your-money.html

[7] http://www.businessinsider.com/how-much-is-netflix

[8] https://www.tomsguide.com/us/what-is-amazon-primenews-18041.html

Impact of Online Insurance Market in Indian Insurance Sector

Parashuram Mishra*

ABSTRACT: We can't avoid the increasing effect of online trade today across the globe as well as in Indian market during present liberalized era. India is the most youth populous country in the world. Every youth of the day is moving their foot in digital world. In India, there are around 371 million mobile internet users, out of which 262 million in urban areas and 109 million in rural areas (Figure 1). Also, our country has more than 450 million internet users. Unlike the other industry, insurance is also one of the booming service sectors and has adopted this new trend of online product selling focusing the future market. The insurer companies know the need of their customers at present. This new trend has benefited the customers in multi ways. It is cost convenient, time saving, easy access, free of documentation and other similar complexities. Online marketing of insurance product has widely changed this industry. In a very short spam of its journey since 2010, it is anticipated that around three fourth of the policies will be influenced by 2020 (A Report by BCG Google). In this paper, it has been tried to describe the scope and impact of online insurance market in insurance sector.

***Keywords:** Online Insurance, IRDA, Digital World etc.*

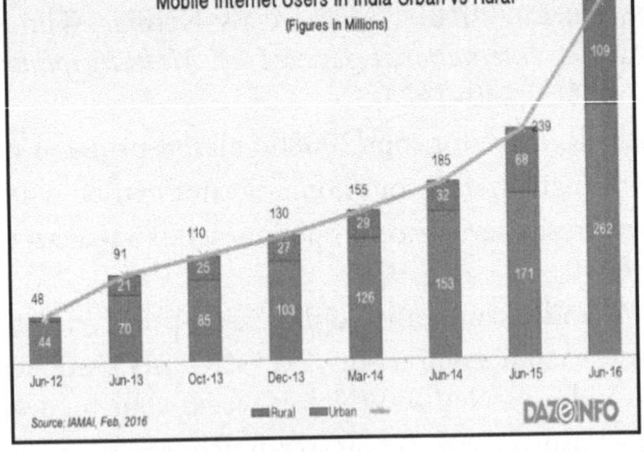

Fig. 1

*Research Scholar, Dr. R.M.L. Avadh University, Faizabad.

1. INTRODUCTION

The insurance industry of India consists of 53 insurance companies of which 24 are in life insurance business and 29 are non-life insurers. Among the life insurers, Life Insurance Corporation (LIC) is the sole public sector company. Apart from that, among the non-life insurers there are six public sector insurers. In addition to these, there is sole national re-insurer, namely, General Insurance Corporation of India (GIC Re). Other stakeholders in Indian Insurance market include agents (individual and corporate), brokers, surveyors and third party administrators servicing health insurance claims.

Out of 29 non-life insurance companies, five private sector insurers are registered to underwrite policies exclusively in health, personal accident and travel insurance segments. They are Star Health and Allied Insurance Company Ltd., Apollo Munich Health Insurance Company Ltd., Max Bupa Health Insurance Company Ltd, Religare Health Insurance Company Ltd and Cigna TTK Health Insurance Company Ltd. There are two more specialized insurers belonging to public sector, namely, Export Credit Guarantee Corporation of India for Credit Insurance and Agriculture Insurance Company Ltd for crop insurance.

Online marketing and services are spreading at a lightning speed to almost all the parts of the world. A developing country like India has also been touched by the online services and now almost everything in India is going online. The limit is not only the online shopping and the social networks. Nearly every service from financial to educational and many more are going online so that you do not have to go out anywhere to fetch a particular service.

Similar to many other services, online insurance in India is also getting famous and is benefitting a number of people.

2. MARKET SIZE

Government's policy of insuring the uninsured has gradually pushed insurance penetration in the country and proliferation of insurance schemes are expected to catapult this key ratio beyond 4 per cent mark by the end of this year, reveals the ASSOCHAM latest paper. The number of lives covered under Health Insurance policies during 2015–16 was 36 Cr. which is approximately 30 per cent of India's total population. The number has seen an increase every subsequent year as 28.80 Cr. people had the policy in the previous fiscal. The market share of all insurance companies regarding insurance premiums received by them in India for the year 2015–16 is detailed as Figure 2.

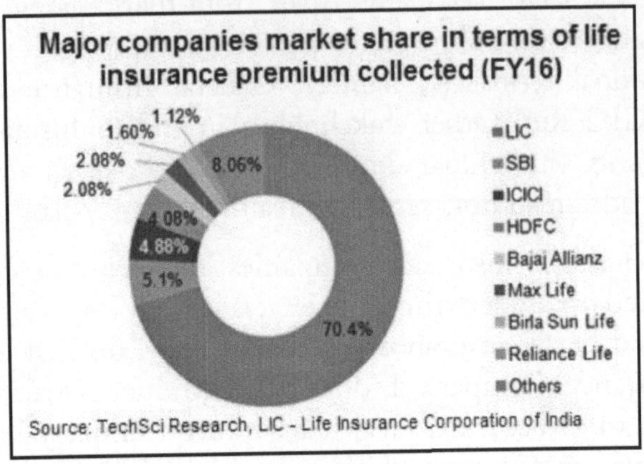

Fig. 2

During April 2015 to March 2016 period, the life insurance industry recorded a new premium income of ₹ 1.38 trillion (US$ 20.54 billion), indicating a growth rate of 22.5 per cent. The general insurance industry recorded a 12 per cent growth in Gross Direct Premium underwritten in April 2016 at ₹ 105.25 billion (US$ 1.55 billion). The life insurance industry reported 9 per cent increase in overall annual premium equivalent in April–November 2016. In the period, overall annual premium equivalent (APE)—a measure to normalise policy premium into the equivalent of regular annual premium—including individual and group business for private players was up 16 per cent to ₹ 1,25,563 Cr. (US$ 18.76 billion) and Life Insurance Corporation up 4 per cent to ₹ 1,50,456 Cr. (US$ 22.48).

India's life insurance sector is the biggest in the world with about 360 million policies which are expected to increase at a Compound Annual Growth Rate (CAGR) of 12–15 per cent over the next five years. The insurance industry plans to hike penetration levels to five per cent by 2020.

The country's insurance market is expected to quadruple in size over the next 10 years from its current size of US$ 60 billion. During this period, the life insurance market is slated to cross US$ 160 billion.

The general insurance business in India is currently at ₹ 78,000 Cr. (US$ 11.44 billion) premium per annum industry and is growing at a healthy rate of 17 per cent.

The Indian insurance market is a huge business opportunity waiting to be harnessed. India currently accounts for less than 1.5 per cent of the world's total insurance premiums and about 2 per cent of the world's life insurance premiums despite being the second most populous nation. The country is the fifteenth largest insurance market in the world in terms of premium volume, and has the potential to grow exponentially in the coming years.

3. NEED OF ONLINE INSURANCE

Today almost everybody who is starting to earn is taking insurance. There are some possible reasons why people are doing so. One of the most common reasons that people give today is to save tax. Apart from tax saving, the other big reason is of course safety. The main benefit of insurance is to provide financial support at times of need.

Some agents and companies offer insurance policies at their office. But people prefer to take online insurance today. Why is it so? Today everyone has become so busy that no one has that much time to visit different insurance offices to check the policies and then buy a plan. In this case, online services can be easily accessed from his home or while on transit and at any suitable time, even at midnight. Also, you get an appropriate amount of time to do proper research before buying the policy. Also, the cost of an online policy is less as compared to an offline one since there is no middlemen involved.

3.1 The Comfort of Online Insurance Process Made it a Big Success in India

Today people are more into comparing things before buying. Even in a case of insurance policy, people like to compare 2–3 companies before settling on one. Comparing becomes hectic when you are confused in between 2–3 brands. To make this easy, there are some comparisons sites that you can make use of. Here you can search for a particular type of insurance and can compare between many brands to get the best deal.

The comparison is based on various parameters like reputation of the company in the market; the services provided by the brand, the benefits and coverage offered by the policy, the price of the policy, returns and many others. After having a look at the various features and companies, you can select the policy that is best suited to you. In fact, this is why the popularity of online insurance has enhanced significantly over the years in India.

3.2 Increasing Demand for Online Insurance in India

There was a time when people in the metropolitan cities such as Delhi, Mumbai, Kolkata among others opted for online insurance services. But with rapid growth of internet and increased penetration, online services have also become quite popular in tier 2 towns as well. Now people in those cities are comfortable in taking help of the online insurance to compare, buy and renew different types of insurance policies.

3.3 Future of Online Insurance in India

With the increase in number of internet users (India has over 400 million internet users; *Source BCG Google Report*), it has also been noticed that the number of people taking up insurance policies online has also increased. There was a time when people with high salaries believed in getting insurance policies and that too, mainly, life insurance policies. But today an individual who has just joined a job starts buying insurance.

People are getting more educated, aware and are trying not just to secure their lives but also their homes, properties, vehicles and even their travel trips. Of course, digitalization has made people more knowledgeable about various types of insurance policies, about how they can be beneficial to them. The most important thing is that people today know how to get the right type of insurance and from where. Buying insurance online is now a trend in India. One of the primary reasons behind this change is the services and benefits offered by the companies and the price benefit that one can avail of while buying online. It might be safe to presume that online is the future for the Indian insurance industry.

3.4 Impact of Online Service in Indian Insurance Market

Gone are the days when people just researched about the particular insurance company and then contacted their agents to buy the policy.

Now the online payment mode is comfortable and safe and you can buy virtually anything online. This feature has boosted the prospects and scope of online insurance in India significantly.

You can make payment through a vast number of choices such as credit or debit cards, internet banking, mobile wallets like Rupay or Paytm and get the policy in your inbox instantly at your reach easily. It is too much cost effective than the cost of traditional insurance policies. Here, the company reduces its cost by reducing the number offices and agents throughout the country. Averagely it has saved around 45% to 60% of cost in various companies.

As per the annual report of IRDA 2015–16, the share of various channels of distribution for direct sales of insurance products under online modes is 2% each for individual as well as group business. In life insurance business the market share of individual new business performance of life insurers is .07% and 1.1% of total premium in LIC and other private life insurance companies respectively or .52% in total industry.

The gateway is also safe and password protected so that your transaction is done successfully and safely. Online insurance also provides a good customer care support, which helps the buyer tackle any tricky situation before or after buying the policy.

3.5 Government Initiatives to Strengthen Insurance Sector

The Union Budget of 2017–18 has made the following provisions for the Insurance Sector:

1. The Budget has made provisions for paying huge subsidies in the premiums of Pradhan Mantri Fasal Bima Yojana (PMFBY) and the number of beneficiaries will increase to 50 per cent in the next two years from the present level of 20 per cent. As part of PMFBY, ₹ 9,000 Cr. (US$ 1.35 billion) has been allocated for crop insurance in 2017–18.
2. By providing tax relief to citizens earning up to ₹ 5 lakh (US$ 7500), the government will be able to increase the number of taxpayers. Life insurers will be able to sell them insurance products, to further reduce their tax burden in future. As many of these people were understating their incomes, they were not able to get adequate insurance cover.

3. Demand for insurance products may rise as people's preference shifts from formal investment products post demonetization.
4. The budget has attempted to hasten the implementation of the Digital India initiative. As people in rural areas become more tech savvy, they will use digital channels of insurers to buy policies.

The Government of India has taken a number of initiatives to boost the digital platform of payments in a mass population preferably in rural areas which will influence the online insurance market at its robust. Some of them are as follows:

1. The Union Cabinet has approved the public listing of five Government-owned general insurance companies and reducing the Government's stake to 75 per cent from 100 per cent, which is expected to bring higher levels of transparency and accountability, and enable the companies to raise resources from the capital market to meet their fund requirements.
2. The Insurance Regulatory and Development Authority of India (IRDAI) plans to issue redesigned Initial Public Offering (IPO) guidelines for insurance companies in India, which are to looking to divest equity through the IPO route.
3. IRDAI has allowed insurers to invest up to 10 per cent in additional tier 1 (AT1) bonds that are issued by banks to augment their tier 1 capital, in order to expand the pool of eligible investors for the banks.
4. IRDAI has formed two committees to explore and suggest ways to promote e-commerce in the sector in order to increase insurance penetration and bring financial inclusion.
5. IRDAI has formulated a draft regulation, IRDAI (Obligations of Insures to Rural and Social Sectors) Regulations, 2015, in pursuance of the amendments brought about under section 32 B of the Insurance Laws (Amendment) Act, 2015. These regulations impose obligations on insurers towards providing insurance cover to the rural and economically weaker sections of the population.
6. The Government of Assam has launched the Atal-Amrit Abhiyan health insurance scheme, which would offer comprehensive coverage for six disease groups to below-poverty line (BPL) and above-poverty line (APL) families, with annual income below ₹ 500,000 (US$ 7,500).

7. The Uttar Pradesh government has launched a first of its kind banking and insurance services helpline for farmers where individuals can lodge their complaints on a toll free number.
8. The select committee of the Rajya Sabha gave its approval to increase stake of foreign investors to 49 per cent equity investment in insurance companies.
9. Government of India has launched an insurance pool to the tune of ₹ 1,500 Cr. (US$ 220.08 million) which is mandatory under the Civil Liability for Nuclear Damage Act (CLND) in a bid to offset financial burden of foreign nuclear suppliers.
10. Foreign Investment Promotion Board (FIPB) has cleared 15 Foreign Direct Investment (FDI) proposals including large investments in the insurance sector by Nippon Life Insurance, AIA International, Sun Life and Aviva Life leading to a cumulative investment of ₹ 7,262 Cr. (US$ 1.09 billion).
11. IRDAI has given initial approval to open branches in India to Switzerland-based Swiss Re, French-based Scor SE, and two Germany-based reinsurers namely, Hannover Re and Munich Re.

4. FUTURISTIC APPROACH

India's insurable population is anticipated to touch 750 million in 2020, with life expectancy reaching 74 years. Furthermore, life insurance is projected to comprise 35 per cent of total savings by the end of this decade, as against 26 per cent in 2009–10. The future looks promising for the insurance industry with several changes in regulatory framework which will lead to further change in the way the industry conducts its business and engages with its customers. Demographic factors such as growing middle class, young insurable population and growing awareness of the need for protection and retirement planning will support the growth of Indian life insurance.

REFERENCES

[1] Annual Report of Insurance Regulatory and Development Authority of India (IRDA), 2015–16.

[2] BCG Google Report.

[3] Media Reports, Press Releases, Press Information Bureau, Union Budget 2017–18, Insurance Regulatory and Development Authority of India (IRDA).

Building Knowledgeable Society through E-Education, Today's Requirements for Better Tomorrow

Shubhendu S. Shukla*

ABSTRACT: Exploring the challenges and opportunities associated with the concepts of communication in online higher education, I tried to re-evaluate in this paper the purpose to replicate face-to-face learning and teaching approaches in online learning environments. Taking an online course should be more than sitting in front of a computer—real engagement involves becoming a part of the community of learners. Being a member of a learning community means engaging in reciprocal learning activities, soaking in new ideas and sharing point of view and experiences to make meaning of the information. An online learning society is a public or private destination on the Internet that addresses the learning needs of its members by facilitating peer-to-peer learning. In an online learning society, people share knowledge via textual discussion (synchronous or asynchronous), audio, video, or other Internet-supported media. Blogs combines personal journaling with social networking to create environments with opportunities for reflection. Types of online learning communities may include e-learning communities (groups interact and connect solely via technology) and combined learning communities (groups utilize face-to-face meetings as well as online meetings). Intentional online learning communities may be categorized as knowledge-based, practice-based, and task-based. Online learning communities may focus on personal aspects, process, or technology. This paper suggests an in-depth analysis of the potential unique requirements associated with online learning platforms. The paper identifies unique ways in which online learning and teaching is different from face-to-face communication, and consequently several ways in which this system can be an advantage for students.

Keywords: *e-Education, Online Education, Online Community, Distance Education, ICT, CRISP, Online Tools, etc.*

*Assistant Professor, SRM Business School, Lucknow, India.

1. INTRODUCTION

The impact of globalization is having substantial effects among various sectors of most nations. We are looking to maximize educational potential in rural areas. Taking this into consideration, government may choose powerful strategies aimed at development of rural area. In other words, encouraging maximum participation in the economic and intellectual life of a community to develop and build knowledge society. Strong agricultural competition and globalization has accelerated rural depopulation. Today the whole world moving towards information based society. After all information is knowledge and knowledge is wisdom. Universal Access of information is essential for 'human resource development' to empower knowledge community through e-Education.

Today there is a need to provide education in rural area for upgrading and building knowledge of marginalised populations. But it is very difficult and costly to provide infrastructure facility in rural area. Providing universal access facility, governments should look to e-Education as a strategy for promotional activity and build knowledge society. Information Technology is changing speedily at which knowledge provides a different challenge in the knowledge society. To upgrade knowledge some of the large companies provide their employees with on-the-job training through electronic. It means that training costs are building knowledge accelerated. In the fastest changing environments the marginilised people are often unwilling or unable to leave either place of work or homes. So there is need to provide education at their doorstep. Basically this is useful for the people namely, students, rural resident, farmers, workers, and others. The need of these peoples is different, so we must focus on suitable or optimal education.

2. NEED OF THE E-EDUCATION

We are using Distance Education for geographically isolated students, those students who are not able to attend the class. There are a number of Open Universities/Institutes which conduct Correspondence courses at various level. At present distance education is delivered by a variety of means including print, radio, television, CD-ROM and Web at various levels. People are not isolated by virtue of geographical location alone but sometimes a culture makes difference. To bridge this gap e-Education can be used and developed to take account of cultural difference (Language). We must account for these kinds of issues through e-Education and develop the rural area. In India ICT (Information and Communication Technology) is playing important role to bridge the digital divide gap. Divide means haves and have not, the poor and the rich, urban and rural, south and north. The cost of e-Education is not affordable to people with low incomes. For this problem we need to share resources through either government or sponsorship or by public provision. e-Education provides group of people to create and develop or to upgrade their knowledge and skills by communicating with others through web. With 40% of the Indian population being illiterate, 100 million of school children not getting a schooling, there is only way India will get educated if e-Education is used to deliver it. But there are the hurdles of cost and technology issues in India.

3. INITIATIVES TOWARDS E-EDUCATION IN INDIA

A phenomenal growth in the Indian Economy primarily fuelled by the service sector has been because of the Information Technology Industry. It is interesting to study the contribution of this growth engine in the lives of about 70% of the 1 billion Indians; the 700 million who live in the rural areas. Major initiatives have been undertaken by the governments in focusing on the issues relating to universal access of information. In most of the country Information and Communication Technologies (ICT) is used as tool for development. It is necessity to provide Universal Access (UA) for rural areas. Universal Service (US) is a different from Universal Access (UA). Universal Service means that every household in the country has communication service. UA means that everyone in a community can gain access to an available telephone. UA may available through pay phones, tele-centers or even single entrepreneurs who market/provides e-Educational services. The emphasis of such services to rural, remote and lower income users thorough e-Education.

The working group recommended several projects for the centre and the states to be undertaken for rural areas. Several schemes were mooted specifically targeted on rural India. For the purpose of spreading e-Education, Modified Vidyarthi Computer Programme was designed and launched. The Ministry of Rural Development also launched programmes like CRISP (Computerized Rural Information Systems Project) and CAPART (Council for Advancement of People's Action and Rural Technology). There have been a few success stories in empowering the rural India with IT. Ministry of Rural development is implementing a countrywide programme for land record computerization in collaboration with states. Infrastructure for this project has been set up in 534 districts. In Rajasthan, An information System for 'mandis' connects 236 'mandis' online providing daily rates of all the 'mandis' by 4 PM. In Karnataka, the Bhoomi project is a major scheme of the government to computerize 190 lakh land records concerning 60 lakh farmers. Gyandoot is a lead project of M.P. government under which 21 rural cyber cafes, called 'Soochnalayas', have been established in the district of Dhar. The services provided by these centres include commodity/mandi marketing information, issues of copies of land records (khatauni and map), online registration for issue of income, caste, domicile certificates, Hindi email etc.

Another major private sector initiatives has been the ITC e-Choupal projects which have created value for the company and provided socio-economic benefits to the farming community by encouraging direct marketing by the farmers. All the information, products and services they need to enhance farm productivity, improve farm-gate price realization and cut transaction costs. M.S. Swaminathan Research Foundation, in an experiment in electronic knowledge delivery to the poor, have connected ten villages near Pondicherry in southern India by a hybrid wired and wireless network that facilitates both voice and data transfer, and have enabled the villagers to get information that they need. The Sustainable Access in Rural India project (SARI) seeks to show that viable markets exist for information and communication services in rural poor areas by inventing and deploying innovative technologies, assessments, and business models. A few groups like TeNet have been developing low cost solution based Business Models for the rural Areas. As is evident from the above facts, the effort thus far has been localized without the focus or backing of a central e-Education policy for the rural India.

In order to ensure that technological innovations, of which e-learning is an example, are diffused and adopted, it is necessary for those involved in projects to have an understanding of the client group who will be using the technologies so that implementation issues are socially and educationally acceptable. In some instances, client groups may feel uncertain or negative about proposed technologies. Exploration of these issues and the subsequent development of positive attitudes to the proposals might enhance the uptake of e-education.

As with many developments, especially in the technology area, new products arrive on the market with remarkable frequency that are capable of increasing the capacity of hardware or the ingenuity of software. Timely and effective communications with intended users enhances their awareness of the benefits e-education systems can bring. Once potential users are awareness of what can be achieved by e-education, then accessible and affordable training has to be provided. Training involves the development and delivery of self-help packages as well as face-to-face contact, with its attendant seminars and itinerancy visits.

Underpinning the e-Education strategies is the assumption that the infrastructural backbone of communications technologies such as cabling, satellite links and bandwidth is available to users. For example, many low-socioeconomic urban places may be well served with fibre optic cables while wealthier rural towns may still rely on copper wires for telecommunications. e-Education strategic planners need to take into account these structural issues when designing flexibly delivered teaching and learning packages.

3.1 Massive Open Online Courses (MOOCs)

Massive Open Online Courses (MOOCs) are free online courses available for anyone to enroll. MOOCs provide an affordable and flexible way to learn new skills, advance your career and deliver quality educational experiences at scale. A massive open online course (MOOC) is a model for delivering learning content online to any person who wants to take a course, with no limit on attendance. It was established back in 2008 and gained momentum in 2012 as a popular learning tool. Many MOOCs have communities that have interactive sessions and forums between the student, professors and Teaching Assistants (TAs) along with the study/course material and video lectures. So, if there is a particular course you want to pursue but cannot, you have an option of considering a MOOC for your chosen higher education path.

The University Grants Commission (UGC) along with the HRD (Human Resource Development) Ministry has launched the MOOC program in India for higher secondary, bachelors and masters degrees. This will cover a wide range of subjects that may or may not be taught in regular campus studies.

There are various notable institutions, both non-profit and commercial, that offer these courses worldwide with the help of MOOC providers. A few of these are listed below.

- **NPTEL (India):** Indian Institutes of Technology (IITs) and Indian Institute of Science (IISc.) offer online courses through this platform which require no registration and are free of cost.
- **Swayam (India):** A new portal for MOOCs named '**Study Webs of Active-Learning for Young Aspiring Minds**', in short, **SWAYAM**, is said to present students with an opportunity to study anything from a list of 2000 courses out of which 200 are currently available for registration. Audio-visual medium, illustrations, research and case studies with self-assessment are few of the mediums chosen to approach the study of these courses.
- **WizIQ (India and USA):** IIT Delhi, India offers this course through this platform which requires registration and fees to study courses offered by them.
- **Open2Study:** The headquarters of this platform for online courses is based out of Australia.
- **Coursera:** The headquarters of this platform for online courses is based out of USA.
- **edX:** The headquarters of this platform for online courses is based out of USA.
- **udemy:** The headquarters of this platform for online courses is based out of USA.

4. E-EDUCATION STRATEGIES

Universal Access of information is an important factor in any strategy of development to empower the rural area (masses). E-Education is a new concept and as with other innovations it will meet with resistance. The following strategies might be considered by those involved with e-Education.

1. **Social Impact:** A social impact of the development the values of upgrading skills and knowledge though e-Education.
2. **Environment and Awareness:** Creating a positive environment and awareness is required. A deep understanding of the culture is needed into which the learning is to be introduced. This takes time, zeal and energy.
3. **Political Support:** Funds are not available without political support.
4. **Pedagogically Sound:** It should be considered that the contents/material of e-Education must be pedagogically sound. Contents especially in the "web based" environment are prepared by using regional language. It carries and attracts community or a specific group of people to create 'knowledge community'. It should be linked with society for successful adoption of e-Education.
5. **Practices:** The delivery and practicalities of e-education, the methods of teaching and learning and the actual delivering strategies suitable for professionals and society.
6. **Change in Technology:** Upgradation of suitable hardware, software, maintenance and technology should be considered.
7. **Technology Infrastructure:** Successful participation in e-Education requires suitable and also personal expenditure on technology (computers, software, packages and network etc.). There are peoples/groups, which it support collective acquisition of the above facilities, especially in rural (low income) areas.

By using the above strategies people can improve economic efficiency, develop skilled workers, upgrade skills, enhanced business communications and access/share to global knowledge.

5. RESPONSE TO E-EDUCATION

Government of India have made educational provision available for all in a variety of people way through schools, teachers and the correspondence system. The Correspondence School provides support to rural area and urban area. Many schools are closing for economic reasons as the population moves from rural to urban areas. Response for e-Education is very good in developed country and underdeveloped country. We need to create awareness about e-Education in undeveloped country.

6. HOW TO BRING E-EDUCATION?

6.1 Remote Students

By using print based system the Correspondence School (CS) has been serving needs of the isolated students. Recently CS used an electronic interface to its students for example Web Based Computer Training or e-mail and chatting system or synchronous/asynchronous methods. e-Education will become global education that will be available to students of all age groups and genders. There is now a move towards a more co-operative learning approach between institutions to service and develop rural area.

6.2 Learners Learning Support

Both government and industry should support for the rural development through funds, creating infrastructure and sponsoring/supporting students specially in rural area.

6.3 People Support

Provide education through radio and television programme in rural area by using regional language. Use of Video conferencing technology to raise achievement standards in rural areas. This type of development helps to build knowledge communities of peoples (learners). Use specific language and culture and give students greater access of knowing.

6.4 Facilitators/Professional

Accountability and quality are the important factors in the professional world for decision making. Facilitators have to adopt the lifelong learning agenda. Through e-Education professional can do lifelong learning. This kind of knowledge is now deliverable using CBT, and web-based training methods; these students can continue to learn while physically staying/being at home or at the workplace. The e-Learning materials developed for learners outside the institution are deliverable anywhere in the world (specially in rural areas).

6.5 Costs and Economic Factors

1. **Standard module:** Today at introductory level it is costly but if we develop standard module, which will serve the need of the rural area at very large scale then it will become cheaper.
2. **Infrastructural costs:** cost of cables, networks and other transmission systems.
3. **Package costs:** cost of the selected software development—package cost. Purchase, upgrade, licensing and compliance costs.
4. **Methods for development:** Quantifying the economic impact of e-education is not yet possible. e-Education costs can be identified using techniques developed for learning packages.
5. **Peripherals costs:** such as computers, scanners, web camera, multimedia kit, modems and printers.
6. **CMS (Content Management System) cost:** cost of developers to develop and trial learning materials; and copyright and other licensing issues.

7. E-EDUCATION BENEFITS

E-education benefits depends on learners and facilitators. It also depends on community, culture and language.

Considering this factor the following benefits would be considered.

- It can be accessed globally through network (Universal Access and Universal Service).
- Build knowledge comminutes by using self-learning or collaborative learning package. It will used for self learning purpose people without instructor.
- It is beneficial for rural areas by preservation of local culture electronically.
- By using e-Education we can transfers knowledge speedily.
- It is useful for dissemination of information through web in rural area.
- It is beneficial for upgrading skills and building knowledge. It is lifelong learning for all who wish to access it.

8. CONCLUSION

Developed and under developed Countries have started adopting e-Education. Government of India has taken strong steps towards e-Education. The idea of building knowledgeable society through e-Education has taken hold. The methods of delivering e-Education are better understood for all levels of people whether they highly educated or they are college students. It is beneficial to those who having universal access. It requires large amount of investment in the technologies and infrastructure and Indian government has taken initiatives on it after 2014. It would be a long term investment for which there may not be immediately economic return but significant social and educational profits. It will be more useful for rural areas those villages located at remote places and people want to educate their ward. It will proved to be the best-suited alternative for rural education and service delivery.

In this context verifying the proposals for governments and education service providers can be highlighted. It is necessary to identify targets communities, their characteristics in terms of attitudes towards e-Education. Characteristics may cross various aspects such as social, technological, personal and community level. Confidence of providers of e-education must be with respect to time and effort, which is definitely a risky business. Both providers and clients of e-Education should have strongly believed in power of information technology as far as its expandability is concerned. In India the infrastructure and initiatives are improving day by day as new technologies and several options are available but it is need to identify specific community and understand their needs.

ACKNOWLEDGEMENT

First, I would like to thank my organization *(SR Group of Institutions, Lucknow)*, who provided me such an academic environment along with special assistance and support by which it would be possible for me. My special thank to *Mr. Pawan Singh Chauhan* (*Honourable Chairman, SR Group of Institutions, Lucknow*), *Mr. Rajesh Chauhan (Deputy Director)* and *Mr. Satranjan Sharma (Assistant Director)*, who encourage me by their thoughts.

Second, a very special thanks to *Kunwar Abhishek Pratap Singh (Librarian)* who made a major contribution to this Paper, their input and support and motivation toward this paper were outstanding.

Last but not the least it were my departmental colleagues who always support me in every dimensions of my professional life.

REFERENCES

[1] Darnell, F. and Higgins, A.H. (1983). Factors and Issues in Australian Rural Education: A Case for New Perspectives, in Browne, R.K. and Foster, L.E. Sociology of Education (3rd ed), Melbourne. MacMillan, p. 29.

[2] Megan Santosus, Leadership training courses target what's different about IT execs.

[3] Pingali, Rajeswari, "Computers on wheels" for people centered development.

[4] Shyamal, Ghosh, Bridging the Digital Divide—Options for India, 3rd National Workshop Hyderabad, CSI Communication, Feb. 2004, p. 4.

[5] Rogers, E.M. (1995). Diffusion of Innovations (4th ed). New York. Free Press.

[6] http://www.emergic.org/archives/2003/08/07/index.html

Growth, Opportunities and Challenges of E-Learning: A Study in the Indian Context

Tripti Barthwal[1] and Aparna Singh[2]

ABSTRACT: E-education or e-learning is the delivery of education or any type of training by electronic teaching methods. This electronic method can be a computer or a smart phone where teaching material is usually accessed by use of internet. Other than internet, CDs, DVDs, television and other similar tools can also be used for e-learning. There are several E-learning portals offering online courses in India and abroad. Many people avail these professional certificate courses to enhance their learning and career.

Online education in its various modes has been growing steadily worldwide due to the confluence of new technologies, global adoption of the Internet, and intensifying demand for a workforce trained periodically for the ever evolving digital economy. E-education is one of the instructional education programmes that can help students in their studies. E-learning has arrived on the education scene, providing solutions on how to create e-learning environments and how to make them useful for students as well as teachers. The purpose of this research is to study the opportunities, issues and challenges of e-learning environment. The major issues discussed in the paper include: the students' level of exposure to e-learning, effectiveness of e-learning, issues related to online learners, transitioning from face-to-face to online, time management, and teaching styles and growth of e-learning.

Keywords: *e-Learning, Opportunities, Issues, Growth, Learner and Teachers.*

1. INTRODUCTION

Today, e-learning offers the solution to many of our problems in education. The term e-learning came into existence in the late

[1]Director, LBSIMDS, Lucknow. E-mail: drtbarthwal@gmail.com
[2]Assistant Professor, LBSIMDS, Lucknow. E-mail: aparnasingh1591@gmail.com

1990s. But before then, some of its aspects were already taking place. First there was correspondence learning. Then came distance learning. The scope and status of e-learning is constantly changing due to continual developments in new technology, hardware and software respectively.

The e-learning activities are important for the development of any country. In modern era everybody is thinking about growth. If it is planned properly then proper results comes. In this research paper e-learning in India is observed. The research paper focused on growth of e-learning and e-learning in India as a main wheel of development of education. Soon after independence in 1947, the Government of India had the challenge of bringing uniformity in educational system and providing education to large segments of the population. Due to various schemes undertaken by India to improve the literacy rate. These measured have resulted in increase in literacy rate from 64.8% in 2001 to 73.0% in 2011. Satisfaction level of learner increase with e-learning compared to traditional learning, along with perceived ease of use and access, interactivity, and user-friendly interface design. It was found that average number of professional courses' teachers in higher education are using e-learning mode whereas only a few non-professional courses' teachers are using e-learning mode.

In the information management systems human agents can be considered one of the most important factors that make system run more smoothly (Peterson & Peterson, 1988). In this manner role of teachers in the e-learning environments are very essential. The questions "Does the growth of technology undermines the significance of teachers?" And "how much e-learning is helpful for students" are very important to answer to analyse the effectiveness of e-learning.

There are numerous advantages and disadvantages of e-learning. Previous research found that e-learning is more cost effective than traditional learning because less time and money is spent by learners on travelling. This means when students embark on e-learning, they can be thrifty. Their spare time could be used to perform other useful activities. Besides, lacking of face to face interaction is a one of the major issue in e-learning. Connectivity issue of internet in semi-urban and rural areas.

2. OBJECTIVES

- To explore the growth for e-learning in Indian higher education scenario.
- To identify the level of exposure of e-learning.
- To explore the disadvantages, issues & challenges that facing by e-learning.
- To identify the role of teacher in e-learning.

3. RESEARCH METHODOLOGY

The basic objective of this study is to understand the concept of e-learning and to identify the growth of e-learning. This paper aims to discuss the exposure and challenges of learning, and tries to identify the role of teachers in this system. In order to fulfil such objective secondary method is adopted. The secondary data was collected through books, periodicals, journal and published material related e-learning for the study.

3.1 e-Learning in Indian Higher Education Scenario

With a very long time traditional learning system had been used in India. But the educational environment needs are changing now a days and a global education standard is imposing and forcing our education system to undergo many changes. The concept of e-learning or education is gaining popularity in the country day by day.

As per Census Report 2018 published by Government of India:

Table 1: Literacy Rates

Year	*Total Population (in per.)*	*Males (in per.)*	*Female (in per.)*
2001	64.8	75.3	53.7
2011	73.0	80.9	64.6

Data Source: Office of the Registrar General & Census Commissioner, India.

The above Table 1 shows that the percentage of literate population in the total population has increased in 2011, from 64.8% to 73%. The percentage of literate male population has increased from 75.3% to 80.9% and the percentage of literate female population has increased from 53.7% to 64.6% in the span of a decade. Still the fact remains that approx 10% of India's total population illiteracy rate has decreased and e-learning can prove helpful to reduce the illiteracy as the advancement in technology and communication has made teaching and training possible anywhere, anytime.

According to a recent study in a global level online learning program, after the United States, India has been reported to have the second highest number of online course enrolments with more than over 1,55,000 students from the country. Of a total of around 1.2 million students worldwide, 32% are from the U.S. while 15% are from India. In higher education, there is a growing demand to create a virtual learning environment (VLE) in which all aspects of a course are handled through a consistent user interface throughout the institution. Some of these programmes are initiated in our country and students need to attend orientation sessions in colleges, but the course content is delivered online. Several universities do offer online student support services, such as online advice and registration, e-counselling, online textbook purchase and student newspapers.

India has one of the largest education systems in the world with a network of more than 1 million schools and 18,000 higher education institutions that are using e-learning because it is ease of use and access, interactivity, and user-friendly interface design. More than half of the country's 1.2 billion population falls in the target market for education and related services.

Digital India and Skill India are among the several government initiatives launched to spread digital literacy in India. Few more such examples are e-Education (all college connected with broadband and free WiFi) in all colleges, development of pilot MOOCs (Massive Online Open Courses), NandGhars (digital tools as teaching aids), NEPTEL, SWAYAM (MOOCs based on curriculum taught in classrooms from 9th class till post-graduation), and India Skills Online (learning portal for skill training). Clearly, the government initiatives go a long way in reaping benefits of online education.

3.2 Opportunities in e-Learning

It is fact that e-learning is growing fast and there is no surprise, because e-learning gives a chance for learning to everyone. Furthermore, most e-learning platforms are not time sensitive, thus no matter where you live, or what time of the day or week best suits to your calendar, you are able to join. It gives a student the opportunity to study at their own pace and a chance for teachers and educational institutions to reach a much wider audience. E-learning gives a chance to study even at night, if that is the preferred choice of the student. All you need is a computer, a good Internet connection and the willingness to learn.

Due to ease of access to information, people with high mobility due to business life are able to access materials so far as they have the prerequisite electronic tools.

One more and a very important advantage is that quality of output information can be adjusted to the required level and are flexible. E-learning emphasizes continuous learning and promotes "just-in-time" and "just enough" learning. Both slow and fast learners can take their own time of learning because they do need separate timings. And hence the overall stress in the classroom environment can be removed.

3.3 Disadvantages, Issues and Challenges of e-Learning

E-learning is not, however, the be all and end all to every educational need, because computers cannot replace human being. The personal touch, eye contacts are missing in e-learning. The impersonality, suppression of communication mechanisms such as body language, and elimination of peer-to-peer learning, reduced social and cultural interactions are major shortcoming associated with e-learning process. There is a limited opportunity to interact face-to-face with professors and other students and this is stimulating and motivating factors in the learning process especially in distance learning courses—difficult to develop relationships with classmates. Possibility of limited local networking opportunities. Most of the communication through email, chat room or discussion groups, but no offline get together. No personalized attentions from instructor with regards to face-to face interactions and feedbacks. No campus atmosphere to create social interaction.

Technology Cost and Scheduling are another drawback. Students may be required to equip the necessary digital system and learn new or enhanced computer and troubleshooting skills. One must have high-speed Internet.

3.4 Role of Teacher in e-Learning

The ability of teachers to communicate through Internet, accessing and publishing information is very diverse. There are some who are pre-e-literate and others who utilise the Internet for day to day school and classroom activity. To make the move toward e-teaching is the next brave step.

Joann Harriso suggested that the e-teacher will not be "the person who knows all the answers and decides what the question will be" but it is the e-teacher who becomes "an expert learner," who can help students solve problems and find answers to their questions. The teacher therefore becomes as much a part of the learning process as their students as they learn to work in a facilitative and collaborative e-learning environment.

There are three main activities that small group teachers have to manage simultaneously: group management, activity management and learning management. There are some role of the teacher is that of facilitator of learning:

- leading discussions,
- asking open-ended questions,
- guiding process and task, and
- Enabling active participation and involvement of learners and engagement with new ideas.

Effective teachers are essential to ensuring that small groups work well. Any event of teaching will be more successful if the teacher:

- is enthusiastic
- has organized the session well
- has a feeling for the subject
- can conceptualize the topic
- has empathy with the learners
- understands how people learn
- has skills in teaching and managing learning
- is alert to context and 'classroom' events
- is teaching with their preferred teaching style
- has a wide range of skills in their teaching repertoire, including questioning, listening, reinforcing, reacting, summarizing and leadership.

4. CONCLUSION

As per research findings we conclude that the rapid increase in internet connectivity the e-learning is important for the growth of the country. A strong internet ecosystem, with a multiple of local and global players, will help online learning make faster. In underdeveloped and developing countries, e-learning raises the education level, illiteracy is reduced and it is helpful for economic development. E-learning can be developed through proper investigate and plan of action. It is proved that the development and adaptation of e-learning will help higher education and as well as government. E-learning is increasing the percentage of literate people in the population of India. E-learning plays a vital role in development of education through e-learning lot of opportunities can be captured and fast development will possible.

This is true that e-learning gives opportunities to learner and country for growth. However, there are some issues related to e-learning like lack of face to face interaction and some technology cost etc.

Facilitating e-learning is empowering for both the learner and the teacher and frees the teacher from much kind of the burdens that having to be an 'expert' or 'perfect'. Making the shift from teacher as expert to facilitator is sometimes seen as diminishing a teacher's power and authority, but this should not be the case.

So, at last we conclude with that e-learning is gift for teacher, learner and as well as for the development of country. For this e-learning needs regular upgradation.

REFERENCES

[1] Arun, Gaikwad *et al.* (2016). E-learning in India: Wheel of Change, 6(1), 40–45.

[2] Bhongade, Devendra *et al.* (2018). Prospect of e-learning in Indian higher education: trends and issues, 5(5), 180–186.

[3] Ndzibah, Emmanel and Ofori, Cephas (2017). Opportunities in developing countries: Case Ghana, ISSN 2489-2386.

[4] Nelasco, Shobana *et al.* (2007). E-learning for Higher Studies of India, 16.1–16.7.

[5] Palvia, Shailendra *et al.* (2018). Online Education: Worldwide Status, Challenges, Trends, and Implications, 21(4), 233–241.

[6] Pushpanathan, T. (2012). The role of a teacher in facilitating e-learning, 2(2).

[7] Sharma, Sunil Kumar *et al.* (2014). E-learning in India, 3(1), 113–117.

Strategy for E-Learning in Higher Education System in India and its Implications

Nisha*

ABSTRACT: Education has accompanied civilization throughout the many centuries. For long time teachers have been teaching and applying applied knowledge to fulfill and to satisfy the expectations of their students. The methods and the tools they applied to assure the need of proper communication have continuously been changing. The time has been changed and the information and technology has afforded it new shape and shine. With the advent of Computer, the advancement of education has made us global pupil who gain knowledge from diverse sources and servers. One of the useful applications of Internet is e-education. It institutes digital classroom anywhere anytime. The term e-learning is widely accepted for E-education. Also terms like online education, virtual education, Internet-based education, web-based education, and education via computer-mediated communication are common in higher education system. E-learning includes numerous types of media that deliver text, images, audio, animation, and streaming video. The "E" letter in E-education may also be applied for the favorable meaning like: "exciting, energetic, enthusiastic, extended, excellent, and educational" in addition to "electronic". E-learning is a part of new dynamics that characterises the educational system. It has become an important part of the society, comprising an extensive array of digitalization approaches, components and delivery methods. The use of e-learning is seen at all levels of educational system, thus in higher education as well. The Academic excellence of Higher education institutions can be maintained and upgraded through E-education system.

In the light of the above, the present study shows the positive effects of e-learning for the higher education system in India. Paper has been divided into four sections. Introductory section explains the concept of e-education. Section II describes the different strategies of education Section and reviews some literature. Section III of the paper analyzes the

*Assistant Professor, Divine International Group of Institutions, Gwalior, India.

impact of e-education, its advantages in education sector especially in higher education system. Last section includes conclusions and suggestion. On the basis of findings we can conclude that E-learning is visualised as the India's license for boosting up its higher education system and the only way to sustain a better future is by educating the younger generation with effective and efficient education methodologies. It optimistic to expose students to the latest technology so that they are not left clueless while they reach the stage at which they will contribute to society.

Keywords: *e-Learning, Higher Education System, Information and Communication Technologies (ICT), Computer Based Training (CBT).*

SECTION I

1. INTRODUCTION

E-learning is a part of new dynamics that characterizes the educational system. It has become an important part of the society, comprising an extensive array of digitalization approaches, components and delivery methods. The use of information and communication technologies (ICT) for educational purpose has increased & the spread of network technologies has caused e-learning practices to evolve significantly. Information and communication technologies (ICT) have become one of the most important factors to the formation of society in the twenty-first century. Their impact is revolutionary. It affects the way of life of people, their work and education. The new paradigm of modern education incorporates primarily the requirement for informatization of education as an important factor for its development. [Tatiana shopava]

Education through internet, network is E-learning. It is the network based transfer of skills & knowledge. E-learning refers to use of electronic applications and processes to learn. The e-learning applications and processes are the web-based learning, computer-based learning, virtual classrooms and digital collaboration. The contents are delivered through the internet, local intranet/extranet, audio or video tape, satellite TV & CD-ROM. E-learning is used by learners and educators in homes, schools, higher education, business and others. In the early days, e-learning received a bad impression, as many people thought bringing computers into the classroom would remove that human element that some learners need, but as time has progressed technology has developed, and now we embrace smart-phones and tablets in the classroom and office, as well as using a wealth of interactive designs that makes e-learning not only engaging for the users, but valuable as a lesson delivery medium. The use of e-learning is seen at all levels of educational system. [Ruma, 2016]

The increasing influence of globalization and the emerging information society, set new requirements for all areas of social life, including to higher education. E-learning became an important instrument in the new Higher Educational Environment in the digital age which creates student-centered learning and educational practice, offering new more flexible learning methods. E-learning has been touted as a way to address some of the challenges higher education institutions face and extol as a tactic for staying competitive. Various external and internal forces have brought about the expansion and growth of e-learning in higher education. External forces such as decreased state funding, tuition increases, technology costs and depressed economies have led to internal pressures to reduce costs and increase revenue in many higher education institutions. Combined, these stressors are influencing and changing the way faculty teach and students learn in higher education (Kuruvilla, Norton, Chalasani and Gee, 2012). Academic leaders expect that e-education will compensate for a decrease in traditional course offerings by saving costs and improving the effectiveness of learning (Allen, Seaman, Poulin, & Straut, 2016). However, in many universities, implementation and initiation of e-education is still in experimental stages, such as combining the new ideas and advanced educational technologies of online education with existing methods (Huron Consulting Group, 2014). Therefore, identifying current trends and issues of e learning and shaping the future of e- education is of importance to senior administrators as well as faculty members. This paper shows recent trends and issues of online learning in higher education through review of literatures and provides recommendations to guide academic leaders in making informed decisions about the future of e-learning in their institutions.

SECTION II

E-learning is classified in two types synchronous and asynchronous. In synchronous learning, teachers and lecturers interact with themselves and each uses communication technologies such as video conferencing, web conferencing, chatting, and telephone conversation. In asynchronous learning, without live interaction the teacher's use technologies such as CD-ROMS, Cassettes, e-mails etc. E-learning in educational institutions follows blended method, i.e. both synchronous and asynchronous. [Eugene Pradeep Kumar & Panchanatham]

Analysis of a sample of such strategies indicates that most universities have adopted a 'bottom-up' rather than 'top-down' implementation policy; they tend to foreground the potential of e-learning to enhance teaching and learning and to foster a wide variety of learning outcomes. In addition, staff training is seen as essential to successful e-learning but flexible support structures and mechanisms are seen as even more important [Mac Keogh and Fox, 2008]. Again this reflects that most institutions are a relatively in early stage of e-learning development. Klink and Jochems suggest that it is time to consider e-learning as an integral part of academic activity and needs to be routinely supported so that e-learning can become almost obligatory to mission statements and strategic plans. The rise of the industrial e-learning paradigm is creating a growing perception for the need of institutional strategies to guide the implementation of e-learning. It is necessary for management to have a clear view of the purpose intended through the introduction of e-learning in order to determine the necessary work. [Klink and Jochems, 2003]

Review of Literature-Nelasco, Arputhraj & Paul (2007) in their paper studied e-learning for Higher Studies of India. The paper concentrates on Indian higher education scenario, eLearning content preparation and presentation tools, application of eLearning in various types of methodologies used in higher studies, pros and cons of eLearning and future of eLearning in India. Technology enabled learning is evolved through a combination of hardware, software, media delivery system and communication systems including networking. eLearning benefits the society by offering integration of all institutions, access to best faculty and quality study material, avoidance of human bias, dust free learning, individualized instruction, learning in experience, unique fast learner—slow learner mechanism, flexibility, cost effectiveness, zero opportunity cost of time etc. But the major challenge faced by eLearning is that it cannot replace human being. e-learning in India has a very big potential and a bright future. Since virtual classroom has got bright future. It is also suggested to attract affordable international students, to utilise the adventurous faculty collaborators, to bring about e-twinning of institutions and to plan more inter-country exchange programs. To conclude global exploration into any branch of knowledge is possible only through technology enabled learning.

Jaiswal (2013) conducted the study to find out the current status of e-Learning in Indian Higher Education of U.P. He says if an educational institution is committed to give high quality education, it should be built on values and ethics, and be innovative in offering its teaching programmes. E-learning is not a single strand but is multi-faceted, covering a wide range of approaches and methods. Thus, in order to study this objective 2919 teachers (839 teachers from professional courses and 2080 teachers from non-professional courses) and 7717 students (4512 students from professional courses and 3205 from non-professional courses at UG & PG levels) were selected as a sample from the eleven state universities of U.P. for the study. It was found that below average number of professional courses' teachers in higher education used e-learning mode whereas only a few non-professional courses' teachers used e-learning mode. He mentioned that there are three modes of e-learning viz. online mode, hybrid/ blended mode and e-enhancement mode but only e-enhancement mode is being used by the professional and non-professional courses' teachers in Indian higher education.

Kalaivani (2014) discussed the role of e-learning in the quality improvement of Higher Education. He says that education is a light that shows the mankind the right direction to surge. The purpose of education is not holds particular relevance to India as the youth constitute its major population and there is no other way to take education in such a scale without the intervention of technology. E-learning includes all the forms of electronically supported learning and teaching including Edutech. In e-learning all lessons can be learned in just one click. Teachers who are giving online lectures are real with vast experiences, without going to school, without spending single rupee for enrolment that is the wisest thing to do if we are not financially equipped. Learning management system and learning content management system is software used for delivering tracking the managing training education Luskin says that the "e" should be interpreted to mean exciting, energetic, enthusiastic, emotional, extended, excellent, and educational in addition to "electronic" that is a traditional national interpretation. This broader interpretation allows for 21st century applications for the improvement of Higher Education. Rapid changes in the technologies are indicating that the role of E-learning in future will grow tremendously in education.

SECTION III

The use of e-learning is seen at all levels of educational system, thus in higher education as well. India has seen a fair amount of progress in e-learning in India for higher education. E-learning is visualized as the India's license for boosting up its higher education system. The increasing fusion of the online education companies and organizations, it is strongly believed that India shall finally cope with the lag in its higher education system. The only way to bridge the growing division in public and private education in India can be tackled by utilizing e-learning and online learning. [Ruma Bhadauriya, 2016]

The adoption of e-learning in education, especially for higher educational institutions has several benefits, and given its several advantages and benefits, e-learning is considered among the best methods of education. Several studies and authors have provided benefits and advantages derived from the adoption of e-learning technologies into schools (Klein and Ware, 2003; Algahtani, 2011; Hameed *et al.*, 2008; Marc, 2002; Wentling *et al.*, 2000; Nichols, 2003).

Some of the advantages that the adoption of e-learning in education, obtained from review of literature includes the following:

1. It is flexible when issues of time and place are taken into consideration. Every student has the luxury of choosing the place and time that suits him/her. According to Smedley (2010), the adoption of e-learning provides the institutions as well as their students or learners the much flexibility of time and place of delivery or receipt of according to learning information.
2. E-learning enhances the efficacy of knowledge and qualifications via ease of access to a huge amount of information.
3. It is able to provide opportunities for relations between learners by the use of discussion forums. Through this, e-learning helps eliminate barriers that have the potential of hindering participation including the fear of talking to other learners. E-learning

motivates students to interact with other, as well as exchange and respect different point of views. E-learning eases communication and also improves the relationships that sustain learning. Wagner *et al.* (2008) note that e-Learning makes available extra prospects for interactivity between students and teachers during content delivery.

4. E-learning is cost effective in the sense that there is no need for the students or learners to travel. It is also cost effective in the sense that it offers opportunities for learning for maximum number of learners with no need for many buildings.
5. E-learning always takes into consideration the individual learners differences. Some learners, for instance prefer to concentrate on certain parts of the course, while others are prepared to review the entire course.
6. E-learning helps compensate for scarcities of academic staff, including instructors or teachers as well as facilitators, lab technicians etc.
7. The use of e-Learning allows self-pacing. For instance the asynchronous way permits each student to study at his or her own pace and speed whether slow or quick. It therefore increases satisfaction and decreases stress (Codone, 2001; Amer, 2007; Urdan and Weggen, 2000; Algahtani, 2011; Marc, 2002; Klein and Ware, 2003).

E-learning, in spite of the advantages that it has when adopted in education, also has some diavantages. The disadvantages of e-learning that have been given by studies include the following:

1. E-learning as a method of education makes the learners undergo contemplation, remoteness, as well as lack of interaction or relation. It therefore requires a very strong inspiration as well as skills with to the management of time in order to reduce such effects.
2. With respect to clarifications, offer of explanations, as well as interpretations, the e-learning method might be less effective that the traditional method of learning. The learning process is much easier with the use of the face to face encounter with the instructors or teachers.
3. When it comes to improvement in communication skills of learners, e-learning as a method might have a negative effect. The

learners. Though might have an excellent knowledge in academics, they may not possess the needed skills to deliver their acquired knowledge to others.

4. Since tests for assessments in e-learning are possibly done with the use of proxy, it will be difficult, if not impossible to control or regulate bad activities like cheating.
5. E-learning may also probably be misled to piracy and plagiarism, predisposed by inadequate selection skills, as well as the ease of copy and paste.
6. E-learning may also deteriorate institutions' role socialization role and also the role of instructors as the directors of the process of education.
7. Also not all fields or discipline can employ the e-learning technique in education. For instance the purely scientific fields that include practical cannot be properly studies through e-learning. Researches have argued that e-learning is more appropriate in social science and humanities than the fields such as medical science and pharmacy, where there is the need to develop practical skills.
8. E-learning may also lead to congestion or heavy use of some websites. This may bring about unanticipated costs both in time and money disadvantages (Collins *et al.* 1997; Klein and Ware, 2003; Hameed *et al.*, 2008; Almosa, 2002; Akkoyuklu and Soylu, 2006; Marc, 2002).

In the present scenario universities had to compete in a global higher education market. E-learning initiatives will not only give universities a new channel of educational deployment, but also will also support strategic objectives by assisting asynchronous discussion consortiums and networked communities. The success of e-learning implementation depends on the institutional Structure that institutional leaders create within their institutions in preparation for the incorporation of any new technological innovations for improving the efficiency of their lecturers and the effectiveness of the pedagogical methods that lecturers use in disseminating educational material to learners. It is therefore necessary to explore HEI organizational structures that enable the adoption of e-learning. [Fry K, 2001]

The students' from non-technical backgrounds or those who are more accustomed to traditional face to face learning environments, experience problems absorbing course material for e-learning, under-graduate students' who are perhaps more assertive and motivated should be given focused training on how they can take full advantage of e-learning environments. IT skills can prove problems of students' on distance learning courses and if the requirement for training is not addressed, students' will not experience the full benefits of the e-learning environment Furthermore, a lack of IT skills is one of the main reasons for students' non-participation in e-learning courses Whilst not looking to replace 'real' paper with technology based resource, it is the process of augmentation and enhancement with the 'traditional' resources to enable reflection, encapsulation, consolidation and extension of the written word. [O'Connell, 2002]

SECTION IV

New technologies and sophisticated learning methods are the symptoms for a major impact in higher education institutions. These institutions need to change to accommodate the impact of e-learning. It is sure that impact of e-learning will require institutions to re-think of the strategies of teaching learning process. Much focus could be given in adopting ICTs and other technological advancements, nevertheless, e-learning certainly has made a prominent beginning in India and there are a quite a few vendors of e-learning as well as e-learning portal developers. This is far surpassed by computer based training (CBT) using CD-ROMs and DVDs used in Indian educational institutions such as schools, colleges and Universities. The students' are encouraged to be actively involved in getting access to the internet, e-mail, World Wide Web (WWW) for information, communication and education (ICE). E-learning and other related learning methods have contributed to the enhancement of the performance of our students' at all levels of our education system, irrespective of individual differences due to heredity and environment. It helps the students' to use pen driver for their purpose of getting their materials in soft copy through e-learning. E-learning involves the delivery and administration of learning opportunities and support via computer, network and web-based technology to help individual performance and development. E-learning can provide the tools to meet that challenge. Retention for a learner varies, based on content type and the delivery vehicle. The better match of content and delivery vehicle to a learner's style, the greater the retention and therefore the greater the results. E-learning activity like pedagogy, curriculum design and development will help to enhance excellence and innovation in teaching and learning, students' achievement, improving employability and skills attracting and retaining learners. The quality will and support enhance benefits of all the students' and faculties in learning. [Eugene Pradeep Kumar & Panchanatham]

The paper underlines that high results cannot be achieved in the learning and the educational process without integrating new information and communication technologies in the education system. The use of enormous integrated set of computer and internet tools and resources allows us to achieve more efficient and effective training. The students are no longer passive consumers of the educational programs and services, but active participants in the educational process. Their skills and competencies to work effectively with digital technologies are prerequisite for successful and responsible solving and presentation of scientific problems and cases.

The only way to sustain a better future is by educating the younger generation with effective and efficient education methodologies. It is optimistic to expose students to the latest technology so that they are not left clueless while they reach the stage at which they will contribute to society. The study shows the positive effects of e-learning for the higher education system in India. In the country like India it is very essential that the e-learning reaches the lowest sections of the society so that in the near future, we have strong and stable labour force in services and agriculture sector.

REFERENCES

[1] Algahtani, A.F. (2011). Evaluating the Effectiveness of the E-learning Experience in Some Universities in Saudi Arabia from Male Students' Perceptions, Durham theses, Durham University.

[2] Allen, I.E., Seaman, J., Poulin, R. and Straut, T.T. (2016). Online report card: Tracking online education in the United States. Babson Park, MA: Babson Survey Research Group. Retrieved from Education Advisory Board.

[3] Amer, T. (2007). E-learning and Education, Cairo: Dar Alshehab publication.

[4] Akkoyuklu, B. and Soylu, M.Y. (2006). A study on students views on blended learning environment. *Turkish Online Journal of Distance Education*, 7(3), ISSN 1302-6488.

[5] Almosa, A. and Almubarak, A. (2005). E-learning Foundations and Applications, Saudi Arabia: Riyadh.

[6] Codone, S. (2001) An E-learning Primer, Raytheon Interactive. Available from: www.faculty.mercer.edu

[7] Eugene, Pradeep Kumar and Panchanatham, "E-learning Strategy in Higher Educational Institutions in India", in the Research & Reviews: *Journal of Educational Studies,* 2016.

[8] Fry, K., E-learning markets and providers: some issues and prospects. *Training and Education,* 2001; 43: 233–239.

[9] Hameed, S. Badii, A. and Cullen, A.J. (2008). Effective e-learning integration with traditional learning in a blended learning environment. European and Mediterranean conference on information system (25–26).

[10] Jaiswal, V. (2013). Current Status of E-learning in Indian Higher Education: A Case Study of U.P., available at SSRN: http://ssrn.com/abstract=2231910 or http://dx.doi.org/10.2139/ssrn.2231910

[11] Kalaivani, A. (2014, November). Role of E-learning in the Quality Improvement of Higher Education, *IOSR Journal of Humanities and Social Science (IOSR-JHSS)* p-ISSN: 2279-0845 e-ISSN: 2279-0837 Vol. 19, No. 11, pp. 15–17.

[12] Klink, M.V.D. and Jochems, W., Management and organization of integrated e-learning. In Jochems W., Merrienbeer J.V. and Koper (edn), Integrated e-learning: Implications for pedagogy, technology and organization: Routledge, 2003.

[13] Keogh, M.K. and Fox, S. Strategies for embedding e-learning in traditional universities; Drivers and Barriers. *7th European Conference on E-learning.* 2008; 2: 135–141.

[14] Klein, D. and Ware, M. (2003). E-learning: new opportunities in continuing professional development. Learned publishing, 16 (1) 34–46.

[15] Kuruvilla, A., Norton, S., Chalasani, S. and Gee, M. (2012). Best practices in initiating online programs at public institutions. *Business Education Innovation Journal,* 4(2), 121–127.

[16] Marc, J.R. (2002). Book review: E-learning strategies for delivering knowledge in the digital age. *Internet and Higher Education,* 5, 185–188.

[17] Nichols, M. (2003). A Theory for E-learning, Educational Technology and Society, Vol. 6, No. 2.

[18] Nelasco, S., Nilasco, A. and Paul, A. (2007, November). E-learning for Higher Studies of India, Fourth International Conference on eLearning for Knowledge-Based Society, pp. 16.1–16.7.

[19] O'Connell, B., A poor grade for e-learning. Classroom students' did better. Workforce. 2002; 81: 1–15.

[20] Rajpal, S. Singh, S. Bhardwaj, A. and Mittal, A. (2008, March). E-learning Revolution: Status of Educational Programs in India, *Proceedings of the*

International Multi-conference of Engineers and Computer Scientists, ISBN: 978-988-98671-8-8, Vol. 1.

[21] Ruma Bhadauriya, E-learning—A boon for Indian Higher Education System International Journal of Engineering Technology, Management and Applied Sciences www.ijetmas.com, February 2016, Vol. 4, Issue 2, ISSN 2349-4476.

[22] Smedley, J.K. (2010). Modelling the impact of knowledge management using technology. OR Insight (2010) 23, 233–250.

[23] Tatiana, Shopova, E-learning in Higher Educational Environment, https://conference.pixel-online.net/edu_future/common

[24] Wagner, N., Hassanein, K. and Head, M. (2008). Who is responsible for E-learning in Higher Education? A Stakeholders' Analysis. Educational Technology & Society, 11 (3), 26–36.

[25] Wentling, T.L., Waight, C., Gallagher, J., La Fleur, J., Wang, C. and Kanfer, A. (2000). E-learning—A review of literature. Knowledge and Learning Systems Group NCSA, 9.1–73.

E-Education: A Splendid Means to Transform Higher Education in India

Nandita Kaushal*

1. INTRODUCTION

Education is a vital aspect of human life. It is a means through which individuals gain knowledge, increase their awareness, enrich their personality and enhance their overall well-being for the benefit of all. The process of education is a life-long one in the sense that individuals start receiving it gradually after their birth and continue to do so throughout their life. However, the interpretation of the word education in common parlance is in the sense of imparting methodic instructions and lessons for indoctrination and enlightenment of individuals. In this narrow connotation the use of the term education is limited to the extent till which individuals are registered with some educational institution for completing a formal course. Education in terms of levels is broadly divided into three categories—primary, secondary and higher. All the stages are significant in themselves but higher education is regarded as a stepping stone to external professional world. The success in professional life is markedly dependent upon appropriate networking and here comes the relevance of information and communication technologies. It is with the application of information and communication technologies the world has been profusely transformed into knowledge world. In the present era of intense competition in all sectors it is important that the individuals should start preparing themselves for it from their school/college/university times. They have to be particularly informed in the higher education stage. That is why in the recent times emphasis is laid on more and more on adoption and use of information and communication technologies at this stage.

Higher education scenario has improved a lot over a period of time in India and technology has played a considerable role in it. The

*Assistant Professor (Stage-2), Department of Public Administration, University of Lucknow, Lucknow, India. E-mail: nanditakshl28@gmail.com

application of information and communication technologies in higher education in the country is radically transforming the scene and is enabling her to gradually realize the dream of becoming a knowledge super-power. According to *All India Survey on Higher Education (2015–16)* there are 799 universities, 39,071 colleges and 11,923 standalone institutions in the country. Gross enrolment ratio in higher education (for 18–23 years of age group) is 24.5% at all-India level, 25.4% for males and 23.5% for females; and pupil-teacher ratio in all institutions both in regular and distance mode is 23.[1] Even though gross enrolment ratio in higher education has improved with times but it is still much low and pupil-teacher ratio is high. The implication of these are that many individuals are not able to reach the higher education stage in their life and due to high pupil-teacher ratio it is not possible for the teachers to give much personalized attention to students. The result is that the human resources of the country are going astray and their talent, which can be easily converted into their strength, is going waste. India has no paucity of human resources owing to her high growth rate of population but in the absence of effective implementation of skill harnessing measures their abilities are either not being utilized or being under-utilized for productive ventures. The information and communication technologies can fill these gaps and their application in higher education has, in fact, started to fill them to a certain extent. This has given rise to e-education in the country.

2. E-EDUCATION INITIATIVES FOR HIGHER EDUCATION IN INDIA

E-education or e-learning is information and communication technology based learning in which formal instructions and eruditions are imparted through electronic means. There is no doubt that application of information and communication technologies in higher education has always been there in one way or the other but the progressive advancements of research in science and technology and their practical relevancy have steadily revamped and contributed in furthering the objectives of higher education in the country.

[1] All India Survey on Higher Education, Ministry of Human Resource Development, Government of India, New Delhi, Higher Education Statistics at a Glance, http://aishe.nic.in/aishe/viewDocument.action?documentId=204

The Government of India and corporate sector have taken several important measures to promote e-education in higher education. Among these measures include EDUSAT satellite, National Mission on Education through Information and Communication Technology, National Programme on Technology Enhanced Learning, Virtual Labs, E-yantra, E-Shodh Sindhu, E-PG Pathshala, Shiksha.com etc.

The launching of *EDUSAT satellite* by Indian Space Research Organization (I.S.R.O.) on *September 20, 2004* from Satish Dhawan Space Centre in Sriharikota (Andhra Pradesh) proved to be a major milestone in advancing the use of information and communication technologies in higher education. EDUSAT or *GSAT-3* (geo-synchronous satellite for communication purposes) was the country's first committed and purposeful educational satellite for distant class room education from primary level to higher education. Through EDUSAT satellite-based two way communication was furnished to the class rooms for disbursement of educational materials.[2] EDUSAT, though de-commissioned, was sweepingly used to provide educational services through all-inclusive reciprocal rendition techniques such as broadcasting of television programmes, video conferencing, web based instructions etc. EDUSAT tele-education programme was meant to attain several objectives like to complement curriculum-based teaching, provide useful and practical training to teachers, introduce quality con-scious resource persons and advanced technologies, and take education to all parts of the country. The programme propped up both formal and non-formal education. After de-commissioning of EDUSAT in September 2010 the traffic of its tele-education networks was deviated to other satellites of I.S.R.O.[3]

Of late a programme of Government of India called *National Mission on Education through Information and Communication Technology (NMEICT)*, launched on *February 3, 2009* by Ministry of Human Resource Development, is assuming immense significance due to the reason that there is a compelling need to make increasing use of

---

[2] Indian Space Research Organization, Department of Space, Government of India, New Delhi, EDUSAT, http://www.isro.gov.in/category-spacecraft/edusat Indian Space Research Organization, Department of Space, Government of India, New Delhi, EDUSAT, http://www.isro.gov.in/category-spacecraft/edusat

[3] Indian Space Research Organization, Department of Space, Government of India, New Delhi, Tele-Education, http://www.isro.gov.in/applications/tele-education

information and communication technologies to successfully overcome the exacting conditions prevailing in higher education sector, spread its ambit, make it more accessible, and meet the education related requirements of students, teachers/academicians and all those who are interested in learning.

The three essential components of NMEICT are broadband connectivity to all colleges and universities, low cost access and computing devices for students and teachers, and high quality e-content generation.[4] The mission seeks to provide phase-wise broadband connectivity to educational institutions, and Bharat Sanchar Nigam Limited and Mahanagar Telephone Nigam Limited have been assigned this task. The funds are being provided under the mission for the evolvement of ultra low cost computing devices called *Aakash* tablet. *Sakshat* is the main one stop portal of NMEICT and all e-contents which have been and will be developed under the mission are being or will be made available through it. There are number of programmes/projects under the mission which are engaged in developing qualitative e-content. These are: National Programme on Technology Enhanced Learning (NPTEL); Consortium for Educational Communication (CEC); E-PG Pathshala; Virtual Labs; Talk to a Teacher; Spoken Tutorial; Free and Open Source Software for Education (FOSSE); E-Yantra; Educational Resource Planning (ERP); Pedagogy; Direct-to-Home (DTH); Study Webs of Active-Learning for Young Aspiring Minds (SWAYAM) – India Massive Open Online Courses (MOOCs); and National Digital Library.[5]

National Programme on Technology Enhanced Learning (NPTEL) is a project in which seven Indian Institutes of Technology (Bombay, Delhi, Guwahati, Kanpur, Kharagpur, Madras, Roorkee); and Indian Institute of Science, Bengaluru are working for developing course contents in engineering and science streams.[6]

---

[4] Sakshat, Ministry of Human Resource Development, Government of India, New Delhi, NMEICT Brochure, Page No. 02–03, http://www.sakshat.ac.in/document/nmeict-brochure-30-11-2015.pdf

[5] Sakshat, Ministry of Human Resource Development, Government of India, New Delhi, NMEICT Brochure, Page No. 05–22, http://www.sakshat.ac.in/document/nmeict-brochure-30-11-2015.pdf

[6] National Programme on Technology Enhanced Learning (NPTEL), Frequently Asked Questions, What is NPTEL?, http://nptel.ac.in/faq.php

Consortium for Educational Communication (CEC) is an inter-university centre established by the University Grants Commission which intends to meet the concerns of higher education through the use of television as well as information and communication technologies.[7] E-content is being developed by it for undergraduate courses.

E-PG Pathshala is a portal under which the University Grants Commission (UGC) is developing e-content in 77 subjects at post-graduate level. The content will be of eminent quality, based on curriculum and interactive in nature and will cover subjects of social sciences, arts, fine arts and humanities, natural and mathematical sciences, linguistics and languages.[8]

Virtual Labs project is for undergraduate and postgraduate levels students and research scholars of science and engineering streams. Its objectives are to provide access to laboratories from a distance, motivate students to do experiments, furnish a thorough learning management system, and mete out valuable accessories and resources. The participating institutions are eight IITs (Bombay, Delhi, Guwahati, Hyderabad, Kanpur, Kharagpur, Madras, Roorkee); Amrita University, Coimbatore; Dayalbagh University, Agra; National Institute of Technology (NIT), Karnataka, Mangaluru; and College of Engineering, Pune.[9]

Talk to a Teacher project is being conducted by IIT Bombay in which Amrita Virtual Interactive E-Learning World (A-VIEW) educational tools being developed by Amrita University, Coimbatore are being used for training the teachers all over the country.[10]

Spoken Tutorial project is being led by IIT Bombay in which an audio-video tutorial of ten minutes in English and all Indian languages is

---

[7] Consortium for Educational Communication, About CEC, http://cec.nic.in/Pages/About-CEC.aspx

[8] E-PG Pathshala, Frequently Asked Questions, What is E-PG Pathshala?, http://epgp.inflibnet.ac.in/faqs1.php

[9] Virtual Labs, Ministry of Human Resource Development, Government of India, New Delhi, Objectives of the Virtual Labs, http://www.vlab.co.in

[10] Sakshat, Ministry of Human Resource Development, Government of India, New Delhi, National Mission on Education through Information and Communication Technology (NMEICT) Brochure, Page No. 13, http://www.sakshat.ac.in/document/nmeict-brochure-30-11-2015.pdf

provided on Free and Open Source Software (FOSS) on significant topics related to the field of information technology to promote self-learning.[11]

Free and Open Source Software for Education (FOSSE) encourages the application of free and open source software for making better the quality of education. It is purported to reduce reliance on commercial or proprietary software in educational institutions.[12]

E-Yantra project is being implemented by IIT Bombay for dissemination of education in embedded systems and robotics with the aim of providing hands-on learning to those engineering students who do not have enough access to laboratories and guides. The intention is to enable these students to relate their learning experiences with real life practical issues and, thus, to bring into being such engineers who have pragmatic perspective and are prepared enough to face the challenges.[13]

Educational Resource Planning (ERP) mission solicits to develop, maintain, regulate and set up web based software system which can be used by educational institutions of the country. The leading institution in this mission is IIT Kanpur and other partnering institutions are IIT Roorkee; Indira Gandhi National Open University (IGNOU), New Delhi; NIT, Hamirpur; Aligarh Muslim University, Aligarh, Amrita *Vishwa Vidyapeetham*, Kochi; Dayalbagh Educational Institute, Agra; Jamia Millia Islamia, New Delhi; and Shri Mata Vaishno Devi University, Katra. A learning management system called *Brihaspati* has been developed by IIT Kanpur for web based e-learning. Other educational resource planning modules are being worked out around *Brihaspati.*[14]

---

[11] Sakshat, Ministry of Human Resource Development, Government of India, New Delhi, National Mission on Education through Information and Communication Technology (NMEICT) Brochure, Page No. 14, http://www.sakshat.ac.in/document/nmeict-brochure-30-11-2015.pdf

[12] Free and Open Source Software for Education (FOSSE), Better Education About Us, http://fossee.in/about-us

[13] E-Yantra, General, http://e-yantra.org/faq

[14] Sakshat, Ministry of Human Resource Development, Government of India, New Delhi, National Mission on Education through Information and Communication Technology (NMEICT) Brochure, Page No. 17, http://www.sakshat.ac.in/document/nmeict-brochure-30-11-2015.pdf

Pedagogy project is concerned with evolving appropriate pedagogical modes and practices for various classes, intellectual calibers and research in e-learning. This project is primarily meant for contriving and making up such curricula for degree courses in engineering disciplines which are learner-centric and will facilitate result-oriented learning. It is a collaborative project in which fifteen educational institutions are participating in the main stage—IIT Kharagpur; IIT Delhi; Birla Institute of Technology and Science (BITS), Pilani; IIT Roorkee; IIT Guwahati; NIT Durgapur; NIT Rourkela; Birla Institute of Technology, Mesra (Ranchi); IIT Bombay; Sardar Vallabhbhai National Institute of Technology, Surat; Shanmugha Arts, Science, Technology and Research Academy, Thirumalaisamudram (Thanjavur); NIT Trichi; NIT Warangal; International Institute of.[15]

Study Webs of Active-Learning for Young Aspiring Minds (SWAYAM) Prabha scheme refers to a collection of thirty-two direct-to-home (DTH) channels which will be telecasting educational programmes of excellent quality on 24 × 7 basis by making use of GSAT-15 satellites. Bhaskaracharya Institute for Space Applications and Geo-Informatics, Gandhinagar uplinks the channels for telecast purposes. For higher education contents based on curriculum of post-graduate and under-graduate courses in different disciplines are telecast.[16]

Study Webs of Active-Learning for Young Aspiring Minds (SWAYAM)—India Massive Open Online Courses (MOOCs) is a digital platform through which online interactive courses are offered free of cost to scholars from ninth class to post-graduation level. These courses can be accessed anytime, anywhere and by anyone. There are seven national coordinators of MOOCs – NPTEL for engineering education (both post-graduation and under-graduation), UGC for post-graduation education, Consortium for Educational Communication for under-graduation education, NPTEL for engineering education (both post-graduation and under-graduation), Indian Institute of

[15] Pedagogy, Ministry of Human Resource Development, Government of India, New Delhi, Project Outline, http://www.ide.iitkgp.ernet.in/Pedagogy1/pedagogy_main.jsp

[16] Swayam Prabha, Free Online Education, Ministry of Human Resource Development, Government of India, New Delhi, About Swayam Prabha, http://www.swayamprabha.gov.in/index.php/about

Management (IIM), Bengaluru for management education (both post-graduation and under-graduation), IGNOU for out-of-school education, and National Council of Educational Research and Training (NCERT), New Delhi and National Institute of Open Schooling (NIOS), Bengaluru for school education.[17]

National Digital Library is an online library of learning resources. Its pilot project has been started by Ministry of Human Resource Development. IIT Kharagpur is developing its framework through which scholars will be able to access these resources in any language from a single window.[18]

E-ShodhSindhu, created by Ministry of Human Resource Development, is a consortium for higher education electronic resources. It provides access to high quality digital educational resources including e-journals, e-books, and large number of bibliographic and factual information bank, to its member academic institutions at affordable subscription rates.[19]

Besides Government of India several private companies have also created their educational portals to serve the rising demands of higher education segment. Some notable such portals are *Shiksha.com*, *Education World.in*, *Edukart.com*, *Brain Buxa*, *Dlpindia.com*, *Campus Hunt.in.*, and *Digitallearning.eletsonline.com.*

3. POTENTIAL OF E-EDUCATION IN TRANSFORMING HIGHER EDUCATION IN INDIA

E-education has tremendous potential to transform the quality, reach and accessibility of higher education in India and to enable the young persons to become knowledge enabled and empowered persons who are inclined to make rewarding contribution in the service of nation. It contributes to the emergence of information rich society which is closely inter-linked with headways made in other countries.

---

[17] Swayam, Free Online Education, Ministry of Human Resource Development, Government of India, New Delhi, About Swayam, https://swayam.gov.in/About

[18] National Digital Library of India, About National Digital Library of India, https://ndl.iitkgp.ac.in

[19] E-Shodh Sindhu, Consortium for Higher Education E-resources, About, http://www.inflibnet.ac.in/ess/about.php

E-education provides a platform where learning resources can be put together, and notions and techniques can be shared. It enables the learners to access them anytime and anywhere at their convenience and thus, makes it possible for them to make best use of their time, money and efforts. All types of essential specific information regarding courses and institutions can be easily made available at one place. Therefore, physical and mental hardships of gaining access to knowledge resources are considerably reduced and their agreeableness is increased. Learners can take more informed decisions promptly, and increase their knowledge and skill levels. This helps in the growth of learning community. It is through e-education only it is possible to create a network of specialists and experts, available within the country and abroad, and utilize their services most effectively. E-education is user-friendly and so learners are able to have more personalized experiences with the course contents and offered information. The effects of e-education, if it is properly utilized, are multiplier in nature which in turn are in a position to spin the growth rate in all sectors of the economy.

Undoubtedly, e-education has tremendous potential to transform higher education scenario but in case of India there are several key issues related to digital literacy, digital divide, infrastructure, internet connectivity, electricity supply and cyber security which are posing numerous challenges to realize its full potential.

4. CONCLUSION

India has come a long way since independence in the education sector. The reach of education has gradually increased as evident in the growth of students, researchers, teachers, institutions and infrastructure. In tune with the philosophy of the government that country has to be digitally transformed in all sectors, the higher education sphere is also getting digitally transformed. There is much of e-education today as compared to the recent past. However, the primary question remains to what extent it is proving to be beneficial. Its worth is being realized but it is limited to few sections of people and regions. Thus, there remains an urgency to increase its desirability by improving its quality and reach.

REFERENCES

[1] All India Council for Technical Education, Government of India, New Delhi, National Mission on Education through Information and Communication Technology, Mission Document, http://www.aicte-india.org/downloads/Mission_Document.pdf accessed on 11.07.2017

[2] All India Survey on Higher Education, Ministry of Human Resource Development, Government of India, New Delhi, Higher Education Statistics at a Glance, http://aishe.nic.in/aishe/viewDocument.action?documentId=204 accessed on 11.07.2017

[3] Consortium for Educational Communication, About CEC, http://cec.nic.in/Pages/About-CEC.aspx accessed on 11.07.2017.

[4] E-PG Pathshala, Frequently Asked Questions, What is E-PG Pathshala? http://epgp.inflibnet.ac.in/faqs1.php accessed on 11.07.2017.

[5] E-ShodhSindhu, Consortium for Higher Education E-resources, About, http://www.inflibnet.ac.in/ess/about.php accessed on 12.07.2017.

[6] E-Yantra, General, http://e-yantra.org/faq accessed on 12.07.2017.

[7] Free and Open Source Software for Education (FOSSE), Better Education about us, http://fossee.in/about-us accessed on 11.07.2017.

[8] Gaebel, Michael, European University Association, New Modes of Delivery...E-learning, http://www.equip-project.eu/wp content/uploads/EQUIP_160509-10_Vienna_pres_GAEBEL.pdf accessed on 11.07.2017.

[9] Indian Space Research Organization, Department of Space, Government of India, New Delhi, EDUSAT, http://www.isro.gov.in/category-space craft/edusat accessed on 11.07.2017.

[10] Indian Space Research Organization, Department of Space, Government of India, New Delhi, Tele-Education, http://www.isro.gov.in/applica tions/tele-education accessed on 11.07.2017.

[11] National Digital Library of India, About National Digital Library of India, https://ndl.iitkgp.ac.in/accessed on 12.07.2017.

[12] National Programme on Technology Enhanced Learning (NPTEL), Frequently Asked Questions, What is NPTEL? http://nptel.ac.in/faq.php accessed on 11.07.2017.

[13] Pedagogy, Ministry of Human Resource Development, Government of India, New Delhi, Project Outline, http://www.ide.iitkgp.ernet.in/Pedagogy1/pedagogy_main.jsp accessed on 12.07.2017.

[14] Sakshat, Ministry of Human Resource Development, Government of India, New Delhi, National Mission on Education through Information and Communication Technology (NMEICT) Brochure, http://www.sakshat.ac.in/document/nmeict-brochure-30-11-2015.pdf accessed on 11.07.2017.

[15] Swayam, Free Online Education, Ministry of Human Resource Development, Government of India, New Delhi, About Swayam, https://swayam.gov.in/About accessed on 12.07.2017.

[16] Swayam Prabha, Free Online Education, Ministry of Human Resource Development, Government of India, New Delhi, About Swayam Prabha, http://www.swayamprabha.gov.in/index.php/about accessed on 12.07. 2017.

[17] Virtual Labs, Ministry of Human Resource Development, Government of India, New Delhi, Objectives of the Virtual Labs, http://www.vlab. co.in/accessed on 11.07.2017.

Digital Entrepreneurship and Skill Development in India: With Special Reference to Uttar Pradesh

A.K. Singh[1] and M.P. Singh[2]

ABSTRACT: Entrepreneurship has been considered as the backbone of economic development. Entrepreneurship and new venture creation has long been a driving force in commercialising new technologies and developing new markets, creating new jobs, and growing economies. It has been well established that the level of economic growth of a region, to a large extent, depends on the level of entrepreneurial activities in the region. In the era of liberalization, privatization and globalization along with ongoing Information Technology revolution, capable entrepreneurs are making use of the opportunities emerging from the changing scenario. However, a large segment of the population, particularly in the industrially backward regions generally lags behind in taking advantage of these opportunities. Therefore, there is a need to provide skill development and entrepreneurship development training to such population in order to mainstream them in the ongoing process of economic growth and development. Government of India has launched National Skill Development Mission and National Skill Development Policy. The national policy on skill development envisages to creating opportunities for all to acquire skills throughout life and specially for youth, women and disadvantaged group, promoting commitment by all stakeholders to own skill development initiatives, developing a high quality skilled workforce, entrepreneurs relevant to emerging employment market needs. The policy has widened the scope of skill training and entrepreneurship development through utilizing the existing educational infrastructure and expansion of institutions engaged in skill training and vocational education. Government of India has also introduced several schemes, programmes and projects for providing training, vocational education and entrepreneurship development to youth, women

[1]Assistant Director, Regional Centre for Urban & Environmental Studies, Lucknow University Campus, Lucknow, Uttar Pradesh, India.
E-mail: awadhesh.rcues@gmail.com

[2]Assistant Prof. Faculty of Management, Shri Ram Swaroop Group of Professional Colleges, Lucknow, Uttar Pradesh, India.

and disadvantaged groups. In view of the high national priority, several state governments have also introduced state Policy for Skill development with mission and strategic plan. Against this view point, present paper purports to review the policy perspective of entrepreneurship and skill development in India.

Keywords: *Digital Entrepreneurship, Skill Development in India, Atal Innovation Mission (AIM), Self Employment and Talent Utilization.*

1. INTRODUCTION

Entrepreneurship has been considered as the backbone of economic development. Entrepreneurship development and training is one of the key elements for development of micro and small enterprises, particularly for the first generation entrepreneurs (Krishna, *et al.*, 2011). Though, India has improved its performance in education, however, there is growing deficit of skilled manpower (Clark, 2005). As per estimates of NITI Aayog, Government of India, more than 700 million Indians are estimated to enter the working age group by 2022, of which more than 500 million will require some form of vocational or skill training. India has skill shortage of 64 percent at present. Large scale skill development is thus an imminent imperative. Entrepreneurship is essential for development and economic prosperity of the nation. Therefore, there is a need to provide skill development and entrepreneurship development youth in order to mainstream them in the ongoing process of economic growth and development (Dahlam, and Anuja, 2005). Entrepreneurship development and training is, thus, one of the key elements for development of micro and small enterprises (MSEs), particularly, for the first generation entrepreneurs.

2. OBJECTIVES AND METHODS

The main objective of the present paper is to examine the profile of candidates perusing skill development programmes, their admission procedure and perception regarding the quality and effectiveness of skill training, and performance of U.P. Skill Development Mission. The present paper is based on a major research study on performance and process audit of U.P. SDM conducted by Bhartiya Institute of Research and Development, Lucknow under the overall guidance and direction of the author of present paper. For the purpose of study, a comprehensive field survey was carried out in 40 districts from all the geographical regions of the state covering 5280 beneficiaries who received skill training. The survey was conducted with the help of structured interview schedules for candidates.

3. DISCUSSIONS

In pursuance of the directions given by the Government of India, Skill Development Mission was launched in October 2008. The state also introduced State Policy for Skill development in 2013 with comprehensive and long term strategy for skill development in the context of the national strategy. U.P. Skill Development Mission program targets women, SC/STs, and other marginalized sections of society. The specific provisions for different categories of people in schemes such as NRLM, MSDP, BOCW, BADP, SCA to SCSP etc. are adhered. The funds available under these schemes are not only used for skill development but also for setting up infrastructure for trainings of these groups. U.P. SDM has empanelled 211 government training partners, 17 flexi training partners, 135 large training partners and 15 small training partners. These partners have established 2202 centres for imparting skill training to youth in the state. Overall, 53 sectors, 654 courses and 11640 batches of students were initiated by U.P. Skill Development Mission. As per information available, 3.78 lakh candidates were enrolled in various courses and out of them, 2.88 lakh candidates completed their training. Moreover, 2.53 lakh candidates were assessed while 1.13 lakh candidates were passed in their training assessment.

Most of the beneficiaries of skill development programmes were from rural background (68.8 per cent). This was found more pronouncing in Eastern Region (83.2 per cent). About 30 per cent respondents were from urban areas in Bundelkhand. Most of the respondents were from the lower age group i.e. less than 25 years. However, a significant proportion of respondents were found belonging to higher age group in Bundelkhand, Eastern and Central region. About 2/5th respondents were females while 56 per cent respondents were males. Again, about 1/3rd respondents were from Scheduled Caste while about 2/5th respondents were from backward classes. A higher proportion of respondents were Scheduled Caste was reported in Bundelkhand while a higher proportion of respondents from backward classes were recorded in Western and Central Region. About 60 per cent respondents were intermediate while about 22 per cent respondents were graduates. The proportion of highly educated respondents was recorded high in Central and Bundelkhand Region as compared to other regions. A large proportion of candidates admitted that they are also pursuing academic courses from college and universities. About 58 per cent candidates further admitted that they are attending their classes regularly in colleges/universities. This was found more pronouncing in Central and Western region. Thus, quality of skill training is being affected as candidates are not taking it seriously and they are pursuing their academic courses from universities and colleges. About 84 per cent candidates reported that they are still pursuing skill training programmes. This was found more pronouncing in Central and Eastern region as compared to Western and Bundelkhand regions. Only 16 per cent candidates have completed their skill training courses. This was found more pronouncing in Western region (22.8 per cent). About 2/3rd respondents reported that they get admission in skill development programmes on first come first serve basis. This was found more pronouncing in Eastern region (83.1 per cent). About 23 per cent respondents further reported that they were selected for skill development programmes on the basis of individual counselling. This was found more pronouncing in Bundelkhand and Central region. UP Skill Development Mission is presently implementing 7 major schemes viz., SDI, VOCW, SCA-SCSP, MSDP, SSDF, BADP, DDUGKY. During 2013–2016, 3.78 lakh students were enrolled in these schemes for skill training and out of them, 84.26 per cent candidates were trained in various sectors and trades. Out of total enrolment, 76.39 per cent candidates completed their skill training. Out of total number of candidates who completed their training, 67.18 per cent candidates were assessed while about 30 per cent candidates were passed. As per field survey, about 2/3rd candidates were found enrolled in SSDF, 25 per cent in SCA-SCSP and 2.6 per cent. As per information available from UPSDM, about 2/3rd candidates were enrolled in the sectors of ICT, banking and accounting, garment making, health care, beauty culture and hair dressing, electrical and retail. The field survey also reveals that candidates were mainly enrolled in the sectors of ICT, security, banking and accounting, health care, garment making, retail, beauty culture and hair dressing, fabrication and courier and logistics in MSDP.

Training partners of UPSDM are including both public and private sector. Some of the major training partners include Raymond, Coffee Global Ltd., G4S India, Future Shart Skills Ltd., Maruti Udyog Ltd., Larsen and Turbo Ltd., Telecom Network Solutions Pvt. Ltd., Karvy, LAVA International Ltd., NISA, Janak Health Care Pvt. Ltd., Jawed Habib Hair and Beauty Ltd., etc. Major placement tie-ups with UPSDP include Café Coffee Day, G4S India, Flipkart, A to Z Hospitality, Apollo, Eureka Forbs, Dominoes, Tech Mahindra, Aegis, Medisure India, Dot on Security, Big Basket, GVK, etc Majority of the candidates of skill training rated the quality of training as good in terms of content of course, time allotted for the course, instructor's knowledge about the subject, illustration by practical examples, interaction of trainer/faculty with training, question handling and communication skills. However, a large segment of candidates rated the quality of training as poor and very poor in terms of available of quality of stock in library, training/teaching aids methods, quality and usefulness of reading materials, and presentation methods. The effecttiveness of overall training programme was rated as good by majority of candidates. This was found high in case of content of training, favourable training environment, domain of training, support of organization, motivation and boosting of confidence, increase of existing body of knowledge and change in techniques and methods of learning. However, a large proportion of respondents rated the effectiveness of training programme as poor and very poor. This was reported high in case of evaluation/assessment, change in behaviour, sharing of information, awareness about competitive exams and job opportunities, training as per need/requirement and expectations.

4. ROLE OF INFORMATION TECHNOLOGY

Human capacity development and entrepreneurship promotion are central issues in bridging the digital divide. Local businesses need to acquire a strong awareness and understanding of the business opportunities these technologies make available. Entrepreneurship plays a particularly critical role during periods of rapid economic change, as small, agile firms increase the ability of an economy to quickly respond to new challenges. Unfortunately, most developing countries have a poor environment for entrepreneurship. In general, there is a lack of knowledge with respect to the new business models that characterize

Internet-centered businesses. People that combine skills and creativity in Internet site creation, business know-how, access to finance and knowledge of local community needs are still relatively rare worldwide, but particularly in developing countries (infoDev, 2000). Nevertheless, as stated in the final report of the Digital Opportunity Initiative it is far from inevitable that ICT will have a negative impact on developing economies; in fact, with the right policies and practical actions, ICT can be a powerful enabler of development (Digital Opportunity Initiative, 2001). Creativity and entrepreneurship in Brazil, India, Thailand, Niger and elsewhere have already developed software for illiterate users and low-cost, solar-powered wireless devices (UNDP, 2001). But two essential conditions for entrepreneurship development are access to architectural tools for business and business knowledge and understanding of the existing opportunities arising out of new ICT. The term 'digital entrepreneurship' refers to the process of creating a new or novel Internet enabled/delivered business, product or service. This definition includes both start-ups which bring a new digital product or service to market but also the digital transformation of an existing business activity inside a firm or the public sector. Digital entrepreneurship may level the playing field in certain sectors, creating opportunities to work from remote areas, at different hours, from the home, or on the go (Wensum, Desirée van (2016). It can play an important role in promoting gender equality and social and economic inclusion, stimulate local development, and contribute to sustainable development, especially when new technologies are combined with the availability of open and public data. Digital entrepreneurship also highlights the scope for the emergence of new digital divides. In many developed countries, the digital divide is increasingly moving from one of (affordable, reliable, safe and high-speed) access (to digital technologies), to the ability to use and exploit them to create new opportunities. Skills issues are extremely important for digital entrepreneurship. From the ability identify the talent that is required and recruiting that talent, including across borders, to having the skills to identify new technology-enabled business opportunities and bringing them to fruition, either as a new venture, or by transforming existing business models, skills issues are key to successful digital entrepreneurship, digital transformations, and even the successful conceptualization and implementation of most IT projects. Business leaders and entrepreneurs need to possess a degree of technological awareness that allows them to identify new technologies that will transform and shape their business model that will allow them to do new things, or do things differently, and to develop new products and services, ways of delivering them, and ways to communicate with their suppliers, customers and employees. At the same time, it is important for technically trained people to have business acumen and skills to identify new opportunities, as well as communication skills to convey them to management and other less technically inclined leaders and decision makers. The emergence of cloud computing over the past decade or so has reduced barriers to entry and increased opportunities for digital entrepreneurs.

Fuelled by the convergence of social, mobile, cloud, data and growing demand for anytime anywhere access to information, technology is disrupting all areas of the business enterprise. Disruption is taking place across all industries and in all geographies. Enormous opportunities exist for enterprises to take advantage of connected devices enabled by the Internet of Things to capture vast amounts of information, enter new markets, transform existing products and introduce new business and delivery models. However, the evolution of the digital enterprise also presents significant challenges, including new competition, changing customer engagement and business models, unprecedented transparency, privacy concerns and cyber security threats. Technology is also changing the ways that people work, and is increasingly enabling machines and software to substitute for humans. Enterprises and individuals who can seize the opportunities offered by digital advances stand to gain significantly, while those who cannot may lose everything (E&Y, 2015). The growth and prosperity of all economies, rapid-growth and mature, remain highly dependent on entrepreneurial activity. Entrepreneurs are the lifeblood of economic growth. They provides a source of income and employment for themselves, create employment for others, produce new and innovative products or services, and drive greater upstream and downstream value chain activities. While some entrepreneurial activity around the world is still driven by necessity, high-impact entrepreneurship, once largely confined to mature markets, is now an essential driver of economic expansion in rapid-growth markets. In some cases, these high-impact entrepreneurs are building innovative and scalable enterprises that capitalize on local needs and serve as role models for new entrepreneurs. The face of entrepreneurship is also changing across the world; entrepreneurs are increasingly young and/or female. Many of these new enterprises are digital from birth. Access to funding remains the primary obstacle for entrepreneurs from all markets. The public and private sector each have an important role to play in creating entrepreneurial ecosystems that, in addition to funding, are essential to promoting entrepreneurial success (E&Y, 2015). Thus, we can say that technology is vital to the entrepreneurial development as it is inevitable in the creation and working of an enterprise. It is present at every step of entrepreneurial development and is the very blood of the process. The modern age cannot even think of establishing an enterprise without Technological aid (Goutam and Sarkar, 2015).

The convergence of technology, integration across diverse fields, distributed architecture and people willing to back an idea, have opened a new world for enterprise. India's first generation e-commerce and mobile entrepreneurs have become angel investors which is a sign of maturing of start-up ecosystem. The government has also come a big way in promoting start-ups. A start-up is a company that is in the first stage of its operations. These companies are often initially bank rolled by their entrepreneurial founders as they attempt to capitalize on developing a product or service for which they believe there is a demand. The start-up and SMEs appear to be of the same size with limited revenues, high cost of operation, job creating but they operate on entirely different business models. The difference between a start-up and a SME unit is that a start-up is new organization designed to search for a repeatable and scalable business model. These start-up needs an appropriate ecosystem thrive which includes adequate funds for start-ups to help them grow; government to create an environment of ease of doing business; ready availability of essential services like office space, location, supplies telecom connectivity etc.; and mentors to provide strategic advice (Times of India, June 30, 2014). In order to simplify the regulatory framework the government introduced the Ease of Doing Business wherein an MSME unit has to fill in a single one page self-declaration online form called Udyog Aadhaar. The Apprentices Act, 1961 was amended to enable even the MSME units' engage apprentices who will enable the units to get trained labour as well as in turn supply skilled labour. Under the Apprentice Protsahan Yojana, 50 percent of the stipend payable to the apprentices would be reimbursed by the Government for the first two years which is an incentive for MSME units to take in more apprentices. In order to give boost to the Make in India programme, the MSME Ministry has launched the ASPIRE scheme in March 2015, a Scheme for Promotion of Innovation, Rural Industry and Entrepreneurship. The objective of the scheme is to set up a network of technology and incubation centers to accelerate entrepreneurship and also to promote start-ups for innovation and entrepreneurship in agro-industry. To ease the credit availability requirements of start-ups the Government had announced Micro Units Development & Refinancing Agency (MUDRA), operated by SIDBI for providing refinance to micro units. This would improve the liquidity of the micro units who right now have to borrow from NBFCs and moneylenders at high rates of interest. Atal Innovation Mission (AIM). The programme operated from NITI Aayog is about an Innovation Promotion Platform involving, academics, entrepreneurs and researchers and draw upon national and international experiences to foster a culture of innovation, R&D and scientific research in India. The platform will promote a network of world class innovation hubs and grand challenges for India. The overarching purpose of this mission is to promote a culture of entrepreneurship and innovation in India. Self Employment and Talent Utilization (SETU) is a Techno-Financial, Incubation and Facilitation Programme to support all aspects of start-up businesses and other self-employment activities, particularly in technology driven areas operated from NITI Aayog. An Expert Committee on Innovation & Entrepreneurship for working out the detailed contours of the Atal Innovation Mission and SETU was constituted by NITI Aayog. The Expert Committee has identified five major drivers for creating a vibrant entrepreneurial eco system viz; (i) catalytic government policy and regulatory framework (ii) easy access to equity capital and debt (iii) businesses as entrepreneurial hubs (iv) culture and institutions which encourage entrepreneurship over careerism (v) adequate and effective collaboration forums. The Ministry of C&IT has launched the Electronics Development Fund (EDF) to promote innovation, research and development, and product development in the field of semiconductors, nano-electronics, IT and associated sectors by bringing in established companies and start-ups on board (Economic Times, 11th June, 2015). The objective is to do research, design and develop electronic products within the country for which the start-up units would be provided supportive financial assistance from the EDF.

Digital India Programme has been launched to provide broadband connectivity in rural and urban areas. Introduction of digital rural connectivity would give a big boost in developing traditional rural arts, crafts or other innovative ideas into business models. With the growing number of start-ups it is essential to protect one's products from impersonators. The start-ups need to go for design patents, trademarks, copyright or trade secrets protection as the need maybe before marketing their product. ₹ 2000 crore India Aspiration Fund (IAF) was launched by SIDBI in August 2015 to boost the start-ups fund of—funds ecosystem in the country. This fund would invest in various venture capital funds for meeting the equity requirement of MSME start-ups. A SIDBI Make in India Loan for Small Enterprises (SMILE) Scheme of ₹ 10,000 crore has also been launched to catalyze tens of thousands of crores of equity investment in start-ups and MSMEs, creating employment for lakhs of persons, mostly educated youth over the next 4–5 years. The objective of SMILE is to provide soft loans in the nature of quasi-equity and term loans on relatively soft terms to MSMEs to meet the required debt-equity ratio norm. The 25 sectors under the 'Make in India' programme' would be the focus with emphasis on financing smaller enterprises in the MSME sector. There will be concessional terms for the enterprises promoted by (SC)/(ST)/Persons with Disabilities (PwD) and women. The scheme is expected to benefit approximately 13,000 enterprises, with employment for nearly 2 lakh persons. These two schemes are in addition to the ₹ 20000 crore MUDRA scheme. Together the three finance schemes should boost the start-ups as well as MSMEs already in the transition phase and create good number of jobs in the years to come. Till date the start-ups have been successful in e-commerce, and other IT based applications of service sector. The start-ups in manufacturing sector are yet to take off in a big way. The launch of the above-mentioned policy initiatives should give a boost to start-ups in manufacturing as well. As of 16th November, 2015, 806 start-ups have taken off during the year and the main sources of funding were seed funding and private equity and the products were mainly IT based applications in the service sector. In the Global Competitiveness Index (GCI) 2015–16 India has scored 16 points and moved up from its earlier ranking of 71 to 55 out of a total of 144 countries. In the World Bank's Ease of Doing Business Ranking 2015 India is placed at 142 places out of a total of 189 economies. But on the start-up front India ranks third position globally with 4200 start-ups. The new initiatives in promoting start-ups would enable India to move up to the top position. Start-up ecosystem has been created through the new policy initiatives which would not only promote start-ups particularly in the manufacturing sector but also the micro units would be able to graduate faster as small and medium units. This process would be fast tracked by the flagship programmes well supported by the Skill India Mission which would facilitate availability of right skilled manpower as entrepreneurs complain about skill mismatch. Start-ups are emerging as major job creators, governments both at the Centre and States need to put in place appropriate policy framework for the start-ups.

5. CHALLENGES IN SKILL DEVELOPMENT

Skill is still not aspirational and is viewed as the last option meant for those who have not been able to progress/opted out of the formal academic system. Currently there is no opportunity of vertical or horizontal mobility within the skill ecosystem. One of the major reasons why skills are not aspirational today is because it is not seen as a stream of education but a decision of circumstances (NITI Aayog, 2017). It is crucial to align skill education with academic education so that it is perceived as an alternate source of education. There is no credit system in skill education or academic education eco-system which would allow someone to use the training done in skill education system in the academic education system. There are no institutes providing high end courses in skilling to provide some one the opportunity to advance his/her skill in order to improve the monetary reimbursement. There are no vertical growth pathways on the lines of the general education system, so that skill education and training is also seen as a valid route to earn degrees and diplomas, and consequently to positions of authority linked to such qualifications. Currently only 30 percent of skilled manpower consist of women. Thus, there is huge deficit in skill training in gender perspective. Indian Institute of Skills will act as higher institutes of skill development similar to IITs for technical education. These Institutions will prepare the workforce of higher order skill courses which will provide progression pathway in skills education equivalent to at least the graduate level in academic education system. These institutes will impart high-end skills with state of the art infrastructure to prepare the Indian workforce for the upper spectrum of skill requirement and also for the job requirement of the future. Five Indian Institute of

Skills are planned to be set up in 5 regions of India. The foundation stone for the first Indian Institute of Skill was laid in Kanpur in December, 2016 (NITI Aayog, 2017).

6. CONCLUSION

There is an urgent need to reorient the skill development to face industry. There is a need for a more objective assessment of the skill gap within the country as well as in the overseas market to provide job opportunities and cash in on the demographic dividend. The curriculum will have to be suitably modified to address the emerging opportunities on account of introduction of technology, higher automation and consequently more and more creative ways of service delivery. The economy has shifted towards knowledge-intensive, service based industries, in which patterns of employment are more flexible and individuals must learn to thrive in a more fluid, unpredictable environment. Focus areas for training would be (1) e-commerce, Internet, cloud computing; digital platforms for providing variety of services; and focus on semi-contractual and self-employment. It is also desirable that Ministry of Human Resource Development should begin the process of aligning the curriculum of technical educational institutions to incorporate needs of industry technologies in order to prepare the future workforce to be ready with right skill sets. There is a need to create a portal for a knowledge repository on the R&D initiatives. The common online database would record the innovations (both process and product) happening across India. There are over 10 lakh institutional buildings which being used less than 40 hours a week. Proper schemes and policy need to be developed to better utilize this tremendous hard and soft infrastructure asset available with us. Skill ecosystem is developing, and with multiple stakeholders getting involved in the ecosystem such as the Ministry, Private training partners, Government training institutions and institutions formed through PPP such as NSDC it is required to have a regulatory authority which is at arm's length. Universities, Colleges and well established institutes of learning, education and research including NGO's may be promoted to start the Training Centers because they have plenty of experienced, qualified and competent faculties well equipped and enriched libraries, hostel and other infrastructural facilities. All the universities, Degree & Post Graduate Colleges, deemed universities should establish a separate section for

Skill Development for facilitating and providing career guidance. Importantly, these centers should be established till for individual career counseling, up gradation of skills, motivation and mobilization of aspirants for various sectors of training. Girls/Women from Scheduled Castes, OBCs and minorities should be given preference in enrolment in such skill training institutions. They should be provided social security, separate toilet facility, and hostel and individual career guidance so that they may join the mainstream and avail the reservation benefits.

REFERENCES

[1] Clark, P. (2005). Technical and Vocational education Systems in Australia and India: An Experiment in Cross Cultural Learning, World Bank, New Delhi.

[2] Dahlam, Carl and Anuja, U. (2005). India and the Knowledge Economy: Leveraging Strengths and Opportunities, World Bank, Washington, DC.

[3] Digital Opportunity Initiative (2001). Creating a Development Dynamic: Final Report of the Digital Opportunity Initiative, Accenture, Markle Foundation, UNDP.

[4] Digital Opportunity Initiative (2001). Creating a Development Dynamic: Final Report of the Digital Opportunity Initiative, Accenture, Markle Foundation, UNDP.

[5] E&Y (2015). Mega Trends, 2015, E&Y, New Delhi.

[6] Goutam, Supriya and Rishiraj, Sarkar (2015). Role of Technology in Entrepreneurial Development: Facilitating Innovative Ventures, *International Journal of Emerging Technology and Advanced Engineering,* Vol. 5, Special Issue 1.

[7] InfoDev (2000). The Networking Revolution—Opportunities and Challenges for Developing Countries, infoDev Working Paper, Global Information and Communication Technologies Department of the World Bank Group.

[8] Krishna, G.R., Nobert Koubek, A.K. Singh, Nagendra, S. (2011). Entrepreneurship and Development, Edited Book, SITA Publications, Mumbai, 2011.

[9] NITI Ayog (2017). Report of the Group of Secretaries on Commerce and Industry, NITI Ayog, Government of India, New Delhi.

[10] NITI Ayog (2017). Report of the Group of Secretaries on Education and Social Development, NITI Ayog, Government of India, New Delhi.

[11] Times of India (2014). Young Entrepreneurs turn Angels for Younger Start-ups', June 30, 2014. UNDP.
(2001). Human Development Report 2001, UNDP, New York.

[12] Welsum, Desirée van (2016). Digital Dividends: Enabling Digital Entrepreneurs, World Development Report, New York.

Benefits of Mobile Application in Differential Educational Planning for Improving the Learning Levels of Students

Pratima Kumari*

ABSTRACT: National Council of Educational Research and Training (NCERT) conducted the National Achievement Survey (NAS) throughout the country on November 13, 2017 for Classes 3, 5 and 8 in government and government aided schools. The attainment of the learning outcomes of 2.2 million students across 701 districts in all 36 States/UTs were assessed through competency-based test instruments. United Nations Children's Fund (UNICEF) in collaboration with NCERT and National Institute of Education Planning and Administration (NIEPA) developed a Data Visualization Application (DVA) on National Achievement Survey to provide quick and easy access to information on the current status of the learning levels at national, state and district level disaggregated by location, school management, gender, social category and learning outcomes. The DVA would serve as an important tool for monitoring progress in the implementation of the Right of Children to Free and Compulsory Education Act 2009 and the progress towards the Sustainable Development Goal 4 (SGD 4) i.e. to ensure inclusive and equitable quality education and promote lifelong learning opportunities for all and target 4.1: by 2030, ensure that all girls and boys complete free, equitable and quality primary and secondary education leading to relevant and effective learning outcomes. This paper will ponder on the benefits of mobile application in differential educational planning by the educational planners for improving the learning levels of the students at upper primary stage in attaining the learning outcomes in Economics which is part of Social and Political Life in class 8.

***Keywords:** National Achievement Survey, Competencies, Learning Outcomes.*

---

*Associate Professor of Economics in Department of Education in Social Sciences (DESS), National Council of Educational Research and Training, New Delhi. E-mail: pratimasingh33@gmail.com

1. BACKGROUND

National Council of Educational Research and Training (NCERT) has been periodically conducting the large-scale surveys of learning achievement in government and government aided school at grade 3, 5 and 8 in different curricular areas since 2001 with an interval of three years. NCERT has been implementing these surveys on sample basis at the State/UT level to provide evidence on health of education system and learning levels of children in key curricular areas at classes 3, 5 and 8. Though the NAS results were shared with the States/UTs through different modes of communication, the findings of these learning achievement surveys were not being used in education policy, planning and teacher professional development.

While planning for new NAS it was felt that these concerns need to be addressed in a more decentralized manner. The NAS (2017) was administered on 13th November, 2017 on nearly 2.5 million children from 120,000 schools across all states and UTs in the country. Being districts as the unit of reporting, the NAS 2017 is expected to help education system to develop differential education plan and need based teacher support system till district level to support learning of children. The test instruments of present National Achievement Survey (2017) are competency based and linked to learning outcomes recently developed by NCERT. In the year 2017, the union government amended Rule 23(2) under the Right to Education (RTE) Act making it compulsory for all state governments to codify expected levels of learning which students in Classes 1 to 8 should achieve in different subjects. The present NAS generated detailed report at the district level on the percentage of students achieving these learning outcomes. This will help the districts to develop evidenced based programmes for improving the quality of education. It is expected that a framework of intervention developed would help to improve the quality of teaching and learning at the schools. The designing and implementation of these interventions is envisaged to include in its ambit the school leaders, teachers and the whole network of officials at clusters, blocks, DIETs, SCERT and the directorate of education at different levels in the States/UTs.

While the NAS has been successful in developing a rich database, the potential for its utilisation has not been fully exploited. In this context, it was felt to develop an online Data Visualisation App for promoting utilisation NAS data at all levels starting from national to district levels through visualisation. The App is expected to promote quick access to all stakeholders on learning levels of children for promoting evidence-based planning, monitoring and pedagogical interventions. UNICEF has developed this Data Visualization App (DVA) to promote utilisation of NAS NCERT data for effective planning and management of school education in the country. The basic purpose is to visualize status and performance of the learning levels. Data visualization has two Apps—Dashboard and Mobile App. Mobile Apps can be downloaded from Google Play Store and Apple Store.

2. HISTORICAL CONTEXT

The National Policy on Education 1986, as modified in 1992, emphasized the need to employ educational technology to improve the quality of education. In 2000, the government media house launched Gyan Darshan dedicated to education. In November, 2001, Gyan Vani, a radio channel on education was launched in the country (GOI Ministry of HRD Press Release, October 21, 2003). National Curriculum Framework for School Education (2000) recommended formulation of plans for integration of computers into the curriculum and creation of a framework for enhancing learning opportunities using ICTs across the curriculum. The report (EQFI 2015) recommended provision of computer systems to all educational institutions up to higher secondary/secondary schools by suitable investments (about 1–3%) of the total budget during the next five years. Beginning with a pilot covering 150 schools, the government proposed to equip each school with a computer lab with internet, intranet and a television to facilitate video-conferencing, web-broad-casting and e-learning. (Kumar, A., October 9, 2002). Edusat was India's first dedicated education satellite launched in September, 2004. NCERT brought out the National Curriculum Framework (2005) recommending inclusion of ICT across the curriculum.

3. MOBILE APP NAS-NCERT

This mobile application provides a quick and an easy access to information on learning outcome. Disaggregated and details learning achievement by management of schools, gender, social groups and

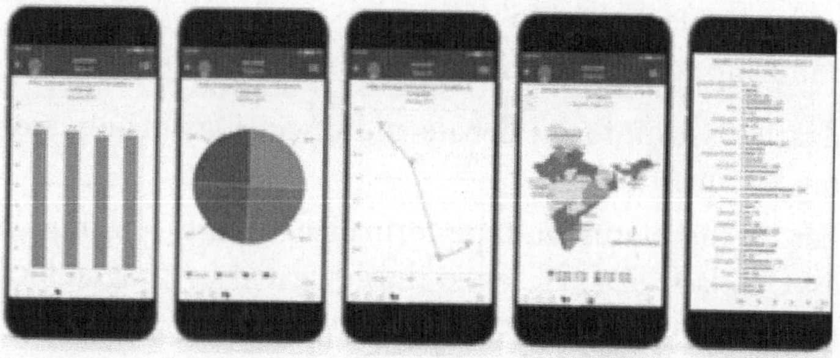

location till district level in classes 3, 5 and 8 and detailed achievement by learning outcomes in classes 3, 5 and 8 are provided in the mobile app. After the selection of indicator and subgroup user can visualize information in charts and maps as per his/her choice and easily share through email or social media to any other user.

4. USING NAS-NCERT MOBILE APPLICATION FOR DIFFERENTIAL EDUCATIONAL PLANNING

The NAS, 2017 collects data on learning levels disaggregated by gender, location, social groups and management of schools, wherever applicable, at various administrative levels such as national, state, and district have been presented in the NAS-NCERT Mobile APP.

Disaggregating data is important to reveal patterns, which are generally masked by large aggregate data. In other words, disaggregating data simply means breaking down information into smaller sub-groups to get a better understanding of trends and patterns. Moreover, disaggregated data analysis is important to inform decisions related to implementation, monitoring, efficiency, effectiveness and equity of a development intervention. Disaggregated data can also be used to advocate specific policy changes, to provide evidence for targeted and differential programming, and to look for patterns over time and see if similarities or differences within and among sub-groups are emerging. The DVA facilitates disaggregated analysis presentation of data collected in NAS for informed decision-making for policy planning, programme management and advocacy. It will help the decision-makers, government officials, academia, researchers and other key stakeholders to:

- identify issues and concerns
- facilitate strategic planning

- effective implementation
- monitoring and evaluation in the school education sector.

DVA for the NAS informs debate and discussions mainly around the following key questions:

- What is the status and performance of the learning levels in Class-3, Classs-5 and Class-8 disaggregated by geographical areas/ administrative units, location, gender, social categories, school management, etc. based on NAS 2017?
- Which are geographical areas/administrative units and social groups lagging behind need to focus and additional resources to achieve the planned targets?
- How is one administrative unit or social group performing as compared to the other administrative units or social group?
- What are the gaps of gender and social disparities in learning levels?
- How are the government managed institutions performing compared to those in government aided?

The following things are important to consider while using DVA:

1. Data presented or used for calculating indicators in the data visualization are based on the National Achievement Survey conducted on November 13, 2017 by States and UTs.
2. When comparing indicators for different administrative units or sub-groups, users should consider the different attributes of each administrative unit or sub-group. Each administrative unit or sub-group has different population size, number of schools and other characteristics that may affect values of indicators.
3. Telangana state reorganized districts in 2016 and increased number of districts from 10 to 31 and similarly West Bengal also increased three more districts. Data are provided for new districts but same will not available in maps due to non-availability of updated shape files for the maps.

The state functionaries can identify the learning levels of students in all districts and accordingly plan out the strategy to improve the learning levels immediately in the districts through training of Key Resource Persons in different subject areas involving the district functionaries. Likewise district functionaries can utilize the mobile app to know the learning levels of students in their districts and accordingly plan the teacher's training programmes and sharing of best practices among the schools. For example there are two learning outcomes in Economics in Class 8. These are:

1. identifies the role of Government in providing public facilities such as water, sanitation, road, electricity etc., and recognises their availability and
2. describes the role of Government in regulating economic activities.

And the pedagogical processes suggested in the Learning Outcome document are given below:

1. share experiences with peers on public facilities and reasons for the disparity in availability of water, sanitation, electricity and
2. organise a debate why Government be responsible for providing public facilities.

Teachers can utilize the mobile app NAS-NCERT to identify the weak areas and take corrective measures. They may use the above mentioned processes as it is or adapt as per the needs of students to improve the learning levels of students in Economics. The district functionaries through training of School Heads and subject teachers can contribute in the endeavor to enhance the learning levels of students in different subjects. The DVA would serve as an important tool for monitoring progress in the implementation of the Right of Children to Free and Compulsory Education Act 2009 and the progress towards the Sustainable Development Goal 4 (SGD 4).

REFERENCES

[1] GOI Ministry of HRD Press Release, October 21, 2003.

[2] http://nas.schooleduinfo.in

[3] Kumar, A. (2002). Department of IT goes to school VIA VIP. Constituencies, Financial Express, October 9, 2002.

[4] Learning Outcomes at the Elementary Stage in Social Sciences, p. 103.

[5] NAS (2017). State Learning Reports and District Reports.

[6] National Curriculum Framework for School Education (2000).

[7] National Curriculum Framework (2005). National Council of Education Research and Training, New Delhi.

[8] Position paper, National focus group on Education Technology, NCF 2005, NCERT, India.

[9] The National Policy on Education 1986, and Programme of Action 1992.

[10] 'The UNICEF today launches data visualisation app' The Hindu Business Line, May 24, 2018 accessed in September 2019.

[11] Use of Information and Communication Technology in Secondary Schools: Study Commissioned by NITI Ayog Govt. of India Conduced by Education Quality Foundation of India, New Delhi (2015).

Economic Value of Blockchain in Healthcare

Nishi Mishra[1] and Rashmi G. Shukla[2]

ABSTRACT: Blockchain is a new digital technology which has been around since the evolution of bitcoin, a new virtual currency which emerged during the last global financial crisis. In the initial stage, the focus remained mainly on cryptocurrency, but its usefulness has been extending to other fields due to its unique characteristics offering advantage to different sectors. Healthcare is no different to the disruption caused by blockchain technology. The elimination of paper trail and making patients records available on a single platform without a threat of hacking or stealing sensitive data will only add to the efficacy of the system. Blockchain gained prominence as a solution offering distributed and trusted systems to perform healthcare transactions. The implementation of blockchain to perform healthcare transactions will not only reduce the overall cost but also ensure safety and security of the patient system. This work will explore the possibilities on how the blockchain technology can enhance the economic value if implemented in the healthcare system for different stakeholders.

Keywords: *Healthcare System, Blockchain, Economic Value.*

1. INTRODUCTION

Blockchain, an underlying technology behind the popular cryptocurrency bitcoin, is a public distributed ledger which can store information pertaining to the transactions happening over a peer-to-peer network (Nakamoto, 2008; Yli-Huumo, Ko, Choi, Park and Smolander, 2016). Ever since the introduction of Blockchain technology in the market, a lot of work has been going in academics and research and its applications have been extended to different industries. Since this technology relies on trust and transparency in a decentralised environment, its application has been extended to different areas like

[1]Assistant Professor, Economics Area, Pt. Deen Dayal Upadhyay Govt. Girls P.G. College, Rajajipuram, Lucknow–226017, India.

[2]Doctoral Candidate, Technology Management Area, MPSTME, NMIMS, Mumbai, India.

Marketing, Operations, Human Resources, Supply Chain etc (Beck, Stenum Czepluch, Lollike and Malone, 2016). Healthcare is yet another industry which has undergone disruptive change due to implementation of blockchain technology (Smith & Dhillon, 2017).

Blockchain is a public distributed ledger developed as a base technology for the cryptocurrency Bitcoin by Satoshi Nakamoto in his white paper (Nakamoto, 2008). With the help of this technology, two parties could transact directly without the involvement of a third party vendor to perform the transaction (Nakamoto, 2008). However, the blockchain technology was equipped with underlying cryptographic capabilities in order to ensure immutability, security and integrity of the transactions performed (Peterson, 2018). The timestamps associated with each transaction in the network intensifies the security thus preventing data infringement. This exclusive properties of the blockchain made the implementation of technology across different domains and industries.

The recent developments of blockchain technology has been extended to non-financial domains like Human resources, Identity Management, Supply Chain Management etc. (Androulaki *et al.*, 2018; Wood *et al.*, 2016). The growing popularity of the technology has broadened its wings to other industries as well. Healthcare poses a significant number of use cases for application of blockchain. Healthcare practitioners suffer with fragmented patient data which becomes difficult to keep track of and thus poses a major challenge in proper diagnosis and treatment of patient. With the implementation of blockchain technology in the Healthcare, the data will be streamlined which will benefit both, the patient and the physicians.

Though, the cryptocurrencies dominate the blockchain industry as a use case, the maintenance of transaction history along with timestamps and encourages other industries as well to move towards implementing the blockchain technology (Crosby, Pattanayak, Verma and Kalyanaraman, 2016). The blockchain technology has evolved beyond the initial case of cryptocurrency. According to a report by Price Waterhouse Cooper (PwC), the technology has disrupted the finance most. The adoption of blockchain by finance is reported to be 46%. Other industries adopting this technology are Healthcare, Industrial products and Manufacturing, Energy and utility and Government. The most popular blockchain application except cryptocurrency is in transforming supply chain management. In particular, agricultural supply chains, from farm to fork have already been transformed by the blockchain. For example, Walmart and IBM have come together in order to enhance food traceability (Galvin, 2017).

Another industry which has gone through a disruption by blockchain technology is Healthcare. Medical data of patients is highly confidential and sensitive in nature (Mettler, 2016). The continuity of the data and medical history of the patient is very important to arrive at proper diagnosis and treatment of the patient. In such cases, blockchain is very beneficial due to its properties like immutability, ease of data sharing and data integrity. A comprehensive blockchain application for this purpose has been developed by Azaria *et al.* (Azaria, Ekblaw, Vieira and Lippman, 2016). One of the most important property which is advantageous to blockchain is decentralisation which makes it possible to develop a distributed network and removes the dependency on one single authority. Thus the loss of data and data corruption is prevented by blockchain technology.

There are many blockchain applications available in the field of healthcare so that the economical aspects are improved once it is implemented. The major economic benefit of implementing the blockchain in healthcare would completely remove the involvement of third party thus reducing the transaction cost. The discrete blockchain applications for each of the functionalities of healthcare would definitely add the complexity but it would improve the overall economic value. This paper mainly throws light on how is the economic value going to be affected once the blockchain in implemented in Healthcare industry.

2. BLOCKCHAIN IN HEALTHCARE

There are relevant areas of applications where blockchain finds its use in Healthcare industry. If the work already done in healthcare with respect to blockchain technology is analysed, it can be observed that most of the conceptual ideation of the work is not implemented into a working prototype. Hence, it becomes important to understand the existing real time prototype of blockchain working in healthcare. This will help in understanding the economic implications of blockchain in Healthcare. The analysis of available prototypes will also help in understanding the potential challenges and limitations of Blockchain Technology in Healthcare.

Ever since the implementation of bitcoin blockchain, the blockchain technology has been tweaked in different ways in order to get a better and efficient model of technology to the industry. In some of the applications of blockchain for different functionalities of healthcare industry, different properties of the technology have been given importance. However, most important use of blockchain technology in the industry has been for maintaining the Electronic Health Records. Patient data is very sensitive in nature, hence, its integrity needs to be maintained for future reference as well as while sharing it to different stakeholders with due permissions. Blockchain comes with a feature of trust, transparency and traceability which is implemented with cryptography and time stamping the transactions happening over the network (Beck *et al.*, 2016; Engelhardt, 2017; Mettler, 2016; Nakamoto, 2008) The blockchain technology is considered to be the most robust technology when secure data exchanges between the stakeholders is involved (Engelhardt, 2017). There also have been researches which analyse the features of blockchain in maintaining the integrity of health data (Smith & Dhillon, 2017).

Drug Supply Chain is yet another important part of the Healthcare industry where data safety, security is vital. Blockchain inspires important innovations with respect to drug supply chain. In this case, the traceability property of the blockchain becomes a key property in avoiding the fake drugs reaching the customer. It also ensures that the genuine drugs are powered for the end users (Tseng, Liao, Chong and Liao, 2018). There are advanced prototypes developed with same theme based on IBM Hyperledger (Androulaki *et al.*, 2018). Implementation of blockchain in the drug supply chain will help in maintaining the records about the originality of the drugs and also makes sure that the genuine information is reached to the end customer.

Another area in Healthcare where the blockchain implementation becomes fruitful is biomedical research especially in the area of clinical trials and maintaining the data sanctity. An Ethereum based blockchain has also been developed in this regard to maintain the data privacy and security (Emanuele & Koetter, 2007). Another area of application is in healthcare training and inferencing through data and insights generated from blockchain platforms. With the blockchain application in biomedical research, the patient data will be available across the network and different formats of the data can be stored without any difficulty. This helps in removing any human borne errors and also avoids any human intervention.

Blockchain also promotes the remote patient monitoring with the help of which the population residing in rural and difficult terrains can also access the best healthcare. Once the patient data is made available on the decentralised blockchain network, it will be accessible to all the physicians who can access this network. Thus, the proper diagnosis and treatment of the patient who are located at the difficult terrains also become possible. However, in order to implement this facility, it is required to synergise the IoT and Blockchain Technology. IoT devices can help in gathering the patient data which can later be stored and analysed and maintained on the blockchain network. Different applications have been deployed in maintaining the bio-medical data through remote sensing with the help of IoTon platforms like Hyperledger, Etherium in order to develop patient centric advanced applications of Blockchain in Healthcare. These applications, in future, will act as robust and reliable source of data monitoring for patients.

The blockchain features like Trust, Transparency, Traceability provide great advantage even in the field of Health Insurance. Maintaining the data privacy of the patients, processing the policy claims, ensuring right accountability helps both, insurers and insurance companies a reliable platform for data exchange (Engelhardt, 2017). There are various prototypes developed for the health insurance based on Ethereum platform. Blockchain technology ensures that the repetitive amount of paperwork is avoided with the implementation. This also ensures that the patients do not face with any problem while claiming their health policies. An illustration of blockchain in health segment is MIStore which is a biomedical insurance system.

An advanced area of blockchain application comes in Health Analytics where blockchain technology is combined with Business Intelligence, Cognitive capabilities and Analytical Power in order to process the data. There have been prominent work done in terms of health records and precision medicine by Moamosihna. Saxena (Saxena, Sanchez and Knuszka, 2018) has designed an intelligent Blockchain framework which helps the stakeholders to encash the power of Artificial Intelligence, Machine Learning and Natural Language Processing.

3. ECONOMIC IMPLICATIONS OF BLOCKCHAIN IN HEALTHCARE

Blockchain technology is often seen as a long time investment in the Healthcare industry. Researchers suggest that the major three areas in which the blockchain technology can bring revolution is Clinical Trials, Supply Chain Management and Quality Control. Though, the initial investment cost is assumed to be high, blockchain technology will increase the economic value of the industry in the long run. The technology will not only reduce the cost of individual transaction, it will also reduce the frequent expenses done by the patient over medical activities. Blockchain technology has got the potential to transform healthcare by placing the patient at the centre of the healthcare system and enhance the overall safety and security of the system.

Blockchain helps in maintaining the patient data over a distributed network. With this facility on board, the physicians and patients can access the data from any location. It also saves the patient time in consolidating all records at one place. In many instances, it happens that the patients consult different doctors for second opinion when they are diagnosed with certain diseases or health issues. In such cases, the medical trials done once can be uploaded over the network instead of repeatedly doing the same tests. This will be cost effective for the patients and hospitals as well and save lot of multiplied effort from the professionals.

Blockchain technology enables patients with a Remote Patient Monitoring. Since, the blockchain technology enables to keep the patient data safely over the distributed network. Due to this advantage, the patients located in remote locations will be able to take opinions of the best of the physicians who might be located at the far off places. This connection saves the travel cost of the patients and also connects the patients and physicians at an economical cost without much trouble. The business of the Healthcare industry increases with implementation of this technology. Remote Patient Monitoring not only enhances the business in the healthcare industry, it also helps in proper diagnosis and treatment of the patients even though located at remote places.

Drug Supply Chain is another prominent area of interest in healthcare industry for the application of Blockchain Industry. Blockchain in drug supply chain helps in tracking the source of the drugs that the patient is consuming. It also helps patients in knowing the complete history of the drugs, its origin, how it was made, what are the allergies related to it, what is the composition, alternate medicines related to it etc. The complete information about the medicine helps patient in deciding the right medicine suited for the patient. This will save the patient with lot of costs involving buying the costly alternate medicine which are prescribed by the physicians for the greed of commission.

Another prominent area in Healthcare Industry for the application of Blockchain is Health Insurance. Implementation of technology for health insurance will remove all the redundant paper work that the insurer and the company has to go through. It also helps in easy and smooth reclaiming of the policies. The availability of all the paperwork over the distributed network will help in maintaining all the documents at a single place so that both the company and the insurers are aware of it. This prevents any fraudulent activities associated in reclaiming of the policies and helps patients in getting their insurance claim if they are entitled to it. This helps in making sure that the insurance claim reaches the right person since proper documentation is available online.

The multi-faceted and inter departmental communication in the Healthcare industry makes it even more necessary for the implementation of the technology in this industry. This also makes sure that the human intervention in these communications is reduced and may lead to proper and correct diagnosis and treatment of the patient concerned.

4. CONCLUSION

Despite all the economical advantages that the blockchain technology facilitates to the healthcare industry, there are limitations associated with it. It obviously comes with a huge initial investment cost to implement the technology in the Healthcare Industry. The hospitals, Insurance Companies or other departments of the industry may not be ready to shell out such huge cost initially. Another problem arises how technology friendly are the stakeholders in operating the entire process over a network. The stakeholders may not be comfortable with using the system unlike they are now with the manual work. One of the most prominent challenge is if the patients are really ready to share their sensitive medical data over a distributed network. Since, the distributed network makes the records available to everyone on the network the initial instalment of the technology has to customise this feature in order give the privacy rights to the patients which comes with an additional cost. Despite such issues, the technology can still be implemented in the industry if the companies and stakeholders are ready to bear the initial investment cost.

REFERENCES

[1] Androulaki, E., Barger, A., Bortnikov, V., Cachin, C., Christidis, K., De Caro, A. and Manevich, Y. (2018). Hyperledger fabric: A distributed operating system for permissioned blockchains. *Proceedings of the Thirteenth EuroSys Conference*, 30. ACM.

[2] Azaria, A., Ekblaw, A., Vieira, T. and Lippman, A. (2016). MedRec: Using Blockchain for Medical Data Access and Permission Management. *2016 2nd International Conference on Open and Big Data (OBD)*, 25–30. https://doi.org/10.1109/OBD.2016.11

[3] Beck, R., Stenum Czepluch, J., Lollike, N. and Malone, S. (2016). *Blockchain—the gateway to trust-free cryptographic transactions.*

[4] Crosby, M., Pattanayak, P., Verma, S. and Kalyanaraman, V. (2016). Blockchain technology. Beyond bitcoin, *Applied Innovation*, 2(6–10), 71.

[5] Emanuele, J. and Koetter, L. (2007). Workflow opportunities and challenges in healthcare. *2007 BPM & Workflow Handbook*, 1, 157.

[6] Engelhardt, M.A. (2017). Hitching healthcare to the chain: An introduction to blockchain technology in the healthcare sector. *Technology Innovation Management Review*, 7(10).

[7] Galvin (2017). IBM and Walmart: Blockchain for Food Safety. Power Point Presentation—Google Search, Retrieved July 24, 2019, from https://www.google.com/search?q=IBM+and+Walmart%3A+Blockchain+for+Food+Safety.+PowerPo int+Presentation&rlz=1C1CHZL_enIN812IN812&oq=IBM+and+Walmart%3A+Blockchain+for+Food+Safety.+Power Point+Presentation&aqs=chrome..69i57j69i60.1539j0j7&sourceid=chrome&ie=UTF-8

[8] Mettler, M. (2016). Blockchain technology in healthcare: The revolution starts here. *2016 IEEE 18th International Conference on E-Health Networking, Applications and Services (Healthcom)*, 1–3. https://doi.org/10.1109/HealthCom.2016.7749510

[9] Nakamoto, S. (2008). "*Bitcoin: A peer-to-peer electronic cash system," http://bitcoin.org/bitcoin.pdf.*

[10] Peterson, M. (2018). Blockchain and the Future of Financial Services. *The Journal of Wealth Management, 21*(1), 124–131. https://doi.org/10.3905/jwm.2018.21.1.124

[11] Saxena, M., Sanchez, M. and Knuszka, R. (2018). *Method for Providing Healthcare-Related, Blockchain-Associated Cognitive Insights Using Blockchains.*

[12] Smith, K. and Dhillon, G. (2017). *Blockchain for Digital Crime Prevention: The Case of Health Informatics.* Tseng, J.-H., Liao, Y.-C., Chong, B. and Liao, S. (2018). Governance on the drug supply chain via gcoin blockchain. *International Journal of Environmental Research and Public Health, 15*(6), 1055.

[13] Wood, C., Winton, B., Carter, K., Benkert, S., Dodd, L. and Bradley, J. (2016). *How blockchain technology can enhance EHR operability.*

[14] Yli-Huumo, J., Ko, D., Choi, S., Park, S. and Smolander, K. (2016). Where is current research on blockchain technology?—A systematic review. *PloS One, 11*(10), e0163477.

Demonetization: Impact on Indian Economy

B.B. Tiwari[1], Puneet Garg[2] and Madhur Mishra[2]

ABSTRACT: In India demonetization has occurred thrice. The first was on 12th January 1946 (Saturday), second on 16th January 1978 (Monday) and the third was on 8th November 2016 (Tuesday). The purpose of this study is to compare and analyze the impact of demonetizations and their significance in the economic development of India by comparing with other countries. Considering the importance and the influence of Indian economy in the global financial markets and the growth rate of India's GDP, this article attempts to document the historical importance of the demonetizations and their impact on the export and import. This article also covers the various other countries who tried demonetization, they are, Nigeria, Ghana, Pakistan, Zimbabwe, North Korea, Soviet Union, Myanmar and Australia. The results of this study provide an insight into the demonetization process and about its impact on the growth and development in these countries. Thus, the findings of this study reveal that, India will achieve a significant growth by adapting the demonetization strategy and it will create a huge positive impact on the entire economy in a long run.

The argument posited in favour of demonetization a—Surgical Strike on Black Money, i.e., the cash that would be extinguished would be—black money and hence, should be rightfully extinguished to set right the perverse incentive structure in the economy. While the facts are not available to anybody, it would be foolhardy to argue that this is the only possibility. Therefore, it is imperative to evaluate the short run and medium-term impacts that such a shock is expected to have on the economy. Further, the impact of such a move would vary depending on the extent to which the government decides to remonetise. The year 2014–15 is known to be the year of financial inclusion with Jan Dhan Yojana, 2016 marked some historic policy changes such as the GST (Goods and Service Tax) and Demonetization much recently, and finally 2017 would be the era of payment banking.

[1]Professor, Department of Management, Shri Ramswaroop Memorial College of Engineering and Management Lucknow, India.

[2]MBA Department, Shri Ramswaroop Memorial College of Engineering and Management Lucknow, India.

Demonetization is the process of withdrawal of a particular form of currency from circulation. Demonetization becomes necessary whenever there is a change in the national currency. The old unit of currency must be retrieved and replaced with a new currency unit. It involves either introducing new notes or coins of the same denomination or completely replacing the old denominations with the new denomination which is usually carried out as an ambush on the black market."

Keywords: *Indian Economy, Paper Currency, Demonetization.*

1. INTRODUCTION

Demonetization is the act of stripping a currency unit of its status as legal tender. It is a process of removing a currency from general usage or circulation of money in a country. Demonetization is an act where the old unit of currency gets retired and replaced with a new currency unit. It can also be considered as withdrawal of a specific currency from market.

1.1 The Birth of a Paper Currency in India

Before we start with the discussion of demonetization which took place on 8th November, 2016 we will look into history of birth of paper currency as how use of paper currency had been started in India.

Until the 18th century, people in India used to use silver and gold coins to carry out their day to day transactions. But then some European companies established their own banks in the region to carry out their business transactions, like the Bank of Hindustan in Calcutta. They introduced the very first versions of Indian paper notes which then boosted the further popularised the use of paper notes.

The Bank of Bengal went on to release notes that featured a small image of a female figure meant to represent the idea of "commerce," as well as the bank's name and the denomination in three scripts: Urdu, Bengali, and Nagri. However, it was only after the Paper Currency Act of 1861 that the British colonial government really got involved in producing money, establishing the paper currency as we know it today. Money was now to be issued by the state alone, not banks.

1.2 Demonetization in India before November, 2016

The act of demonetization 2016 is not happening for the first time in India, but before it, has happened twice, first in the year of 1946 and then in the year of 1978. In January 1946, ₹ 1,000 and ₹ 10,000 banknotes were withdrawn but the same ₹ 1,000, ₹ 5,000 and ₹ 10,000 notes were reintroduced in 1954, and were again demonetized in January 1978.

The second demonetization has taken place in the year of 1978 by the Janata Party government. It had decided to withdraw ₹ 1,000, ₹ 5,000 and ₹ 10,000 notes by issuing an ordinance on the morning of 16 January that year.

The objective behind the all the acts of demonetization happened in past and happened recently is common reduction of black money, corruption and removal of fake currency.

1.3 Demonetization—November, 2016

On Tuesday, 8th of November, 2016 Prime Minister of India Narendra Modi announced the demonetization of ₹ 500 and ₹ 1000 notes with effect from midnight, making these notes invalid. The major reasons behind this move were controlling black money, controlling fake currency and controlling corruption.

Following are the main impacts

1. Demonetization is not a big disaster like global banking sector crisis of 2007; but at the same time, it will act as a liquidity shock that disturbs economic activities.
2. **Liquidity Crisis:** Liquidity shock means people are not able to get sufficient volume of popular denomination especially ₹ 500. This currency unit is the favourable denomination in daily life. It constituted to nearly 49% of the previous currency supply in terms of value. Higher the time required to resupply ₹ 500 notes, higher will be the duration of the liquidity crunch. Current reports indicate that all security printing press can print only 2000 million units of ₹ 500 notes by the end of this year. Nearly 16000 mn ₹ 500 notes were in circulation as on end March 2016. Some portion of this were filled by the new ₹ 2000 notes.

Towards end of March approximately 10000 mn units will be printed and replaced. All these indicate that currency crunch will be in our economy for the next four months.

3. **Welfare Loss for the Currency Use People:** Most active segments of the population who constitute the 'base of the pyramid' uses currency to meet their transactions. The daily wage earners, other labourers, small traders etc. who reside out of the formal economy uses cash frequently. These sections will lose income in the absence of liquid cash. Cash stringency will compel firms to reduce labour cost and thus reduces income to the poor working class. There will be a trickle up effect of the liquidity chaos to the higher income people with time.
4. **Consumption will be Hit:** When liquidity shortage strikes, it is consumption that is going to be adversely affected first. Consumption ↓→ Production ↓→ Employment ↓→ Growth ↓→ Tax revenue ↓
5. **Loss of Growth Momentum:** Risks its position of being the fastest growing largest economy: reduced consumption, income, investment etc. may reduce India's GDP growth as the liquidity impact itself may last three-four months.
6. **Impact on Bank Deposits and Interest Rate:** Deposit in the short term may rise, but in the long term, its effect will come down. The savings with the banks are International Journal of Commerce and Management Research 74 actually liquid cash people stored. It is difficult to assume that such ready cash once stored in their hands will be put into savings for a long term. They saved this money into banks just to convert the old notes into new notes. These are not voluntary savings aimed to get interest. It will be converted into active liquidity by the savers when full-fledged new currency supply take place. This means that new savings with banks is only transitory or short-term deposit. It may be encashed by the savers at the appropriate time. It is not necessary that demonetization will produce big savings in the banking system in the medium term. Most of the savings are obtained by biggie public sector banks like the SBI. They may reduce interest rate in the short/medium term. But they can't follow it in the long term.
7. **Impact on Black Money:** Only a small portion of black money is actually stored in the form of cash. Usually, black income is kept in the form of physical assets like gold, land, buildings etc. Hence

the amount of black money countered by demonetization depend upon the amount of black money held in the form of cash and it will be smaller than expected. But more than anything else, demonetization has a big propaganda effect. People are now much convinced about the need to fight black income. Such a nation-wide awareness and urge will encourage government to come out with even strong measures.

8. **Impact on Fake Currency:** The real impact will be on counterfeit/ fake currency as its circulation will be checked after this exercise. Demonetization as a cleaning exercise may produce several good things in the economy. At the same time, it creates unavoidable income and welfare losses to the poor sections of the society who gets income based on their daily work and those who doesn't have the digital transaction culture. Overall economic activies will be dampened in the short term. But the unmeasurable benefits of having more clearness and reduced quantity of black money activities can be pointed as enduring benefits.

1.4 Impact on the Poor

Two ideas have been offered in the claim that the adverse impact upon the poor will be small:

1. **Cash Savings as Predictors of Impact on the Poor:** Estimates based on national surveys show that cash earnings of the poor are small, and they usually lack cash savings. So, it is argued, they are likely to seldom visit a bank branch or post office, and they are not particularly inconvenienced.
2. **Credit as a Mitigant of the Impact on the Poor:** It has been argued that since the rural economy is significantly credit-driven, the impact on rural poor will be small. If transacting parties know each other, they would be willing to extend credit, which would make short-term non-availability of cash less costly. Given the practices in rural markets, many commercial relationships are indeed credit-driven, and cash calls are only made periodically.

1.5 India's Financial Markets Fall down in Case of Demonetization

Indian equity markets have been on a near secular falling trend since the government demonetized the 500 rupee and 1,000 rupee currency notes after midnight on November 8, 2016. The two benchmark equity indices—the Nifty 50 and the S&P BSE Sensex—fell on each trading day since the demonetization except for November 10 and November 22. While the Nifty 50 fell 6.3% from November 8 until November 22, the S&P BSE Sensex fell 5.9% during the same period. Due to the rise in the US dollar, the dollar equivalents of the Sensex and the Nifty fell more than 8% each.

The S&P BSE 100 Index, which is comprised of 100 stocks compared to the Sensex's 30, fell 6.6% during this period. Mid and small-cap indices have been hit much harder than broader market indices. Even after a rise on November 22, the S&P BSE MidCap and the S&P BSE SmallCap indices fell 8.2% and 10.9%, respectively, in the previously mentioned period.

Apart from concerns about demonetization, Donald Trump's victory and concerns about his restrictive trade philosophy led to foreign investors pulling out of Indian equities. According to Bloomberg, foreign investors have net sold Indian equities (PIN) (INDA) worth $1.4 billion from November 9–17.

However, once the short-term impact of demonetization is over, Indian equities will likely bounce back sharply. A rate cut from the Reserve Bank of India would be helpful and easy monetary conditions are generally beneficial for equities. Consumption-driven sectors and stocks (TTM) (VEDL) will continue to be hit in the short term.

1.6 Indian Rupee Fall Down

The Indian rupee fell against the US dollar. It mainly fell due to Donald Trump's victory in the US presidential election. Given the pressure on the local unit and its relative stability, it seems like the Reserve Bank of India has been working hard to keep the currency stable.

India's tech companies (INFY) (WIT) saw a sharp correction since the demonetization was announced. However, the rupee's weakness can benefit these stocks. For now, Donald Trump's trade philosophy will be the main driver of the Indian unit.

1.7 Mutual Funds Perform Better

In the long term, the mutual fund industry will benefit from scrapping of 500 and 1,000 rupee notes. Banks will soon reduce the fixed deposit rates. Some banks have already reduced fixed deposit rates. With fixed deposits offering less interest, citizens will shift money to mutual funds, to get returns more than inflation. Investments in mutual fund schemes will increase. When interest rates are falling in the economy, debt mutual funds do well. Many debt mutual fund schemes, have given more than 2% returns in a week. This could continue for some time. Good equity mutual funds, invest in fundamentally strong stocks. Stocks with good fundamentals, do well in the long term. With stock markets falling due to demonetization uncertainty, you can invest in good equity mutual funds, at a low price. Expect to get good returns, from your equity mutual funds, in the long term.

2. ADVANTAGES AND DISADVANTAGES OF DEMONETIZATION

2.1 Advantages of Demonetization

1. The greatest favorable position of demonetization is that it helps the legislature to track individuals who are having expansive totals of unaccounted money or money on which no pay charge has been paid in light of the fact that many individuals who acquire dark cash keep that cash as trade out their homes or in some mystery put which is extremely hard to discover and when demonetization happens all that money is of no esteem and such individuals have two choices one is to store the cash in financial balances and pay assesses on such sum and second choice is to let the estimation of that money diminished to zero.
2. Since dark cash is utilized for illicit exercises like psychological warfare subsidizing, betting, IRS evasion furthermore blowing up the cost of significant resources classes like land, gold and because of demonetization all such exercises will get lessened for quite a while furthermore it will take years for individuals to produce that measure of dark cash again and consequently in a way it helps in putting an end this hover of individuals doing unlawful exercises to gain dark cash and utilizing that dark cash to accomplish more illicit exercises.
3. Another advantage is that because of individuals revealing their pay by storing cash in their financial balances government gets a decent measure of duty income which can be utilized by the administration towards the improvement of society by giving great

foundation, doctor's facilities, instructive organizations, streets and numerous offices for poor and destitute segments of society.

2.2 Disadvantages of Demonetization

1. The greatest weakness of demonetization is that once individuals in the nation becomes more acquainted with about it than at first for few days there is disorder and free for all among open as everyone needs to dispose of demonetized notes which thusly infrequently can prompt to International Journal of Commerce and Management Research 76 lawfulness issue and clamorous circumstance particularly in banks and ATMs which are the main medium to change the old cash units to new money units.

   Another hindrance is that annihilation of old coin units and printing of new cash new units include costs which must be borne by the legislature and if the expenses are higher than advantages then there is no utilization of demonetization.
2. Another issue is that dominant part of times this move is focused on towards dark cash however in the event that individuals have not kept money as their dark cash and pivoted or utilized that cash as a part of other resource classes like land, gold thus on then there is no certification that demonetization will help in getting degenerate individuals. As should be obvious from the over that demonetization has both points of interest and disservices and it is up to the administration to see and dissect every one of the upsides and downsides and after that choose whether it is helpful to proceed with demonetization or not.

2.3 Reasons of Demonetization

According to The Reserve Bank of India, the most important reason for the demonetization of 500 and 1000 rupees note was the rise of fake currencies of the same notes, and also the higher occurrence of black money in the economy. "The fake notes are being used for illegal activities by anti-nationalists like terrorists and India being a nation of a cash-based economy, the circulation of fake currency continues to be a threat. But it has been taken care by Government that the public that a person who changed his higher value cash will get exactly the equal amount in lower denominations.

Demonetization affects the economy through the liquidity side. Its effect will be a telling one because nearly 86% of currency value in circulation was withdrawn without replacing bulk of it. As a result of the withdrawal of ₹ 500 and ₹ 1000 notes, there occurred huge gap in the currency composition as after ₹ 100; ₹ 2000 is the only denomination. Absence of intermediate denominations like ₹ 500 and ₹ 1000 will reduce the utility of ₹ 2000. Effectively, this will make ₹ 2000 less useful as a transaction currency though it can be a store value denomination.

3. CONCLUSION

Demonetization though it has created some positive and some negative impacts on different sectors but in long run it definitely will have positive impact in controlling black money and fake money Demonetization technically is a liquidity stock; a sudden stop in terms of currency availability. It creates a situation where lack of currencies jams consumption, investment, production, employment etc. In this context, the exercise may produce following short term/long term, consumption/investment, welfare/growth impacts on Indian economy. The intensity of demonetization effects clearly depends upon the duration of the liquidity shocks.

REFERENCES

[1] Demonetisation of ₹ 500 and ₹ 1000 notes: RBI explains. The Hindu, 2016. Retrieved 10 November 2016. Here is what PM Modi said about the new ₹ 500, ₹ 2000 notes and black money. India Today, 2016. Retrieved 9 November 2016.

[2] Demonetisation: Chaos grows, queues get longer at banks, ATMs on weekend, 2016.

[3] India demonetisation: Chaos as ATMs run dry. Al Jazeera. Retrieved 9 November 2016.

Read more

[1] http://www.businessdictionary.com/definition /demonetization.html

[2] Investopedia http://www.investopedia.com/terms/d/demo netization.asp# ixzz4PhFwOAeH

[3] http://www.investorguide.com/definition/demonetization. html

Technology Adoption in Context of E-Payment System in India after Demonetization

Ram Singh[1] and Musheer Ahmad[2]

ABSTRACT: In order to make India Corruption free, The Prime Minister of India took the step of demonetization by banning the currency of 500 and 1000 as legal tender. The demonetization brings the new revolution in the Indian Economy in terms of e-Payment System. The present paper aims to study the acceptance of the Technology Adoption model for e-payment system in the context of Demonetization. The study used the Technology Adoption model introduced by Davis in 1986. The study uses the five dimensions i.e. Perceived Usefulness, Perceived ease of use, subjective Norms, Behavioural intentions and Perceived Usefulness (PU), Perceived ease of use (PEU), Subjective Norms (SN), Behavioural intentions (BI) and Voluntarily use of Technology (V). The survey was carried among 200 e-Payment users in the Lucknow City. The hypotheses were formulated in order to know the significant correlations between these dimensions to measure the extent of acceptance of the e-Payment after demonetization. The conclusions of this paper will help policy makers to take initiatives about promoting e-Payment system in India.

***Keywords:** E-payment, Technology Acceptance Model, Demonetization.*

1. INTRODUCTION

The rapid development in the IT sector in India transform the society radically. With the advent of world wide web in India, the traditional method of payment is replaced by electronic payment system. Electronic payment refers to make payment online. In Mid eighties, and early nineties RBI introduces the technological solution to improve the existing mode of payments. In order to handle the bulk

[1]Senior Research Fellow, Department of Business Administration, University of Lucknow, Lucknow India.

[2]Associate Professor, Department of Business Administration, Khwaja Moinuddin Chisthi Urdu Arabi Farsi University, Lucknow, India.

payment requirement the Bank introduces the e-Clearance system during 1990s for the first time in India. During the year 2008 RBI Launches the National Electronic Clearing service to facilitate multiple credit to the beneficiary accounts.

In 2005, RBI launches the National Electronic Fund Transfer to promote one to one fund transfer. Further Real Time Gross Settlement system initiated by the Government of India, where the money is transfer in 'real time' and Gross basis.

With the advent of mobiles in Country, RBI issue guidelines to use Mobile phones as a medium for providing banking services. In order to make India Corruption free, The Prime Minister of India took the step of demonetization by banning the currency of 500 and 1000 as legal tender. It is for the first time in Indian history when no one was spared from this move whether from rural or urban, industrialist or common man. The demonetization brings the new revolution in the Indian Economy in terms of e-Payment System. The present paper aims to study the acceptance of the Technology Adoption model for e-payment system in the context of Demonetization.

2. LITERATURE REVIEW

The e-payment and mobile payment system make the payment more convenience and make purchase faster than traditional mode of payment. At the same time there is always a issue of safety and security while making such payments. The study conducted by sumanjeet (2009) found that credit card payment system is prominent among e-payment mode of system. The success of e-payment system depends on the effective technological support. Ashish Das & Rakhi Agarwal (2010), concluded that Cash mode of payment is found to be expensive proposition for the Government and Government should move from Cash to Cashless economy. The adoption of e-payment system will help in long term reduction in the working capital of the companies (Balkrishan, 2007). User acceptance of technology is one of the prime area of study during the last decades. Fishben & Azjen (1975) proposed the model of Theory of reasoned action. In their theoretical model they suggested that persons 'actual behavior could be determined by his prior intentions and the belief that person has for the given behavior. They defined intention as the behavioral intention of the person. Further they defined subjective norms associated with the behavior as the person's perception that most people who are important to him.

They further concluded that subjective norms should be the summation of the person's normative beliefs and his motivation to comply. Finally the Behavior intention is the sum total of Attitude and Subjective Norms.

Ten years later Davis (1985) took the same model and adapted the model in context of technology acceptance and take only perceived usefulness and perceived ease of use enough to predict the attitude of a user towards the use of a system.

The Technology Acceptance model was developed by Davis in the year 1989 with the objective to assess why performance gain was often inhibited by users' unwillingness to accept new technology (Davis, 1989). The study conducted by Davis *et al.* (1989) compared the effectiveness of the Technological model and concluded that TAM model is and adaptation of Theory of Reasoned Action (Fishbein & Ajzen, 1975) tailored for modelling user acceptance of information systems" (Davis *et al.*, 1989, p. 985). The scholar concluded that Hybrid model consist of TRA and TAM may produce more beneficial determinants of the Behavioural intentions of the technology users.

The Present study uses the modified TAM model by including the Demonetization variable in the subjective norms. The proposed model is shown in Figure 1.

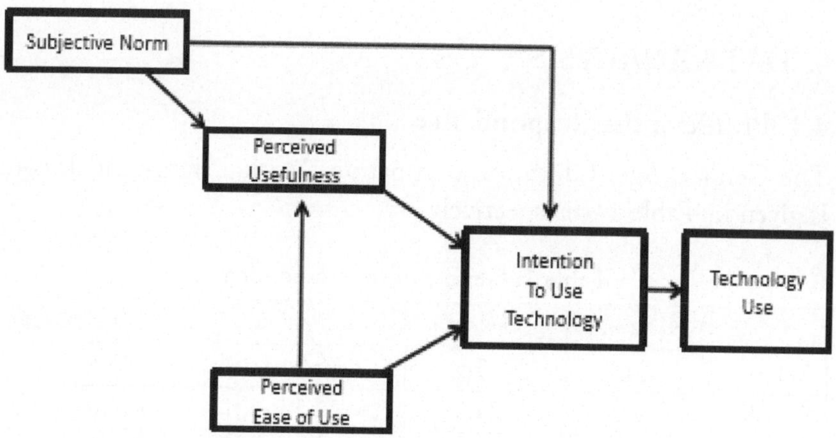

Fig. 1: Technology Acceptance Model (Davis 1989)

3. RESEARCH METHODOLOGY

The study uses the five dimensions i.e. Perceived usefulness, Perceived ease of use, Subjective norms, Behavioural intentions and Technology use.

3.1 Population and Sample

The hypotheses were formulated in order to know the significant correlations between these dimensions to measure the extent of acceptance of the e-Payment after demonetization. The survey was carried among 200 E-Payment users in the Lucknow City. The survey was conducted using structured Questionnaire administered to 300 respondents. Only 200 responses were received.

3.2 Survey Instrument

The questionnaire used in the study consists of overall 19 items. All items were measured on six point Likert scale ranging from strongly disagrees to strongly agree. The chronbach alpha test was conducted to assess the reliability of the instrument used in the study. The overall reliability of the scale was found to be .760 for all of the 19 items.

3.3 Objective of the Study

The main objective of the study is to study the significant correlations between the dimension of Technology acceptance model.

4. DATA ANALYSIS

4.1 Profile of the Respondents

The Gender, Age, Education occupation, Marital status and Income is given in Table 1–6 respectively.

Table 1: Gender of the Respondents

	Frequency	*Percent*	*Valid Percent*	*Cumulative Percent*
Male	151	75.5	75.5	75.5
Female	49	24.5	24.5	100.0
Total	**200**	**100.0**	**100.0**	

Table 2: Age of the Respondents

	Frequency	*Percent*	*Valid Percent*	*Cumulative Percent*
less than 25	123	61.5	61.5	61.5
25–35	42	21.0	21.0	82.5
35–45	7	3.5	3.5	86.0
>45	14	7.0	7.0	93.0
11.00	14	7.0	7.0	100.0
Total	**200**	**100.0**	**100.0**	

Table 3: Education of the Respondents

	Frequency	*Percent*	*Valid Percent*	*Cumulative Percent*
Graduate	137	68.5	68.5	68.5
Post Graduate	56	28.0	28.0	96.5
Professional	7	3.5	3.5	100.0
Total	**200**	**100.0**	**100.0**	

Table 4: Occupation of the Respondents

	Frequency	*Percent*	*Valid Percent*	*Cumulative Percent*
Self employed	96	48.0	48.0	48.0
Government Employed	34	17.0	17.0	65.0
Student	70	35.0	35.0	100.0
Total	**200**	**100.0**	**100.0**	

Table 5: Marital Status of the Respondents

	Frequency	*Percent*	*Valid Percent*	*Cumulative Percent*
Single	172	86.0	86.0	86.0
Married	28	14.0	14.0	100.0
Total	**200**	**100.0**	**100.0**	

Table 6: Income of the Respondents

	Frequency	*Percent*	*Valid Percent*	*Cumulative Percent*
Less than 5 lacs	111	55.5	55.5	55.5
10–15 lacs	47	23.5	23.5	79.0
15–20 Lacs	14	7.0	7.0	86.0
more than 20 lacs	28	14.0	14.0	100.0
Total	**200**	**100.0**	**100.0**	

4.2 Analysis and Interpretation

The purpose of this study to explore the relationship between the factors which influence the willingness to accept the e-payment system after demonetization.

The present study find the correlations between the dimensions of the Technology acceptance model viz. Perceived Usefulness (PU), Perceived Ease of Use (PEU), subjective Norms (SN), Behavioural intentions (BI), and Voluntarily use of Technology (V) and impact of demonetization on these dimensions.

4.2.1 *Correlation among Variables of TAM in Context of E-payment*

In order to know the correlation among the variables of TAM following null Hypothesis were formulated:

1. There is no significant relations exist between variables of TAM in reference to e-Payments.
2. There is no significant impact of Demonetization on the customers Technology Acceptance in reference to e-payment.

4.2.2 *Hypothesis Testing*

4.2.2.1 *There is no Significant Relations Exist between Variables of TAM in Reference to E-Payments*

The correlation analysis was conducted in order to test the hypothesis. The correlations among variables of TAM and significant value is shown in Table 7.

Table 7: Correlations between Dimensions of TAM in Context of E-payment

		PU	*SN*	*PEU*	*BI*	*V*
PU	Pearson Correlation	1	.333**	.493**	.422**	.320**
	Sig. (2-tailed)		.000	.000	.000	.000
	N	200	200	200	200	200
SN	Pearson Correlation	.333**	1	.412**	.406**	.432**
	Sig. (2-tailed)	.000		.000	.000	.000
	N	200	200	200	200	200
PEU	Pearson Correlation	.493**	.412**	1	.419**	.452**
	Sig. (2-tailed)	.000	.000		.000	.000
	N	200	200	200	200	200
BI	Pearson Correlation	.422**	.406**	.419**	1	.401**
	Sig. (2-tailed)	.000	.000	.000		.000
	N	200	200	200	200	200
V	Pearson Correlation	.320**	.432**	.452**	.401**	1
	Sig. (2-tailed)	.000	.000	.000	.000	
	N	200	200	200	200	200

**. Correlation is significant at the 0.01 level (2-tailed).

It can be interpreted from Table 7 that there is significant relations exists between perceived usefulness and subjective norms. It implies that in case of e-payments, the degree to which a person believes that using a particular system would be free from effort is affected by subjective norms. The study also found the significant correlation between perceived norms and intention to use technology. The perceived use and perceived ease of use is also found to be significantly correlated. **Overall all of the variables of TAM are significantly correlated so our null hypothesis was rejected.**

4.2.2.2 *There is no Significant Impact of Demonetization on the Customers Technology Acceptance in Reference to E-Payment*

In order to know the impact of Demonetisation on Technology Acceptance in context of E-payment the correlation analysis was conducted and the results are deciphered in Table 8.

Table 8: Impact of Demonetisation on Technology Acceptance in Context of E-payment

		Demonetisation	*PU*	*SN*	*PEU*	*BI*	*V*
Demonetisation	Pearson Correlation	1	.190**	.520**	.091	.148*	.081
	Sig. (2-tailed)		.007	.000	.202	.037	.254
	N	200	200	200	200	200	200

It can be seen from the Table 2 that there exist a significant relations between the Demonetisation and perceived usefulness, Subjective norms, Behavioural intention to use technology and volunteer use of technology. The impact of Demonetization on PEU is insignificant (**p = 0.202**). Overall. The study did find overall impact of demonetisation on Technology acceptance in e-payments. Thus, our null hypothesis was rejected.

5. CONCLUSION

The present study concludes that in case of e-payments, there is significant relations exists between all of the dimensions of TAM. The study also found that Demonetization significantly affects the acceptance of e-payments among Indian Customers.

REFERENCES

[1] Aparna Iyer (2013). The new "Face book of Indian banking", The Financial Express, March, p. 6.2.

[2] Ashish, Das and Rakhi, Agarwal (2010). Cashless Payment System in India—A Roadmap Technical Report, http://dspace.library.iitb.ac.in/jspui/handle/10054/1732.

[3] Balakrishnan, M. (2007). "Working capital management—Impact of emerging electronic payment Options in India." The Indian Banker, Vol. 2 (.6) pp. 18–26.

[4] Davis, F. (1989). Perceived usefulness, perceived ease of use, and user acceptance of information technology. MIS Quarterly, 13(3), 319–340.

[5] Davis, F., Bagozzi, R. and Warshaw, P. (1989). User acceptance of computer technology: A comparison of two theoretical models. *Management Science*, 35(8), 982.

[6] Fishbein, M. and Ajzen, J. (1975). Belief, attitude, intention and behavior: An introduction to theory and research. Addison-Wesley, Reading, MA, 302.

[7] Sumanjeet, S. (2009). "Emergence of payment Systems in the Age of Electronic Commerce": The state of Act" *Global Journal of International Business Research,* Vol. 2(2), pp. 17–36.

From a Cash Economy to a Less-Cash Economy

Dinesh Kumar Gupta*

"We want to have one mission and target: Take the nation forward—Digitally and economically".

—Narendra Modi
(Prime Minister of India)

A Cashless Economy is a system in which all types of transactions are carried out through digital resources. It includes e-banking, debit and credit cards transactions, card-swipe or point of sales (POS) machines and digital wallets also. The government has been sowing the seeds of a cashless economy: In 2014, the government launched the Jan Dhan Yojana. The best method to reduce corruption and black money in the economy is to move to electronic transfers which needs universal banking access and facility. The idea of a cashless economy is a revolution from the fiat money to digital money with increasing transparency of the flow of cash.

1. OBJECTIVES OF THE STUDY

1. To know the concept of Cashless Economy.
2. To understand the modes of Cashless transactions.
3. To understand the advantage and disadvantage of Cashless transactions.

Concept: Cashless Economy is when the flow of cash within an economy is non-existent and all transactions have to be through electronic channels such as direct debit, credit and debit cards, electronic clearing, and payment systems such as Immediate Payment Service (IMPS), National Electronic Funds Transfer.

*Astt. Professor (Economics), Govt. Degree College Banbasa (Champawat).

2. ADVANTAGES OF A CASHLESS ECONOMY

In India only 10–15 per cent of the population is estimated to have ever used any kind of non-cash payment instrument, compared to 40% of people in Brazil and China.

1. As of 2014 India's ratio of currency in circulation outside of banks to GDP was 11.1% which is higher than other emerging economies like Russia, Mexico and Brazil.
2. Cashless society offers the government and the public many advantages:
3. ***Convenient mode of payment***: The cashless economy offers enormous benefits including reduction in transaction cost of carrying and doing business in cash.
4. ***Lower risk***: With proper cyber security, online payment is relatively risk free, whereas there are always safety issues with physical cash.
5. ***Reduction in the cost of printing money***: In 2015, printing currency cost the RBI ₹ 27 billion. The cost can be reduced if the economy moves towards a cashless economy.
6. ***Decrease in crime rate***: Many anti-social and illegal activities like drug trafficking, prostitution, terror financing and money laundering are carried out only in cash. A cashless economy will make it difficult to carry out such operations.
7. ***Good for the banking sector***: Once people get used to digital payment and transfers, there would be less demand for cash holding or cash hoarding; this would leave more cash in the banking system and thereby enable more savings.
8. ***Transparency and accountability:*** It becomes a lot easier to track the flow of money with every transaction being recorded with the buyer, seller as well as regulatory bodies, making the system much more transparent and compliant. In the long term it leads to better business and investment prospects for the economy as a whole.

3. THE SWEDEN EXPERIENCE

Sweden is one of the top five cashless economies in the world. It has already adopted effective policies to facilitate transactions using mobile or plastic payments through digital infrastructure. Sweden is the first country to promise to go 100% cashless by 2020, and leads the race to become a cashless society. As on December 2015, the population of Sweden was estimated at 9.85 million people literacy was almost 100%. India had a population of 1,260 million; literacy was only 75%. The population of illiterate people in India was almost 30 times the entire population of Sweden.

It is difficult for India to think along the lines of Sweden; nonetheless, India has started the movement towards cashless economy now. The RBI and commercial banks need to come up with an innovative idea that enables cashless transactions which is safe and easy to perform.

4. DISADVANTAGE OF CASHLESS TRANSACTIONS

1. Many of the rural people and even some urban people still do not have a functional bank account in order to make online payments.
2. A large number of India's population is in rural areas, and there are no proper internet facilities available to make online payments.
3. People in rural locations are not well educated about the digital mode of payment system.
4. Even today some places which take paper cash and do not accept debit and credit cards. Making a purchase at such places with card becomes very difficult to customers. Small retailers in India still deal only in paper cash as they cannot afford toinvest in digital infrastructure facilities.
5. Cash is not under our control, people will spend excessive amount for purchase of goods and services.
6. If you lose your debit/credit card, it takes some time to get a new one.
7. Hacking and cyber theft are major and challenging problems which can be caused by online transactions. Cyber Security measures have to be brought in place to avoid money going into wrong hands.
8. Even in big cities, sometimes online transactions cannot be made because of poor internet facilities or network problems.

5. CHALLENGES AHEAD

In rural areas, there are only 20.8% of ATMs of the public sector banks and 8.5% of the ATMs of private sector banks. So it is difficult to find an ATM in rural areas. E-wallets and mobile payment systems need a smart phone and an internet connection, but less than a quarter of the population owns a smart phone. Fast and reliable internet connection is expensive and it is difficult to find public wifi hotspots and mobile phone battery charging stations. Issues like cyber security and online frauds are key concerns. In a democratic system of government, political party funding is one of the major sources of corruptions. Therefore, any attempt at fighting corruption that does not first involve bringing transparency to the funding of political parties cannot be meaningful or successful.

6. BENEFITS OF LESS CASH ECONOMY

If all transactions are electronic then all transactions can be chased, can be recorded and checked. This will be possible to curb the menace of black money which has been denting the tax base, tax collections, encouraging terror financing, drug distribution, generation of fake

Table 1: Payment System Indicators—Annual Turnover

Item	*Volume (million)*			*Value (₹ billion)*		
	2015–16	*2016–17*	*2017–18*	*2015–16*	*2016–17*	*2017–18*
1	*2*	*3*	*4*	*5*	*6*	*7*
Systemically Important Financial Market Infrastructures (SIFMIs)						
RTGS	98.3	107.8	124.4	8,24,578	9,81,904	11,67,125
CTS	958.4	1,111.90	1,138.00	69,889	74,035	79,451
Non-MICR Clearing	138	94.8	32.6	11,972	6,923	2,442
ECS DR	224.8	8.8	1.5	1,652	39	10
ECS CR	39	10.1	6.1	1,059	144	115
NEFT	1,252.90	1,622.10	1,946.40	83,273	1,20,040	1,72,229
IMPS	220.8	506.7	1,009.80	1,622	4,116	8,925
Unified Payment Interface	–	17.9	915.2	–	69	1,098
National Automated Clearing House (NACH)	1,404.10	2,057.30	2,503.30	3,802	7,916	10,736
Total Card Payments	2,707.30	5,450.10	8,207.60	4,483	7,421	10,607
Credit Cards	785.7	1,087.10	1,405.20	2,407	3,284	4,590
Debit Cards	1,173.60	2,399.30	3,343.40	1,589	3,299	4,601
Grand Total	9,002.90	14,473.90	20,633.50	181,748.00	107,246.00	122,575.00

Source: RBI Annual Report 2017–18.

currency and much more. It will also reduce real estate prices because of curbs on black money as most of the black money is invested in real estate prices which inflates the prices of real estate markets. Less cash economy will also pave the way for universal availability of banking services to all as no physical infrastructure is needed other than digital which can be facilitated by the government very easily. Digital payments bring in greater efficiency and transparency in welfare programmes as money is wired directly into the accounts of recipients. Payments can be easily traced and collected, and corruption will automatically drop, so people will no longer have to pay to collect what is rightfully theirs.

7. FINDINGS AND SUGGESTIONS

The findings of the study show that India in terms of using digital payment methods is still very poor in comparison to other developed countries in the world. As many countries are already adopted payment system in an economy, India is in its developing phase and most of the population are dependent on cash based transaction because of unavailability of proper internet connectivity, lack of information and knowledge of financial transaction, charges on card payments and un operational bank accounts. India needs to come up with the new policies of electronic transactions. It is recommended that government should promote their agencies and private sector service providers to spread financial literacy at a great extend especially in rural areas. Government should provide extra benefits on digital transaction payments and offer extra incentives or interest rate on cash saving in bank accounts. At the same time reduction in charges of digital transaction or exemption completely on digital banking should be offered for few initial years which can be more helpful for speeding up the process of digitalization of payments in India.

8. CONCLUSION

By doing away the exemption of cash donations to political parties below ₹ 20,000 will take care of the non-transparency of 80% of political funding. The unprecedented step of demonetisation may hopefully turn out to be a blessing in disguise for conducting free and fair elections, where cashless transactions will ensure higher level of transparency and scrutiny. RBI has also recently unveiled a document—"Payments and Settlement Systems in India: Vision 2018"—setting out a plan and mood to encourage electronic payments enabling India to move towards a cashless society or economy in the medium and long term. A cashless economy is secure, it is clean. We have a leadership role to play in taking India towards an increasingly "digital economy". Thus, as citizens and youths of India it is in our hands to promote this magnificent India encouraged by our PM Mr. Narendra Modi who has a bright vision towards the upcoming of future India. Big success and it will help to attain vision of "DIGITAL INDIA".

REFERENCES

[1] Anthonima, K. Robin *et al.*, India Moving towards Cashless Society. *International Journal of Engineering & Scientific Research (IJMRA Publications)*, Vol. 6, Issue 5, May 2018.

[2] Das, A. and Agarwal, R. (2010). Cashless Payment System in India—A Roadmap, Technical Report, *Indian Institute of Technology Bombay, Department of Mathematics*, Bombay.

[3] Fatimah, M.A., Kusairi, M.N. and Mohd, F.A. (2000). E-commerce adoption in Malaysia: Problems and Barriers from the firms' perspective, *Proceedings of International Conference on Electronic Commerce.*

[4] Khosla, S. (2017). India is far away from being a cashless economy. Here's why. http://www.hindustantimes.com/ Retrieved 14 March 2017, from http://www.hindustantimes.com/analysis/india-is-far-awayfrom-being-a-cashless-economy-here-s-why/storyybFui5M53JPFyD1MGvHigJ.html

[5] Mahor, N., A Study of the Customer Perception of the Risk of cash and cashless transaction, Kaav International *Journal of Economics, Commerce & Business Management*, 4(4), 2017, 103–119.

[6] Mellon, B.N.Y., Global payments 2020: transformation and convergence, New York, 2014, retrieved on April 26, 2018.

[7] Nielsen, Mobile Money: From shopping to banking to payments, how mobile is transforming commerce around the world, Global Mobile Money Report, 2016, retrieved on April 26, 2018, http://www.nielsen.com/be/en/insights/reports/2016/mobilemoney.html

[8] Rajanna, K.A., Perception and Awareness of Customer towards Cashless Transaction; A Case Study, *International Journal of Application or Innovation in Engineering & Management (IJAIEM),* Vol. 7, Issue 3, March 2018, ISSN 2319-4847.

https://www.bnymellon.com/_globalassets/pdf/business-insights/global-payments-2020-transformation-and-convergence.pdf

[9] https://www.rbi.org.in/SCRIPTs/AnnualReportPublications.aspx?Id=1236

Insights into Board Size and Composition in the Indian Corporate Sector

J.K. Sharma[1] and Sukhmani Gandhi[2]

ABSTRACT: This paper attempts to examine the compliance with Clause 49 of SEBI Regulations, 2015 by the Indian companies in respect of Board composition. A survey of Large cap companies (companies with the average market capitalisation of more than 100000 million) comprising of 161 companies revealed that more than 75% of large cap companies do not comply with the requirement of minimum 50 percent of board independence and have preponderance of executive directors controlling the decision making process. Further, the results also point out inadequate representation of women on the Indian boards. This raises the serious questions on corporate governance issues in India. Hence, not only mere compliance of governance mandates and provisions is essential, but also its compliance with full letter and spirit is the need of the hour in the Indian firms.

Keywords: *Board Size, Board Independence, Executive Directors, Women Directors, Clause 49 of SEBI Regulations.*

1. INTRODUCTION

Corporate governance has become an imperative issue in the emerging economies and is gaining momentum worldwide. Corporate governance is such a comprehensive term, that it is not only limited to the "systems by which businesses are directed and controlled" (the Cadbury report, UK), but also encompasses a transparent and efficient administration so that the operations of a company are directed towards achievement of long-term strategy and goals and in the interest of its various stakeholders.

[1]Professor, Department of Business Administration, University of Lucknow, Lucknow. E-mail: jkbaba@gmail.com

[2]Assistant Professor, Navyug Kanya Mahavidyalaya, Lucknow. E-mail: sukh.gandhi@gmail.com

The recurrent series of corporate scams that took place in India, were mainly due to mis governance, fraudulent practices adopted, financial statement manipulation, income smoothing, lack of transparency and efficiency on the part of Indian firms. This discredited the confidence of the investors of the listed firms. The grave consequences of similar corporate misdemeanors worldwide, made it indispensable on the part of Indian corporates to adhere the mandate governance practices and laws so as to bring more transparency and integrity into their business operations. For stricter adoption of governance practices, SEBI introduced the Clause 49 of listing agreement and several other committees were constituted for the purpose to review and improve the governance practices of the Indian listed firms from time to time. The recommendations given by these committees were amended in the SEBI regulations, and their compliance was made mandatory for the listed firms. Over the last two decades now, revolutionary change has been observed in the governance framework of the Indian corporates due to compliance of mandate governance provisions.

It has been revealed in the survey of literature that different dimensions to study corporate governance of firms are Board size, Board composition, Ownership concentration, CEO duality etc. (Bachiller *et al.* (2015); Castro *et al.* (2013); Kota and Tomar (2010); Adam *et al.* (2015)).

In this paper, using the Clause 49 of SEBI regulations, 2015, we try to gather the insights into the compliance of governance provisions by analysis of the corporate governance dimensions of the firm, namely, Board size and Board composition of the Indian firms.

The second part of the paper deals with the thorough survey of literature. The third part outlines the objectives of this study. The fourth part of the paper explains the methodology of research used in the paper followed by the analysis of the results as well as the findings in the fifth part. The discussions and conclusion of the study appear in the last part.

2. LITERATURE REVIEW

2.1 Clause 49 of the SEBI Regulations: Background

In order to prevent the corporates failures, SEBI initiated to raise and promote the governance standards of the Indian firms, listed on stock exchange. For this purpose, SEBI appointed the ***Kumar Mangalam Birla Committee*** in the year 1999. The recommendations by the committee in the year 2000 were indeed a remarkable move in terms of progression of governance practices among the Indian corporates.

Later, in the year 2000, upon considering the recommendations of the committee, SEBI introduced the Clause 49, so as to encourage better governance practices by ensuring disclosures and transparency among the listed firms, in the context of following:

1. The Board of Directors and their remuneration details
2. The details of Audit committee
3. Details of shareholder and management
4. Corporate governance report
5. Certificate of compliance by the auditors.

Further, in order to review and analyze the clause 49 and also to improve the existing governance framework of the firms, SEBI set up a new committee, the ***Narayana Murthy Committee*** in 2003. Few key mandatory recommendations by the committee were related to:

1. Audit Committee
2. Related Party Transactions
3. Code of conduct
4. Excluding nominee director from the *definition of independent directors*
5. Whistle Blower Policy
6. Risk Management Structure etc.

Later, in the year 2014, SEBI amended the clause 49 of the listing agreement. The amendments comprised of new elements of governance as well as improving the existing provisions.

Some of the important elements explained were.

2.1.1 *Board of Directors*

(a) *Composition of Board*

The clause states that the board of directors of a company must comprise of an optimum combination of executive and non-executive directors, where it is mandatory to have at least one woman director. In this case, at least 50% directors on the board must be non-executive.

The number of independent directors on board may vary depending on the chairman of the board. If the chairman of the board is the non-executive director, then in that case, the board must comprise of at least one third independent directors. But if the chairman besides being a non-executive director, is also one of the promoters of the company or related to any of the promoters or any person occupying key managerial position in the company, in that case the board shall consist of a minimum one half of the independent directors. Similarly, if the chairman of the board is an executive director, then the board shall have at least one half of the independent directors.

(b) *Independent Directors*

The clause defines the term "independent directors". The clause defines the term "independent directors" as any director who is not a non-executive director and not a nominee director. You should possess the relevant expertise, skills and experience in his area. The limit on number of directorships, Maximum tenure of independent directors, Performance evaluation of independent directors are also stated in detail.

(c) *Audit Committee*

It explains:

1. Qualified and independent audit committee
2. Meetings
3. Power of audit committee
4. Role of audit committee
   (a) Subsidiary Companies
   (b) Risk Management
   (c) Related Party Transactions
   (d) Disclosures
   (e) CEO/CFO Certification
   (f) Report on Corporate Governance
   (g) Compliance.

2.2 Board Composition

2.2.1 *Board Size*

Existing literature on corporate governance reveals that firms can use board restructuring as one of the tools to avoid any governance failures on their part. Bachiller *et al.* (2015), point that composition of board as well as its size are important factors of the board structure. The Indian companies act, 2013 does not authorize any ideal size of the board. On the other hand, Clause 49 SEBI regulations, 2015 stipulate on having a board, comprising of balanced mix of non-executive directors and executive directors. Every company is free to determine its board size, depending upon its requirements.

It is assumed that the smaller boards function in a cohesive manner, meet more frequently and expedite the strategic decision making process of the organization. On the other hand, Clause 49 SEBI regulations 2015 stipulate on having a board comprising of balanced mix of non-executive directors and executive directors. Every company is free to determine its board size, depending upon its requirements. It is assumed that the smaller boards function in cohesive manner, meet more frequently and expedite this strategic decision making process of the organization. This also supports the view given by Dey & Chauhan (2009) that smaller boards function more effectively. Empirical literature reveals that expanding boards beyond an acceptable limit, impacts the value of the firm and its decision making in a negative manner day (Dey & Chauhan, (2009); Ghosh, (2006); Kumar & Singh, (2013)).

On the other hand Agency theory assumes that larger boards work in a more efficient manner. In this regard Mehrotra (2016) corroborates the view by pointing that larger boards are more vigilant monitors of the actions of the firm. The report on India board Index, published by Spencer Stuart in 2015, revealed in their empirical findings, that the average board size of BSE-100 listed firms was 10.3.

2.2.2 *Independent Directors*

The SEBI regulations, mandate the number of independent directors that are necessary to be present on the board. The Clause 49 of SEBI Regulations states, ***board of directors of the company shall have an optimum combination of executive and non-executive directors with not less than fifty percent of the board of directors comprising of non-executive directors. The number of independent directors would depend whether the Chairman is executive or non-executive. In case of a non-executive chairman, at least one-third of board should comprise of independent directors and in case of an executive chairman, at least half of board should comprise of independent directors.***

None of the laws or regulations prescribe the role or duties of independent directors. Moreover, lesser commitment on the part of the board was one of the main reasons behind the increasing importance of the independent boards. Uzun *et al.* (2004) discovered that boards with lesser independent directors are more prone to occurrence of fraud activities.

Castro *et al.* (2013) & Kota and Tomar (2010) describe independent board as a key governance variable. However, it is expected that the duty of independent directors is to align the interest of the various stakeholders of the organization and to mitigate any conflicts that arise between them. Daily *et al.* (2003) also support the view that independent board structures reduce any sort of conflict between the shareholders and management.

It is also the duty of directors to exercise judgement and opinion on the various strategic, operational and other matters of the company. Maseda *et al.* (2015) assert that a balanced board in terms of inside and outside directors contributes in value creation, improved performance of the firm and a well functioning board.

2.2.3 *Executive Directors*

Executive directors, also called as inside directors are employed by the forms on a "full-time basis". They are supposed to assist the firm in their routine business operations in an effective and efficient manner. Executive directors their expected to perform fiduciary duties and work in the best interests of the organization. They also function as strategic planners of the organization. Maseda *et al.* (2015) consider that such directors have comprehensive and in-depth knowledge about the details of the business, their operations and also other technical details. Sarkar (2009) discovers that inside directors as 'credible source of information', that can provide the necessary information about the company.

Empirical evidence from the extant literature does not highlight the role of executive directors as far as the corporate performance is concerned. Lodh *et al.* (2014), claimed that executive directors of family firms expropriate money from the organization for their personal monetary benefits. They are involved in 'tunneling of resources', since they are usually under the pressure of promoters of the organization. In simple words, executive directors might prioritize self-interest over the organizational interests.

2.2.4 *Woman Directors*

The Indian Companies Act, 2013 has made it mandatory for every listed and other specific public sector firms to have at least one woman director on board. The empirical evidence of existing literature on women directors on board points out the prevailing gender imbalance that is observed in the top management of the corporate boards. Bhalla (2012) asserts that board diversity increases the strength of the board. Adam *et al.* (2015) highlighted the relevance of diverse boards for better and quality decision-making. Ample evidence from past studies support the view that diverse boards along with diverse management are found to be more effective. It will also bring more innovation and creativity needed to stay competitive (ET team (11 February 2019), "Diversity Sparks Creativity and Innovation in Companies", The Economic Times).

3. OBJECTIVES OF THE STUDY

The objective of the paper is to analyze the data of the boards of the selected sample of companies for the financial year 2016–17, on the lines of clause 49 of SEBI regulations, 2015 in the context of the following dimensions of corporate governance:

(a) The board size
(b) The board composition—The board composition shall be examined using the following sub-components:
    1. Independent Directors
    2. Executive Directors
    3. Women Directors.

4. METHODOLOGY FOR RESEARCH

The steps for selection of final sample used for the study and the research strategy adopted, are as explained below:

1. CMIE's (Centre for monitoring Indian Economy), Prowess database, was used for extraction of the BSE listed companies along with a market capitalization figures for 5 years, from the years 2013 to 2017.

2. The average market capitalization of all the extracted firms was calculated.
3. On the basis of the average market capitalization figures, the firms having average market capitalization of 100000 million and above were categorized as Large Cap Firms. A total of 219 such firms were found.
4. Out of all the firms categorized as Large Cap, Public Sector Undertakings (PSU), banking firms and firms with non-availability of relevant information were eliminated.
5. Thereafter the final sample of Large Cap companies used for the study consisted of **161** firms.
6. The Annual reports of the company for the relevant financial year, extracted from their official websites, were used to supplement the required financial as well as other data related to the company boards.

Lastly SPSS, which is the statistical software package, was used for application of statistical tools on the data.

5. ANALYSIS OF THE RESULTS

5.1 Board Size

Table 1: Statistics Summary of Board Size (Descriptive Statistics)

	N	*Minimum*	*Maximum*	*Mean*	*Std. Deviation*
Board Size	159	7	24	13.33	2.944
Valid N (listwise)	159				

Source: SPSS.

Table 1 depicts the descriptive statistics, calculated for the board size. The minimum value of the board size in the sample was found to be 7, whereas the maximum board size was 24. The Mean board size calculated for the sample was 13.33 and the Standard Deviation for the same is 2.944.

Low Standard Deviation indicates that most of the data values of the board size of the sample are close to the mean size of the board.

Figure 1 represents a histogram of the board size values of the sample. It can be observed that board size values of the sample spread across the size of 7 to 24 members. However, it can also be observed from the histogram that the majority data is clustered around the board size range of 10 to 17.

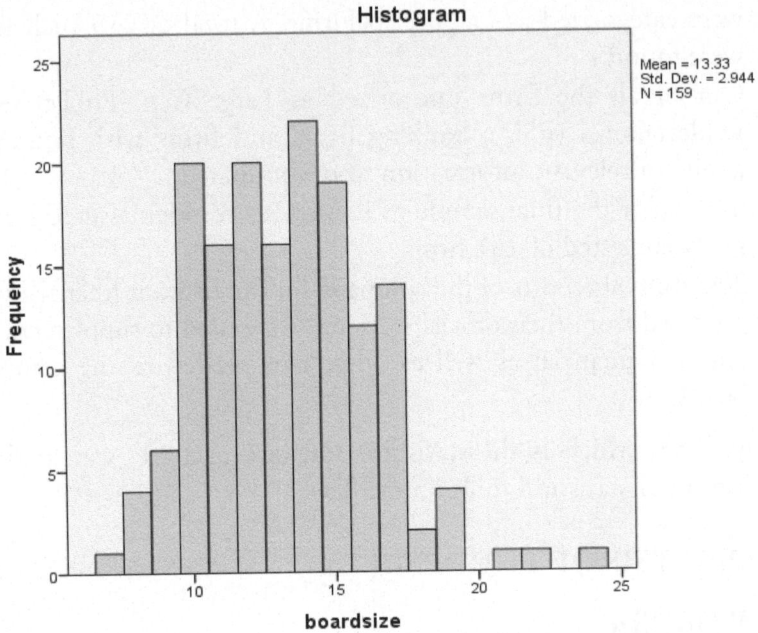

Fig. 1

Source: SPSS.

5.2 Independent Directors

Table 2: Number of Independent Directors on Board

Percentage of Independent Directors on the Board	*Total Number of Companies Matching the Criteria*
70 %	01
60% to 69%	08
50% to 59%	28
Less than 50%	120

Table 2 reveals the analysis of the number of independent directors present on the board. The results point that out of the 161 sample companies, approximately 22% sample companies (37 companies) had the boards which comprised of at least 50% or more independent directors on their Boards. Approximately 5% of the sample companies had 60% or more independent directors on its board.

5.3 Executive Directors

Table 3: Number of Executive Directors on Board

Percentage of Executive Directors on the Board	*Total Number of Companies Matching the Criteria*
Less than 50%	132
50% to 59%	20
60%	04
64%	01

Table 3 shows the analysis of the number of executive directors present on the board, it is evident from the results that only approximately 15% of the sample size (25 companies) had one-half or more directors as executive directors, whereas the remaining sample taken for study, had less than 50% executive directors on their boards.

5.4 Women Directors

Table 4: Number of Women Directors on the Board

Total Number of Women Directors on the Board	*Total Number of Companies*
No Women Director	02
One	81
Two	55
Three	15
Four	04
Five	02

Insights into Table 4 reveal the analysis of board structure in the context of number of women directors present on the board of 161 sample Large Cap companies. It is evident from the results that one-half of the companies had a single woman director on board. 97.5% of the sample (157 companies) was found to have at least 1 women director on their boards. The maximum number of women directors revealed in any sample company was found to be 5 directors.

6. FINDINGS AND DISCUSSION

The overall findings of the study reveal that although governance compliance by the Indian corporate sector has gained impetus but the outcome or its progress is still fragmentary. It is a matter of concern, that even after a decade, 100% compliance to governance provisions of Clause 49 of SEBI Regulations is yet to be achieved. Board Composition is stressed upon as one of the key variables of governance. The board size analysis of the study reveals an average board size of 13.33. The findings of the study point lesser independent directors on the board of the majority sample companies, indicating the need of an improved oversight role by the directors of the firms. Only 22% approximately sample companies were found to comply with the provisions of having at least 50% independent directors on the board. Majority data sample was found to be in non-compliance with the provisions of independent directors on the board as per the clause 49 of SEBI regulations, 2015. The results suggest the realization of the importance of an independent board. Clause 49 of SEBI regulations, 2015 has mandated the presence of women directors on the board to bring more diversity in terms of talent and expertise. One-half of the sample was found to have mere formal compliance to clause 49, SEBI regulation 2015, by having a single woman director on the board. This suggests that inadequate representation of women on board, implying that lesser significance is given to reduce the gender disparity on the board.

A snapshot of the results is as follows:

Provision/Regulation	*Required Compliance*	*Percentage of Companies Found Compliant*
	Atleast 50% independent directors on the board	22%
Clause 49 of SEBI Regulations, 2015	Less than 50% of executive directors on board	15%
Clause 49 of SEBI Regulations, 2015 and Indian Companies act, 2013	At least 1 women director on board	97.5%

Size of the sample-161.

7. CONCLUSION

The results of the study indicate that even after decades, it is a cause of concern for the Indian corporate sector that 100% compliance to governance provisions of Clause 49 of SEBI Regulations is yet not achieved. Not only mere formal compliance of the governance provisions, but its compliance with full letter and spirit is the need of the hour among the Indian firms. Commitment of the companies towards stronger governance compliance practices helps them achieve competitive advantage, enhances their goodwill and boosts the trust of its investors and helps them in sustainable growth of the business. Firms with better governance structures tend to bring cohesiveness, expedite the strategic decision making process of the organization and increase the effectiveness of the board. Moreover, a balanced and effective board can help to foster a conducive organizational culture within the organization, which can be aligned strategically with the business, thereby creating value for the firm and maximizing the shareholder's value in the long-term.

REFERENCES

[1] Adams, R., Haan, J., Terjesen, S. and Ees, H. (2015). Board diversity: moving the field forward, corporate governance: An international review, 23(2):77–82.

[2] Bachiller, P., Giorgino, M. and Paternostro, S. (2015). "Influence of board of directors on firm performance: analysis of family and non-family firms", *International Journal of disclosure and governance,* Vol. 12, 230–253.

[3] Cadbury Committee Report, 1992.

[4] Castro, R., Aguilera, R. and Arino, M. (2013). "Bundles of Firm Corporate Governance Practices: A Fuzzy Set Analysis", *Corporate Governance: An International Review*, 21(4), 390–407.

[5] Clause 49 of Listing Agreement, SEBI Regulations.

[6] Daily, C., Dalton, D. and Cannella, A. (2003). "Corporate governance: Decades of dialogue and data", *Academy of Management review*, Vol. 28(3), 371–382.

[7] Dey, D. and Chauhan, Y. (2009), "Board composition and performance in Indian firms: a comparison", *The IUP Journal of corporate governance,* Vol. 8(2), 7–19.

[8] ET team (11 February 2019). "Diversity Sparks Creativity And Innovation In Companies", The Economic Times.

[9] Ghosh, S. (2006). "Do Board Characteristics Affect Corporate Performance? Firm Level Evidence for India", *Applied Economic Letters,* 13(7), 435–443.

[10] Kota, H. and Tomar, S. (2010), "Corporate governance practices in Indian firms", *Journal of management and organisation*, Vol. 16, 266–279.

[11] Kumar, N. and Singh, P.J. (2013). "Effect of Board Size and Promoter Ownership on Firm Value: Some Empirical Findings from India", *Corporate Governance*, 13(1), 88–98.

[12] Lodh, S., Nandy, M. and Chen, J. (2014). "Innovation and Family Ownership: Empirical Evidence from India", *Corporate Governance: An International Review*, 22(1), 4–23.

[13] Maseda, A., Iturralde, T. and Arosa, B. (2015). "Impact of outsiders on firm performance over different generations of family-owned SMEs", *Journal of small business management,* Vol. 53(4), pp. 1203–1218.

[14] Mehrotra, S. (2016). "The nature of corporate board structure and its impact on the performance of USA listed firms", *The IUP Journal of Corporate Governance,* Vol. 15(1), 30–46.

[15] Sarkar, J. (2009). "Board Independence and Corporate Governance In India: Recent Trends and Challenges Ahead", *The Indian Journal of Industrial Relations*, 44(4), 576–592.

[16] Uzun, H., Szewczyk, S. and Varma, R. (2004). "Board Composition and Corporate Fraud", *Financial Analysts Journal,* 60(3), 33–43.

[17] Spencer Stuart Report, 2015.

[18] The Indian Companies Act, 2013.

Author Index